The New York Times

SUNDAY AT THE SEASHORE CROSSWORDS
From the Pages of *The New York Times*

Edited by Will Shortz

ST. MARTIN'S GRIFFIN ☙ NEW YORK

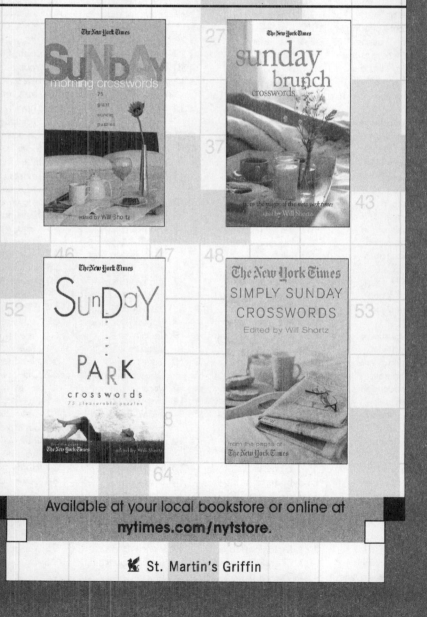

1 WHAT THE PROFESSOR MEANT TO SAY

ACROSS

1 Takes off
6 Blurted (out)
10 Track runner?
14 Mona ___ smile
19 Parts of hearts
20 Docent's offering
21 Sarah Josepha ___, who wrote "Mary Had a Little Lamb"
22 Seven-time French Open winner
23 Melodramatic
24 "The Aviator" actor, 2004
25 Marine killer
26 The Beatles, once
27 "Have a nice weekend . . . heh-heh"
31 Cousin of Muhammad
32 Babealicious
33 E'en if
34 Part of a speller's clarification
35 Having four sharps
36 Cry of success
37 Pound with a metric system?
39 First name in modeling
42 Cantillated
44 "You, in the front row!"
47 Cracked
50 Family
51 Stamp letters
52 Controversial 50's event
56 Element in magnetic alloys
59 Caesarean delivery?
61 Apples can be compared to them
64 Quadrennial White House administration

65 "My lecture's done, but we still have five minutes"
68 Crowd attractor
70 Riddle-me-___
71 Like some effects
72 Last lines
74 The lonely goatherd, in a "Sound of Music" song
76 Feminine suffix
77 Slate, e.g., for short
79 "I can't read your handwriting!"
81 Track event
83 Record problem
85 Behind
86 Listening to Muzak, maybe
87 German coal city
89 Uncle ___ rice
91 Inlet
93 Some bills
94 "Your grades aren't what they should be"
100 Inhuman
103 Meat loaf serving
104 50-Across's partner
105 Father or son Joad in "The Grapes of Wrath"
108 It lacks 93-Across
109 Port container
111 Its musical ID is just the notes G, E and C
113 Brian of rock
114 Govt. org. with a flower in its logo
115 "If I could digress for a moment . . ."
121 Diplomat Deane of early America
122 Start of a decision-making process
123 "Good ___!"

124 Netanyahu's successor
125 Sharp
126 Philosopher Descartes
127 Ending of many toothpaste names
128 Steamed
129 Heads of états
130 River of W.W. I
131 Ziegfeld Follies costume designer
132 Spaced (out)

DOWN

1 Proceed nonchalantly
2 "High Spirits" star, 1988
3 Literary dueler
4 Opportune
5 Pourer's request
6 Successful film franchise starting in 1979
7 San Francisco street named for a president
8 Not take for credit
9 Certain guilty pleasure
10 Ten Commandments word
11 "For the ___ and radiant maiden": Poe
12 Reynolds Wrap maker
13 Isn't joking
14 Sore throat remedy
15 One of six Russian rulers
16 Submit
17 French satellite-launching rocket
18 Was a good dog, perhaps
28 Go through slowly

29 "Dig?"
30 Dig
38 Cutting down, after "on"
40 Old literary inits
41 Car maker whose name is Latin
43 "___ take arms against a sea of troubles": Hamlet
44 Like some Bedouins
45 Like Charlie Chaplin
46 Gets
47 Professors' environs
48 Objects of envy
49 Black holes, e.g.
53 In the initial phases
54 Index fingers, in a children's hand game
55 Great American Ballpark team
57 Siren
58 Is multitudinous
60 Any of TV's Simpsons
62 Polite question
63 Technique for viewing some slides?
66 Neb. neighbor
67 Old German duchy name
69 Fall locale
73 Best replacement
75 Set of values
78 Ridicule
80 Trojan horse
82 Hardy girl
84 Some have black eyes
88 Bottom lines
90 Vikings' org.
92 Turn off
95 Verve
96 Open case
97 Good time to collect seashells
98 27 for 56-Across, e.g.: Abbr.

by Ethan Cooper and Michael Shteyman

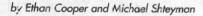

99 "That's ___!"
100 Serenades, as the moon
101 Le soleil, par exemple
102 It works like a charm
105 W.W. II conference site
106 Endorphin, e.g.
107 Like raccoons
110 Cap sites
112 Spy's gizmo
116 Beard
117 Feminine suffix
118 Appraiser
119 County of Dover, Delaware . . . or Dover, England
120 Relative of a potato

ACROSS

1 A list of the A-list
6 Polish port
12 Footwear name
19 Gazetteer data
20 With freedom of tempo
21 "Dunno"
22 Source of a little laughter
24 Nether world
25 General breakout
26 Off course
27 Old propaganda source
28 List
29 Driver's opportunity
31 People aren't usually drawn to this
33 Make out
34 Yule decorations
40 Place in a Robert Redford flick
41 Foofaraws
45 Godiva product
46 One working close to Washington?
48 Breakfast cereal
49 Learn via a third party
50 Berth place
52 Excessive suavity
54 Off
56 Doo-wop syllable
59 Virginia, once
60 Terse truths
63 Drew on
64 Coeur d'___
65 Almond Joy nuts, perhaps
67 Waiting for a pickup
68 Diner on "Alice"
69 Backyard game
70 Red and blue
71 Big Ten inits.
72 Makes right
73 Unwrap impatiently
75 Son of Mary Stuart

77 "Good grief!"
80 Give a little
81 Health, in Le Havre
82 Free
84 Paris pops
85 Start of a 1940's–60's world leader's name
86 Vehicles that may be under the Yuletide tree
90 Director Jean-___ Godard
91 Blowing away
92 Not even
97 Cultural character
99 Creaky, maybe
100 Prepares, as chestnuts
105 History chapters
106 Prepares for a ride
108 Season's greetings
110 Laments loudly
111 Capital of Somme
112 Render helpless
113 Old dinero
114 Fly with a long proboscis
115 Pounding parts

DOWN

1 Attended
2 Poet who wrote "I have executed a memorial longer lasting than bronze"
3 Saint-Germain's river
4 Drops off
5 Multitude
6 Cubism pioneer Juan
7 Way in or out
8 Can't take
9 Simba's love in "The Lion King"
10 Doesn't touch again
11 Levels, briefly

12 Thistlelike plant
13 Winter frosts
14 Mohawk-sporting actor
15 Hurdle for future docs
16 Present seeker
17 Juju and mojo
18 Popular drink mix
21 Stable place
23 Cold war side
27 Chevrolet model
30 Quoits pegs
32 Sports org. north of the border
35 Chief Jack House and others
36 Foie ___
37 "Ben-___"
38 West Coast airport inits.
39 Fishermen bring them back to shore
40 Suffix with Ecuador
41 Bum place to stay?
42 1983 World Series winners over the Phillies
43 Handel bars?
44 About half of table salt, chemically
47 "Capeesh?"
49 "Get your hands off me!"
50 Richie's mother, to the Fonz
51 Sights
53 Calgary-to-Edmonton dir.
54 Director ___ C. Kenton
55 New York City park name
57 Greek
58 Sum parts
60 Breezed through
61 Get by
62 Merry sound of the season
63 Strip

65 Mus. increase in volume
66 First name in Egyptian politics
67 "It is the night of ___ dear Savior's birth"
69 Course for course preparers
70 Speaker systems, briefly
72 Invoice no.
73 Garb for 2-Down
74 "I kiss'd thee ___ kill'd thee": Othello
76 Nickname for the young Darth Vader
77 Some credit card security features
78 Snake in the grass
79 Elementary school trio
81 Sink
82 Biting
83 Ending with tele-
84 Ltr. afterthoughts
85 Lies low
87 Heroes
88 1936 Olympics star
89 Pelé's org., once
93 Mantel
94 Hold forth
95 Contribute
96 Lots of sissies?
98 16-Down's desire
99 Fictional wirehair
101 Mayberry kid
102 In ___ (worked up)
103 Assn. and org.
104 "Just hear ___ sleigh bells jingling . . ."
107 Too rehearsed
108 Santa has a red and white one
109 Restaurant chain since '58

by Nancy Salomon and Harvey Estes

ACROSS

1 Failures
7 Strolled
13 Mob action
20 Foothold facilitator
21 Annual October event, with "the"
22 "That really touched me"
23 Scene of some disgraceful one-nighters?
25 Traffic caution
26 Longtime Syrian president
27 Singer Redbone
28 Business honcho Perelman, who was once the richest man in America
29 Bad testimony
30 Headline about a philanthropist's settled loan?
37 Several periods
40 Bribe
41 Vacationer's destination
42 Rudy's coach in "Rudy"
43 Take off (on)
45 Wife of Saturn
47 Like a piece of cake
49 "That'll do, thanks"
53 "I'll say it again — I'm outta here"?
58 A
59 Slows
60 Slow
61 Largest island in the Cyclades
62 It may blow when it's hot
63 Prefix with angular
65 Pour
67 Made privy to

69 Darning some smelly socks?
75 Early French settler in the Maritimes
76 "Oxford Blues" star, 1984
77 Fitness centers
78 Meticulousness
79 "Julius Caesar" role
83 When repeated, a South Seas getaway
85 Tattered Tom's creator
88 D.C. setting
89 Item on a busboy's to-do list?
92 Donne, for one
94 Spent
95 Behind
96 Bygone time
97 Notebook maker
99 Can't stand
102 Diving bird
104 Grp. with some crack staff
105 Retrieves a phone message again?
111 Had something
112 Kicks
113 Ill-gotten gains
114 Old Russian ruler known as "The Moneybag"
118 Big cheese?
121 Drive Dali back?
125 Occupied, as a saddle
126 Irish P.M. Ahern
127 Calm
128 Running out of gas
129 Vital ratings period
130 Password preceder

DOWN

1 Bologna bread, once
2 First-rate
3 Perks (up)
4 Skater Hughes
5 Moving experience?
6 It makes waves
7 Bloodless
8 Recounted account
9 "The Professor: A Tale" novelist
10 Turned on
11 Clown's foot spec, maybe
12 Cable alternative
13 Wisconsin college town
14 Egyptian god of the universe
15 Mid-millennium year
16 Curse
17 Walled city near Madrid
18 Contents of lamps, maybe
19 Just beat
24 Played pat-a-cake
28 Blue
31 Secure
32 ___ mgr.
33 Actor Atkinson, player of Mr. Bean
34 "The Faerie Queene" character
35 Faerie land
36 One of TV's Ewings
37 Work units
38 Go wild
39 Opening-night celebration
44 Md. town near Baltimore
46 Reject
48 Fairy tale character
50 "O.K. by me"
51 TV journalist David

52 Minute
54 PC character system
55 Slate, e.g.
56 Put ___ on (go for at auction)
57 ___ directed
62 "It's about time!"
64 Bit of evidence
66 Frequent English football score
68 Late name in rap
69 Toy on a track
70 Online shoppers might use it
71 Unsuitable
72 Gen. ___ E. Lee
73 Old draft category
74 ___ Buena, Calif.
80 Came home dusty?
81 "Put it here," basically
82 Prefix with nitrile
84 Farm plant also called lucerne
86 To be over there?
87 Mother of Hades
89 Country name
90 Place at the start
91 Pin holder
93 .001 inch
98 "Ri-i-i-i-ight!"
100 City connected to the Sunshine Skyway Br.
101 Nickname of baseball's Leo Durocher
103 Hibachi chef's pride
105 1969 Hoffman role
106 Novelist Canin
107 Senior Tour golfer Calvin
108 Bright
109 Someone ___ problem
110 Dodge
115 Purim month
116 Denier's comment

by Joe DiPietro

117 Hot
119 Queen ___
120 Across the street from: Abbr.
121 N.F.L. ball carriers
122 "That's gross!"
123 School opening?
124 The Fighting Tigers, for short

ACROSS

1 Quakers or Shakers
5 Old film magnate Zukor
11 Bill collector?
15 Low-___
19 1940's–50's actress Raines
20 State bordered by the Colorado River
21 "It is my suggestion . . ."
22 Baseball star born in Santo Domingo
23 The marijuana dealer tried to . . .
25 Confidentially
27 Wasted
28 The veterinarian tried to . . .
30 Goes off
34 Title for a 50-Across
35 Clinton or Dole: Abbr.
36 Crosstown rival of the Bruins
39 Store outside a city?
41 "When I was young . . ."
44 What markers may represent
48 Actress Vardalos
49 Bette Midler and others
50 All-wise one
52 Bird feeder fill
53 Canasta plays
56 Budapest-born conductor
58 Flattens
60 Core of a PC
61 Radiant
62 Almost too much
64 Awestruck
66 Bottom line figure
69 The arsonist tried to . . .

71 Shades of red
73 Srs. may take it
74 Shakespearean term of address
75 The demolitions expert tried to . . .
79 Fuel
82 Use over, as tea leaves
83 Sonata finales
84 Tragic figure in Greek myth
85 Ending with rest or fest
86 Wheel on a spur
88 Slip by
91 All-purpose connector
92 Baklava ingredients
94 RCA competitor
96 Give a lift
98 It may get into deep water
99 Old-fashioned adventure
101 Food for thought?
102 Forward
104 Urban gridwork: Abbr.
105 42-Down users, for short
107 "Now I get it"
109 Baseball Hall-of-Famer Fox
111 The artist tried to . . .
117 Keyboard commands
121 National park in Colorado
122 The hair stylist tried to . . .
126 Angle (off)
127 Patient wife of Sir Geraint
128 Big bookseller
129 Somalia-born supermodel
130 Louver feature
131 Somewhat, to Salieri

132 Counters
133 Miss

DOWN

1 1999 war combatant
2 Ben-Gurion arrival
3 Sister in myth
4 Refinement
5 Bowl over
6 Cry made with a head-slap
7 What I will always be?
8 Prune
9 T.A.'s superior
10 Is averse to
11 Related to
12 "___ It Time" (1977 hit)
13 Plaster base
14 Instruments played by 3-Down
15 Denture parts
16 Tremendously
17 50–0, e.g.
18 In use
24 Verb origin of suis and sont
26 Scratched (out)
29 Taker of a bow?
31 Electric flux symbols
32 Modern subscription service
33 Zigzag
36 Frighten
37 War tactic
38 The telemarketer tried to . . .
40 One of the ones waiting in "Waiting for Godot"
42 Manuscript marks
43 Offshoot of punk rock
45 The rodeo rider tried to . . .
46 Crow's home

47 Gives an electric jolt
51 Supplement
54 Place marker
55 More stylish
57 Go where one's not welcome
59 Title girl in a 1979 #1 hit
63 Start of a full house declaration, maybe
65 Luke Skywalker's father
67 Paired up
68 "No dice"
70 Part of H.R.H.
72 Big name in women's tennis
75 Raise, with "up"
76 Song-and-dance special
77 "Unbelievable!"
78 Alternative education institute since the 1960's
80 W.W. II menace
81 Salon jobs
87 Ton of money
89 Broad
90 List ender
93 Popular late-night host
95 Home of the superhighways H1, H2 and H3
97 Actresses Fulton and Brennan
100 Ron Howard flick of 1999
103 "The Mod Squad" role
106 Wolf's prey
108 "And the ___ goes to . . ."
110 Web biz
111 Auto lic. bureaus
112 Part of a Hollywood archive
113 Fishing, perhaps

by Michael Ashley

114 ___ Laszlo skin
    care products
115 It helps prevent
    runs: Abbr.
116 Philosopher David
118 First name in
    newspaper humor

119 Vitamin bottle
    info, for short
120 Personal ID's
123 Keyboard key
124 China's
    Lao-___
125 In

5 E-TAIL

ACROSS

1. __ once
6. Blood-related
11. Spot on a horse
17. Not as nice
19. Oscar winner who made his film debut in "Me, Natalie," 1969
20. One who works on walls
21. Chant
22. Patch type
23. Go from worse to bad?
24. Female competitor in springboard competition?
26. Personal points of view
28. Pouchlike part
29. "House of Incest" author
30. Smidgen
31. Breathing space?
32. Cooped (up)
33. Decree
34. Where the smoke rises in a sty's chimney?
37. Sounds of impact
39. Cardboard pkg.
40. Suit to __
41. Wal-Mart rival
42. Normandy city
43. One of the Borgias
45. Film role played by both Vincent Price and Bill Cosby
47. They have quarters downtown
50. Newspaper no.
52. Without carrying charges?
55. Be-bopper
56. Start of the second quarter
59. It fits in a lock
61. On a high
62. Notable #4 with a stick
63. Lionize
64. Cashew family member
66. Contents of a diamond bag
67. Theater org.
68. Cross promotion?
69. Fellini's "La __"
70. Part of T.G.I.F.
71. Not quite right
72. Solo in space
73. Where Brahmans build their houses?
76. Hard to believe
78. Get moving
80. Addition symbol
82. Imp
86. Barbering area
87. Produce plays, say
89. Grate
91. Corrosive chemical, to a chemist
92. Protractor measurements
94. A choice between cinnabar and galena?
96. Rush
97. One and only
98. Fraternal letters
99. School since 1440
100. Puerto Rico hrs.
101. Mexican Mrs.
102. Baltimore's Enoch __ Free Library
104. Command to a gardener?
108. Maximilian, for one
110. Handle an F-15, e.g.
112. It may zip out
113. Chefs, at times
114. Gave birth on a farm
115. Sound setup
116. Underhanded, to put it nicely
117. President born in Charles City, Va.
118. It may be rolled up in a bun

DOWN

1. In the thick of
2. Early Russian Communist
3. Modern-day inhabitants of old Livonia
4. Apply chrism
5. Home of Ft. Donelson Natl. Battlefield
6. Author Ellison
7. Green subj.
8. Go for the gold
9. She rescued Odysseus
10. Topographic map feature
11. British title
12. Computer programs, briefly
13. In accordance with
14. What you'll find at a prison library?
15. Mediterranean region
16. Puts up
18. Make an impression
19. Devout acts
20. Toll road
25. Heavyweight champ Riddick
27. Lover of Aphrodite
31. Appointment book
32. Bargaining factor
33. TV overseer: Abbr.
35. Last word of Missouri's motto
36. Alarm
37. Show in theaters
38. Roughly measured (off)
40. Seed coat
44. 91-Across, e.g.
46. Wear away
47. Oil worker
48. What Shakespeare called "the little O"
49. Leave the straight and narrow
51. Student's selection
53. Kay Thompson character
54. Firmly secured
56. Kind of star
57. Song of joy
58. Miler's mistake?
60. Latin 101 word
64. Union members
65. Chalk or marble
67. Needs a doctor
69. Land's end?
71. Uproar
74. Word of honor
75. Leaves home?
77. Weapons collections
79. __ bonding
81. Stepped lively
83. Cheese type
84. Some solvents
85. Letters after a barrister's name
87. Shed tears
88. Reading to the unruly
90. Lined up
92. Stocks and such
93. Everyday
95. One who's lying
96. One of the original Not Ready for Prime Time Players
98. Components of some codes
102. Veep's boss

by Richard Silvestri

103 Calhoun of TV's
"The Texan"
104 Mental power
105 Overhang
106 "Norma Rae"
director
107 Vanity cases?
109 Greek vowel
111 "Oy __!"

THE SOUND OF MUSIC

When this puzzle is completed, the circled letters, read in order from left to right (column by column), will reveal the name of a Mystery Person.

ACROSS

1 Oliver Twist, e.g.
5 Little fight
10 Squawker
14 Advanced
18 Some chorus voices
19 Run ___ of
20 Father-and-son name in football coaching
21 Modeler's need
22 As a toddler visiting a farm, Mystery Person heard a pig squeal and . . .
26 Dorothy's transport to Oz
27 Aardwolf features
28 Puncture
29 "Comin' ___ the Rye"
31 Blunderbuss
32 Francis, e.g.
33 After a single hearing of a sacred piece in the Sistine Chapel, Mystery Person . . .
44 Continental money
45 One of Alcott's "Little Men"
46 Privy to
47 Concept embodying yin and yang
48 Founded: Abbr.
49 Jawbreaker?
51 Less loco
53 Mythical creature
55 Mystery Person once composed a piano piece that, to be performed correctly, required the . . .
59 One pole: Abbr.
60 Hematite component
61 Song from on high?
62 Med. specialty
63 Use for support
65 Massenet opera
66 Jewish sect
70 Back
71 Trowel wielder
72 Uncommon
73 Singer with a palindromic name
74 Mystery Person would sometimes compose symphonies . . .
80 Assailed
81 Revere
82 Well
83 Cars once advertised as "The Gold Standard of Value"
84 Loosen up, maybe
85 Org. with an acad. near Colo. Spr.
86 ___-mo
87 Country north of Tonga
88 Scholars believe that "A Musical Joke" by Mystery Person was . . .
95 Tribe with a state named after it
96 Part of l'année
97 Carrier whose name means "skyward"
98 G-rated
101 Whine-making?
105 Throw
110 Mystery Person once wrote a waltz in which the choice of measures played was determined . . .
113 Suffix with switch
114 12 on a cube
115 "Whole ___ Love" (1969 hit)
116 Gusto
117 Buzzed
118 Gregor Mendel research subject
119 Northernmost county of Massachusetts
120 Cuts off

DOWN

1 "Hold it!"
2 Fashion executive Gucci
3 Path of Caesar
4 Spender of markkas, once
5 Greeted informally
6 Pains
7 Vous, familiarly
8 January 27, 1756 (Mystery Person's birthdate), e.g.
9 Chicago district
10 Bloke
11 Deceit
12 "___ the heavy day!": "Othello"
13 Catch
14 Celebratory toast
15 Gusto
16 Buster?
17 Family
20 Working ___
23 "Soap" family
24 Part of Bush's "Axis of Evil"
25 ___-eyed
30 Favored
32 He outpolled H.H.H. in '68
33 Tots
34 Brown shade
35 Sandinista head
36 List heading
37 Swear words
38 Finished cleaning
39 Youngest Oscar winner in history
40 Poetic time of day
41 1931 Medicine Nobelist Warburg
42 Some stingers
43 Days of ___
49 1960's TV series set at Fort Courage
50 Exuberant casino cry
51 Ice treat
52 Simple arithmetic
53 U.S.-born grandchild of Japanese immigrants
54 Nay sayer
56 Act antsy
57 Reply to a captain
58 So very much
64 Simba's mate, in "The Lion King"
65 Furlough
66 Campus building
67 Long green
68 Away from the elements
69 Israeli intelligence group
71 Letter salutation
72 Five-carbon sugar
74 "Hold your horses!"
75 Locks
76 Furloughed
77 Use a surgical beam
78 "Road" picture destination
79 ___-American
85 One-eighty
86 Doctor's signboard
87 Canonized fifth-century pope
89 Edible clam
90 Minneapolis-based magazine
91 Old Dodges
92 Game stopper
93 Missouri feeder
94 Swab target

by George Barany and Michael Shteyman

98 "Good buddy"
99 Neighbor of Draco
100 ___ jacket
101 Fashion
102 "Eugene Onegin" girl
103 Pub quaffs
104 Gunks
106 Chisellike tool
107 It means nothing to the French
108 Golden State sch.
109 Understands
111 Agt.
112 Basketball stat.

ACROSS

1 Printing array
6 Eats
10 Not very bright
14 Eighty-six
18 Like tinned fish
19 Pointer's pronoun
20 Sommelier's prefix
21 Fixes holes, say
22 Important part of mayo
23 Site for stretchers
25 U-shaped river bend
26 Raise money using heavenly messengers?
29 "Romanian Rhapsodies" composer
30 Something may be taken in it
31 TNT alternative
32 ___-Seltzer
35 Defense grp. formed in Bogotá
36 Farm workers
40 Like a phobic longshoreman?
45 Suffix with ranch
46 Mid-seventh century date
47 Tip, in a way
48 Appetizer or entree
49 Geiger with a counter
50 Here, in Juárez
51 Cross inscription
52 Close encounter
54 Tax check
55 Portrait of an explorer with his timepiece?
58 One expressing the same thoughts
59 ___ Clemente
60 Kind of pass
61 Agcy. spawned by the Manhattan Project

62 Brewpub staple
63 F.D.R. program
64 Erasers?
66 Force a physician and a "Star Trek" officer into a plane?
71 "Stand and Deliver" star, 1987
72 Hydra, for one
73 Dash
74 Can. money
75 Sangre de Cristo Mountains resort
76 "It's Impossible" singer
77 Middle: Prefix
78 "Rocks"
79 Onetime Jeep mfr.
80 Result of wires down in a blizzard?
85 Prepare for firing
87 Cock and bull
88 Restrain
89 Québec's Côte-St.-___
90 Works together
93 Not fooled by
98 Brews in an elm instead of an oak?
102 The Wall Street Journal visual
104 Draft, basically
105 "Them" author
106 European capital, in song
107 ___ B'rith
108 Alternative to Breyers
109 Surgical tube
110 Blown away
111 Short pans
112 Secretary, for one
113 Wiesbaden's state

DOWN

1 Archives unit
2 Bagel flavor
3 Time being
4 Seconds on a watch
5 Toy racer
6 It's found on a lid
7 "Whoops!"
8 House gofers
9 Begin
10 Akin to Ken?
11 Check the total
12 Looped handles
13 Cap'n's underling
14 Accountant's concern
15 Planets, to poets
16 ___-Globe (common paperweight)
17 Jacksonville-to-Tampa dir.
21 Makes out
24 One of diamonds?
27 Guadalajara greeting
28 Deep ravine
33 Take illegally
34 Sew on sequins, say
36 Fancy-schmancy
37 Herd containment device?
38 1944 Pulitzer-winning journalist
39 Cosa ___
40 Ridicule of a foreign speaker?
41 It might be only a scratch
42 "The Wizard ___"
43 Cabinet dept.
44 Poker chip, e.g.
46 1989 Peace Prize recipient
49 "Say what?"
51 "The fix ___"
52 One may replace an oath

53 Fabled fliers
54 Super-duper
56 "Concord Sonata" composer
57 Encrusted
58 Sommer of "The Prize," 1963
59 Like clay pigeons
62 Buttonhole
65 Calendar pages: Abbr.
66 N.Y.C. cultural center
67 Like crazy
68 ___-à-porter (ready-to-wear)
69 Havens
70 Bank regulating org.
72 Work with feet
76 Pain in the neck
77 1960's TV show set on a farm
80 Lacking tact
81 Thingy
82 Author/screenwriter Ben
83 Chopped down
84 Valley Girl exclamation
86 Chose the window instead of the aisle?
90 Giving a line to
91 Book club name
92 Nobel, for one
94 Condition
95 Some Deco works
96 Cold temps
97 270° from norte
98 Stripped
99 Indian-born actor in "A Tiger Walks," 1964
100 They're caught at the shore
101 City on the Irtysh River
102 Univ. stat
103 Damp and chilly

by Rich Norris

CENTRAL INTELLIGENCE

The eight theme answers in this puzzle are clues to common words. When the grid has been filled, guess these missing words, whose letters correspond to the numbers shown. Every number from 1 to 25 is used exactly twice. When you're done, arrange the letters in order from 1 to 25 to reveal a bit of advice about getting ahead.

ACROSS

1 Father of Magnus the Good
5 "Uh-huh"
8 Pressure: Prefix
12 "There ___ goes . . ."
15 Mrs., in Madrid
18 Auto with a trident logo
20 Far from home, perhaps
22 "If only ___ listened . . ."
23 17-20-24-12-8-9-13
25 Latin 101 word
26 Suffix with violin
27 Radio advice-giver
28 "Outta here"
29 Quarrel
30 Corp. bigwig
31 5% of a C-note
32 Like many adherents to 55-Down
34 17-9-19-10-2-12-22-7
39 Loonies
40 Smells
41 Charlemagne's realm: Abbr.
42 English exclamation
43 Foot soldiers: Abbr.
44 Classic gas brand
45 Level
46 Baby kisser, maybe, in brief
47 Hard times
51 Fraction of a min.
53 Parisian article
54 "___ Baby" ("Hair" song)
55 Suffix of approximation
58 Seize

60 Like many sports interviews
62 Place for Us and Them
64 How bananas are bought
65 Breaking news
66 Mighty boss's opposite
67 River at Ghent
68 Actor Guinness
69 "Brat Farrar" mystery writer
70 Turning point?
72 Place on a TV?
74 Woman in a personal ad: Abbr.
77 Hang
79 Road ___
83 Good times
84 Code in which many Web pages are written: Abbr.
85 Suffix with Capri
86 Bit of Gothic architecture
87 Bite-the-bullet type
89 1-15-6-11-5-22
92 Followers of philosopher René
94 Make like
95 Youngster
96 Common conjunctions
97 Joker, e.g.
98 Roils
100 Lawyer: Abbr.
103 Original "King Kong" studio
104 25-14-2-19-7
107 Hosp. readout
108 Ethiopian river
109 Discharge into the air
110 Crown maker: Abbr.
111 Mormons: Abbr.
112 Restaurateur Toots
113 Like some ears
114 Leisure

DOWN

1 Popular hotel chain
2 Vientiane's land
3 Secy.
4 Whimsical
5 Peter who wrote "Puff the Magic Dragon"
6 Elec., e.g.
7 Garment worn like an apron
8 Ludlum protagonist
9 Reebok rival
10 Lawyer's thing
11 Something that gets copied
12 Fishing nets
13 ___ cow
14 Compass point
15 24-8-20-16-11
16 Observation
17 Prettifies
19 Places for clowns
21 Hip's opposite
24 Arrow's place
29 It started about 2½ million years ago
30 Storage medium
32 Japanese soup
33 It may leave its mark
34 The "vey" of "oy vey!"
35 They often have photos
36 Rebuffs
37 Red squirrel named for the sound it makes
38 Upholstery problem
45 4-23-14-10-3-18-25
47 How many proposals are delivered
48 15-21-13-1-18-6
49 British tar
50 Burpee product

52 Slow-cooked meal
53 Start of Superman's catchphrase
55 See 32-Across
56 Reach the top of
57 4-23-16-21-5-3
59 Vortex
61 "___ 'clock scholar"
63 New members
71 Weave
73 Some time ago
74 Subs
75 One rationale for the 2003 invasion of Iraq: Abbr.
76 "Alice" waitress
77 Baked entree
78 Kind of cable for a computer
80 Stomach muscles, for short
81 Day-___
82 Poetic time of day
84 Car known for its storage space
86 Staples of annual reports
87 One way to run
88 Bloody drunk
89 Break
90 "Our ___ . . ."
91 Connect, in a way
93 Say "tsk" to
98 Historic Normandy town
99 California's ___ Valley
100 Three oceans touch it
101 Ring wins, briefly
102 Actress Daly
104 Two-bagger: Abbr.
105 Biomed. group
106 Lao-___

by Eric Berlin

LADIES' FINISHING SCHOOL

ACROSS

1 Staff
5 Test group?
10 La Scala cheer
15 Germ jelly
19 "I smell ___!"
20 Financial mogul Carl
21 Indian bread
22 Plain and simple
23 Nostalgic person's utterance
24 Why the convent's head couldn't find information on the nun?
27 Basilica of San Francesco site
29 "Er-r . . ."
30 First step in addicts' treatment
31 Kind of school
32 Merged coastal access?
36 Gives more than a licking?
38 Social sort
39 Wall protector
40 Victory: Ger.
42 Staple of Italian cuisine
44 Unilever?
47 Mexican Mrs.
49 Reason for school cancellation
50 "Ouch!"
51 Canadian Club and others
52 Henhouse sounds
54 Iceland is part of it: Abbr.
57 Pops
60 Accepts oppression no longer
63 Reason to lube a tube?
69 Certain canine
71 Tape, for short
72 Surrender

73 Artist's board nearby?
76 Circular
77 Cast
78 Word said with a tip o' the hat
80 Stomach and intestine, e.g.
81 View from the Gulf of Catania
85 Speaker of the line "Help me, Obi-Wan Kenobi; you're my only hope"
87 Spanish flower
90 French connections?
91 Cabaret singer in the style of an old pope?
97 Square things
98 "Cut it out!"
99 "___ take arms against a sea of troubles": "Hamlet"
100 Knock over
103 Second-stringer
104 Top knot?
107 Mil. address
108 Washersful
112 Accelerate, for short
113 Lesser hit locations
114 Rubber mania?
119 Stakes
120 Moscato d'___ (Italian wine)
121 Lion's home, to Hercules
122 Dander
123 "Waiting for the Robert ___"
124 Sound before "Your fly's open"
125 Dagwood and Blondie's dog
126 ___ Foods, Fortune 500 company
127 Cat with tufted ears

DOWN

1 Winter melon
2 Up
3 Bothers
4 Standard of living?
5 They're easy to park
6 "Baudolino" author
7 Time out?
8 Fuchsia, e.g.
9 Belief of many Africans
10 Cold comment
11 Felt sorry about
12 Area with a curved wall
13 Flak jacket, e.g.
14 Like some exercises
15 Cinemax competitor, for short
16 Class of planes?
17 One in handcuffs
18 Funny Foxx
25 "___ vincit amor"
26 Have a place in the world
28 Big Apple park
33 It takes the cake
34 Quark-plus-antiquark particle
35 Counting-out starter
37 See the sights
41 Kind of room
42 Unfair treatment
43 Surgeons' sites, briefly
44 Philip Seymour Hoffman title role
45 Substitute
46 Pays, as a bill
47 "Bye"
48 Make merry
52 Princeton Review or Kaplan study
53 Exertion aversion

55 Modern recording option
56 It's addictive
58 ". . . so long ___ both shall live"
59 Crouch
61 Carry
62 Enter quietly
64 "So Big" author Ferber
65 In chains
66 Acclaim
67 Smart guys?
68 Etta of old comics
70 "___ heart" ("Be kind")
74 Power to control
75 Put in stitches
79 Tool along
81 Ingredient in a flip
82 Poach
83 Bases from which profits are figured
84 Golden or teen follower
86 Isn't naturally
88 Novi Sad resident
89 High-speed roadway
92 Seed-to-be
93 Get well fast
94 Time of operation
95 "Bon ___!"
96 Propagates
100 In many places
101 50 to two
102 Setting for many Thomas Hardy novels
105 Part of EGBDF
106 Defamation
107 "Do I need to draw you ___?"
109 Well off the coast
110 Half: Prefix
111 "___ Gotta Have It"
115 Do nothing
116 "Way to go!"
117 Bradbury's "___ for Rocket"
118 Prefix with morphic

by Manny Nosowsky

ACROSS

1 Small turnover
7 Careless
15 Gut feeling?
20 Preener's partner
21 Color similar to turquoise
22 Shades
23 "Now!"
25 Make into law
26 Stephen of "Breakfast on Pluto"
27 Thought some more about
28 Gas company known for its toy trucks
30 Gas company known for its tiger slogan
31 Tiny __
32 Ceremonial burner
33 Gob
34 Crescent point
36 "A Passage to India" woman
38 Bawdy
40 One way to chop peppers
42 For one
45 Certain turtle
48 One with a thin skin?
50 "I'm not impressed"
53 Jacket style
54 "Make __ away"
55 Vice
56 Cry of distress
60 What the connected may have
62 The D.A. probably took it once
63 Dear ones
65 Graph component
66 Pension recipient
68 Afternoon hour in Italy
69 Puts on a coat
71 Bother
72 Cartoon collectible
75 Worked up
77 It may be met or filled
78 2002 Olympics venue
80 Musical opening
82 Gran Canaria, for one
83 Support
85 Blood designation, for short
86 Old sports org. featuring the Minnesota Kicks
87 Florida Rep. __ Hastings
89 Theseus abandoned her
91 Fugard's "A Lesson From __"
93 Not just lean
96 Shelters
97 "Yeah, right"
99 Angelo's instrument
100 Trac II alternatives
104 Off-white
105 It has nine figures: Abbr.
107 Markets of yore
111 Greeting of yore
112 Carl Sagan's subj.
114 Popular insulator
116 Dyemaking material
117 Raiders' org.
118 Old war story
120 Debt cause
123 Describes
124 "Just a little bite?"
125 Crumbly Italian cheese
126 Symbol of strength
127 Certain math sign
128 Staggered

DOWN

1 Ancient military hub
2 Work recounting Dido's suicide
3 Butterfly, e.g.
4 An omega stands for it
5 Specialty of Russian painter Aivazovsky
6 A joint that's hopping?
7 Short cuts
8 Leaves something behind
9 Loser
10 __ Station
11 Under the name of, as a co.
12 Part of many stars' names
13 A-one, or one living in 1-A, perhaps
14 Attention getters
15 Had a beef?
16 Declined
17 Instantly
18 P.I.'s
19 Concerning
24 Poetic time of day
29 Genetics, e.g.: Abbr.
33 Use keys
35 Afternoon hour in Italy
37 Dish out the beans?
39 Punishes, in a way
40 Healthful dessert
41 Eastern discipline
43 Alliance created in 1948: Abbr.
44 Not take risks
46 Ikhnaton, for one
47 Automaker Maserati
49 "Hardly"
50 Swig
51 Actor Novello
52 "Be a little more patient"
57 & 58 Common cake ingredient
59 Fire starter?
61 Nothing that plays a prominent role in this puzzle
64 Resting place
67 Ad salesman, informally
70 "__ was saying . . ."
71 March word
73 Knotted up
74 Ticket choice
76 Character on "Frasier"
77 Quite odd
79 Not just poke fun at
80 Santa in California
81 Cartel city
84 "__ Day" (1993 rap hit)
88 Dash
90 Just partly
92 It's 94-Down for south
94 See 92-Down
95 The Arrow constellation
98 Coke's partner
101 Michelin offering
102 Get payback for
103 Neptune, e.g.
105 Display
106 Vaults
108 Football Hall-of-Famer Merlin
109 Splitting image?
110 Something lent or bent, in a phrase
112 Hurts

by Joe DiPietro

113 Opening
115 Object of worship
116 Room to swing ___
119 Cable alternative
121 Letters within the theme entries that are, literally, next to nothing
122 Quit working

11 WRITING LESSON

ACROSS

1 Constitution
8 "___ 70's Show"
12 Operating
17 "How dare they?!"
18 Darn it
19 Uranium-exporting country
20 Infinitives . . . it's ___
23 Word we share
24 Daily Planet worker
25 Reach
26 Beverage served with le dessert
27 More, in music
29 Big fish, to a fisherman
31 Paleontologist's discovery
32 Frat party detritus
34 The passive voice ___
38 Agcy. once involved with fallout shelters
40 Carrier with HQ in Tokyo
41 Gift on "The Bachelor"
42 N.F.L. linemen: Abbr.
43 Ambiguity ___
49 Trip planning org.
51 Pub order, maybe
52 Rhetorical questions . . . ___
57 Fantastic
58 Author's desire
59 Pope after John X
60 Org. that rates members of Cong.
61 C-worthy
64 Cold capital
66 Latin foot
67 Meshlike
70 ___ Life ("Porgy and Bess" character)
74 1997 title role for Demi Moore
77 Subject-verb agreement ___
79 One in the fast lane?
81 Deface
82 Contractions ___
84 Show whose theme song is "Who Are You"
86 Shortstop Chacon of the 1962 Mets
88 Malodourous room?
89 84-Across airer
90 Prepositions are not good ___
97 Sad poets
98 Creator of "All in the Family"
99 Mule alternative
103 Outworn
104 Scratch (out)
105 Not much
106 Daydreaming, say
108 Word said with a salute
109 Exaggeration is among the ___
114 Put back at zero
115 Ticked
116 Toughened
117 Macho types
118 Proceed slowly
119 Reporter's purchase

DOWN

1 Vacuuming, e.g.
2 Setter
3 Perspectives
4 Comeback
5 Adviser of Capt. Picard on "Star Trek: T.N.G."
6 When to call, in some ads
7 M.L.K. Jr., e.g.
8 Seat of power
9 Inexpensive place to stay
10 Brand in a can
11 Bus. card info
12 Ahead
13 Bistro, informally
14 "I don't like it"
15 Overlook, as someone's weaknesses
16 Fine furs
17 Steadfast
20 Bowl-shaped pan
21 They may be stroked
22 Receipt listings
28 Mt. Rushmore State sch.
30 Apparel company Evan-___
31 Round end?
32 Part of a talk show staff
33 Work for a museum
35 Spanish eyes
36 Restaurant waiting areas
37 Lecture badly
38 In pieces
39 Abu Dhabi, e.g.
43 Creature in a Tennessee Williams title
44 Cellular stuff
45 Elusive swimmers
46 Member of the flock
47 Doo-wop syllable
48 Piece of property
50 Communication for the deaf: Abbr.
53 Night school subj.
54 Not hoof it, perhaps
55 Planes
56 Lowest state?
58 Tree trauma
62 Jardin zoológico attraction
63 Trainers treat them
65 Meanie
68 Comic's asset
69 Singer Sumac
71 "The Facts of Life" actress
72 Spike TV, formerly
73 Cousin ___ of "The Addams Family"
75 Collection agcy.
76 Heifetz heard at Carnegie Hall
78 Media handouts
79 Big suits
80 "Don't have ___!"
83 Pgh. Pirate, e.g.
84 Nabs
85 Tiny start
87 Wings hit "___ In"
90 Formula One driver Fabi
91 Lost on purpose
92 What a picador pokes
93 Got warm
94 Bad boyfriends
95 "Perhaps"
96 Do some fancy footwork
100 Counterfeited
101 Spotted
102 Hi-___
105 What a soldier shouldn't be
106 "___ Angel" (Mae West movie)
107 Force
110 Baton Rouge sch.
111 Medium ability?
112 Whip
113 ___ king

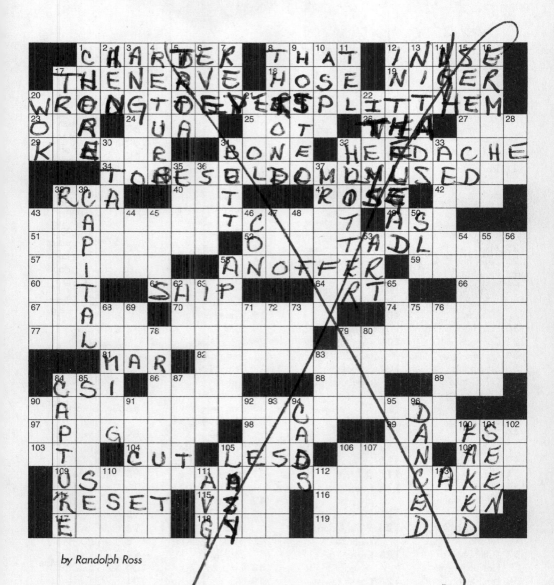

by Randolph Ross

ACROSS

1 Country that won its first Olympic medal in 2004
8 1959 Ricky Nelson hit
15 Summons
20 Nay sayers
21 Tennis star Zvereva
22 Essence
23 Shady accountant's April 15 work?
25 Allied (with)
26 Saxophonist Al
27 Racer Al
28 Director of "Chicago" and "Dancin'"
30 Hula hoop
31 Connects with
34 Chinese "way"
36 Smash hits
38 G.R.E. takers
39 Caroler's reward?
44 Kind of D.A.
45 Rolodex no.
46 Pad site
47 Handy-andies
49 Unsmiling
51 Slip in a pot
53 1940's–50's All-Star Johnny
55 Pilot announcements, for short
57 "Little Shop of Horrors" dentist
58 Persistent photographers?
61 Sorority letters
63 Main entrances?
65 Wisecracker
66 Analyze
68 Turkey part
69 Mischief makers
73 Deep Throat, e.g.
74 Owls
76 Vandal
77 Comparatively small
79 Late 80's sitcom
80 Unfolding view for a hapless hang glider?
84 Summer cooler
85 Summer coolers
87 Art containing 4-Down
88 Elvis or Madonna
89 Honeyed drink
90 Tens, e.g.
92 Cry of eagerness
94 Et ___ (following)
95 Asunción assent
97 "Faucet drips ahead"?
101 Nutrition info, for short
104 Graffitist's addition to a face
106 Org. that drafts guards
107 School zone requirement
109 Goals in 106-Across, quickly
110 "Cool!"
113 Runner
116 Served past
117 Dull
119 Roller coaster inventor?
123 Top guns
124 Waist reducer, perhaps
125 Current contraption
126 Comic Lewis
127 Sits atop
128 Fancy parties

DOWN

1 Puts out
2 "La Loge" artist
3 Feels irritated
4 Kids' TV staples
5 Like some sleep, for short
6 ". . . ___ he drove out of sight"
7 Not dull
8 "Need You Tonight" group, 1987
9 Weight allowance
10 Catch off-guard
11 Ontario, par exemple
12 Request
13 Dutch filmmaker ___ van Gogh
14 Packs away
15 Old Toyota
16 Jackie's "O"
17 Concern for Rev. Falwell?
18 Gulf State V.I.P.'s
19 Tormentor
24 Soon
29 Sports venue seen from the Grand Central Parkway
32 Twosome
33 King's org.
35 Hairy Halloween costume
37 Fountain order
40 30's migrant
41 M.D.'s who may cure snoring
42 "Got it"
43 Like city land, usually
45 Soldier's helmet, slangily
48 Instruction unit
49 Nutritious nosh
50 Where the ice skater fell?
51 "Evita" narrator
52 English pianist who was made a dame
54 Works of Michelangelo
56 Follow
57 Hold 'em variation
58 Mild cigar
59 Part of the 1992 Olympic Dream Team
60 Knolls
62 Metric measure
64 ". . . and I mean it!"
67 1968 hit with the lyric "I like the way you walk, I like the way you talk"
70 Dr. ___
71 Shoos
72 W.W. II site
75 Projecting part at the foot of a wall
78 Dark time in poetry
81 City south of the Salt River
82 Stylish gown
83 Yearn
86 Get to work on Time?
89 29-Down team
91 One way to turn
93 Rural valleys
94 Liverpool-to-Plymouth dir.
95 Military V.I.P.
96 Halogen salt
98 Comic Don
99 Staff leader
100 Main lines
101 Say poetry, say
102 Political pundit Myers
103 Puff ___ (Old World menaces)
105 Other side
108 Kitchen implement
111 Way off
112 Yarn
114 Chocolaty treat

by Ashish Madhukar Vengsarkar

115 No-no on office computers
118 Salt
120 Plenty steamed, with "up"
121 Wellness grp.
122 Recording giant

ACROSS

1 Professional bouncers' org.
5 "Chicago" star, 2002
9 Ne plus ultra
13 Significance
19 Omelette ingredient
20 Lena of "Havana"
21 Gymnast's worry
22 Charlotte ___, Virgin Islands
23 Rabbit cliques?
26 "Phèdre" playwright
27 Caffeine-free drink
28 Foreign title of respect
29 Poker prize
30 Elect
31 "The Godfather" actor
33 Word before "dear" or "sir"
35 Parenting author Eda
37 Training with building strips?
40 Ex followers
44 Desktop feature
46 "Scram!"
47 Prairies
48 ___-kiri
49 Old troupe member
52 Dr.'s order?
53 Autobiographer of "Speak, Memory," 1951
55 Did lunch, say
56 Extreme admirer of a Poe poem?
60 "Oh, really?"
61 Way to address a sweetheart
63 Saturn model
64 Saturn model
65 More fitting
66 Closet feature

69 Spacecraft that began orbiting Saturn in 2004
71 "This time ___ me"
74 Basis of illegal discrimination
75 Disperse, with "out"
76 Driving a nail obliquely
80 1953 film or the last word spoken in it
81 Pics featured at Dollywood?
85 "." follower
86 Certain NASA craft
88 According to
89 Pharmaceutical plant
91 1947 romantic comedy "The Egg ___"
92 Times up
95 National League city: Abbr.
96 Rug source
97 Imbroglio
98 Fees for removing dead animals?
102 Not caring anymore
104 Site for 125-Across, with "the"
105 Sleep: Prefix
106 Money may be held in this
109 Prefix with system
111 Speed
113 He was cast into the lion's den by Nebuchadnezzar
117 Bowls
118 Permit from the Nuclear Regulatory Commission?
121 Very much
122 Within: Prefix

123 Gunfight time, maybe
124 Concessions
125 Performances at 104-Across
126 Saxophone, e.g.
127 Bygone fliers
128 Graceful fliers

DOWN

1 Blows away
2 Tide type
3 Vice president under Jefferson
4 Just over 6% of U.S. immigrants nowadays
5 Attacked
6 Trickster
7 Shore indentations
8 Make secret
9 "___ was saying . . ."
10 Walking sound
11 Olympus competitor
12 Brian who managed the Beatles
13 Italian noblewoman
14 Creighton University site
15 Cry of joy in Georgia?
16 Bush and Kerry, once
17 Small square
18 Adolescent
24 Conseil d'___
25 Class
32 Israeli desert
34 Author Rushdie
36 Wall fixtures
37 Filleted
38 West ___ virus
39 Ones sharing a crest
41 Siberian people
42 Weaken
43 Relish
44 Prayer leader
45 Washington or Madison

50 Apprentice
51 "Bloody"
52 One way to have gone
54 Close
57 Warmer and sunnier
58 Several czars
59 Part of the E.U.: Abbr.
62 Commotion at an English school?
67 Tupac, for one
68 Turkish title
69 Marriage site in a Veronese painting
70 "Sock ___ me!"
71 Submission, literally
72 Feudal aristocrat
73 Bygone Las Vegas hotel
75 ___ Prison, setting for the 1979 film "Jericho Mile"
77 Ones who take the cake?
78 "A Doll's House" wife
79 Fed
82 Comical Jacques
83 "Hell ___ no fury . . ."
84 Southwestern crocks
87 Harness tracks
90 Like some waltzes
93 Intelligence officer, at times
94 Classy French theater
95 Behavior
99 ___ Corp., former name for Royal Crown Cola
100 "The Thinker" and "The Kiss," e.g.
101 Auto financing co.
103 "There!"
106 Old station name
107 Period in English literature

by Daniel C. Bryant

108 Kind of package
110 Bone: Prefix
112 Slaughter in Cooperstown
114 "___ out?"
115 ___ Zone
116 Minus
119 It has roots
120 Builder's purchase

ACROSS

1 Item on a chain
7 Deep water
14 Microwaveable lunch sandwich
18 3½ million square mile expanse
19 Lapse
20 Antarctica's Prince ___ Coast
21 Diethyl ether, to butanol
22 Medium, maybe
23 Bone: Prefix
24 Whizzes (by)
25 "Go!"
26 Prepare, as leftovers
28 Authorize
30 Renaissance family name
31 Playground retort
32 ___ given
34 1998 British Petroleum acquisition
36 It has frozen assets
42 Constellation next to Telescopium
43 1969 N.H.L. M.V.P., familiarly
47 Tree with pods
48 Undo, as binder rings
51 Hua's predecessor as Chinese premier
52 Many
54 Starting
55 Recliner feature
57 Brand X
59 Hit, in Variety slang
61 Not far from
62 Bit of editing
64 Big name in construction
66 One making calls
67 Powerful handheld electronic devices
70 Game played on a 49-Down
72 Avalanche victim's salvation
73 Spectra maker
74 Radiate
75 Popular candy since the 1780's
77 Like King Gyanendra
79 "Quién ___?"
81 "Aha"
85 Place to see a camel
87 Scandal
89 Must
90 Spore producer
91 Aunt Chloe's husband, in literature
94 Ethelbert who composed "Mighty Lak' a Rose"
95 Classic brand whose symbol is a tiger
96 "___ bad"
97 Kitchen fixture
99 "Understand?"
101 O's predecessors
102 Simple itinerary destination
106 Interstate sign
109 Old 280Z's and 280ZX's
115 Covered
116 Temperatures
118 Capital that's the home of Lenin Park
119 Distant
120 Lecture
122 Blasted, with "at"
123 See 103-Down
124 Exposed to oxygen
125 Object in le ciel
126 Subtle thieves
127 Big fish, say
128 Lint collector?

DOWN

1 Miniature
2 Had a base in baseball
3 "What ___ !"
4 1960's singer Terrell
5 Procter & Gamble brand
6 Laugh sound
7 Vintner's prefix
8 Turn out
9 Some Art Deco works
10 Tokyo airport
11 Road atlas part
12 Port. is part of it
13 Language that favors "sedans" to "saloons"
14 To-do
15 Half of a 1930's vaudeville duo
16 Byes
17 Presidential prerogative
25 Mojave Desert vista
27 Green: Prefix
29 Family pooch
33 Actress Karina who played Scheherazade
35 City SSW of Moscow
36 Heroin, slangily
37 Anemic-looking
38 Coll. major
39 Judges
40 Longtime Lone Ranger player
41 Old section in Algiers
43 Prophet who led Jews back to Jerusalem
44 L.P.G.A. star ___ Turner
45 Campaign need
46 Like some expenses
49 Image this puzzle grid is supposed to suggest
50 Mistaken
53 Quick timeout
56 Prefix with centric
58 Early second-century year
60 Lacking sparkle
63 Cpls.' superiors
65 Morlocks' prey in "The Time Machine"
67 Handy-dandy tool
68 Shares
69 Tricks
71 Farm cries
72 Complimentary closing
74 Roth who directed the 2005 horror flick "Hostel"
76 Silas ___, emissary of the Continental Congress to France
78 River to the Ligurian Sea
80 Half of a noted 1955 merger: Abbr.
82 River that flows by the Hermitage
83 Suffix with neur-
84 Overstudious sort
86 Rope expert's favorite radio station?
88 Poet who wrote "To err is human . . ."
92 Do
93 Smart set?
98 Org. for Va., but not Md.
99 Sporty Pontiac

by Michael Shteyman

100 Kicker's aid
102 "Fingersmith"
103 With 123-Across, pleading, perhaps
104 Lazybones
105 Lymphatic system parts
107 Like quaking aspen leaves
108 Stop
110 Angle denoter, in math
111 Permanent site?
112 Pitch-black
113 Seasonal music
114 Start of 67-Across or end of 72-Across, literally
117 Some roulette bets
121 Low mark
122 Rural affirmative

ACROSS

1 Military academy freshman
6 Cowbell sound
11 Fingerboard ridge
15 Weaken
18 "___ Gets Drafted" (1942 Disney cartoon)
20 Much-climbed Alpine peak
21 Actor Jared
22 Hamas rival grp.
23 California, compared to Kansas?
25 Kiss
27 Call's companion
28 ___ Ark
29 ___ polloi
30 Jeweler's unit
31 Tweak
33 Silk undies, compared to cotton undies?
37 White-collar worker?
39 Dance to 1920's–40's jazz
40 Big time
41 "We've been ___!"
42 1990's sitcom based on the British series "One Foot in the Grave"
45 Having seniority
47 Claim valuables
51 Strong suit
52 A waistcoat worn in summer, compared to one worn in winter?
54 In addition
56 Subject in religion class
58 Hero of Tom Clancy novels
59 Jai alai basket
60 Some H.S. math
61 Clinton cabinet member Hazel
63 Dolly of Dollywood
64 Naval base?
65 A one-milligram tablet, compared to a five-milligram tablet?
70 Employee of M
71 Chevrolet sedan
73 Land created by C. S. Lewis
74 "QB VII" novelist
75 Froth
76 Small indentation
80 Go ___ length
81 Formal vote
82 Potatoes and cucumbers, compared to apples and eggplants?
85 Rows on a calendar page
87 Actor Omar of TV's "House"
88 Hang it up
89 1996 Olympic gymnast Strug
90 Spoon-___
93 ___-pitch
94 Tribe of the Amistad slaves
96 Intense, as a gaze
98 Dog show winners, compared to dog show also-rans?
105 Africa's largest country
106 Benefit
107 Wise actions
108 Get the better of
110 Novelist Jaffe
111 Measureless
113 SpongeBob SquarePants's pants, compared to Humpty Dumpty's?
116 Dead heat
117 Stylist's creation
118 Cliff's edge
119 Pass on
120 Airport checkpoint needs
121 Palindromic girl's name
122 Napster downloads
123 Some Southwest scenery

DOWN

1 Pseudonym of musician Peter Schickele
2 Gossipy Parsons
3 Passed
4 Televangelist paroled in 1993
5 Priest in 1 Samuel
6 French film award
7 How ballerinas dance
8 Tennis star with a shaved head
9 Human cannonball's destination
10 Test for M.A. seekers
11 Elevator stop
12 Is an integral part of
13 "You know the rest" abbr.
14 Bird on a Kellogg's Froot Loops box
15 Slash on a scorepad
16 Here comes the bride
17 They're "born, not made," according to an old saying
19 TV room
24 Pistol, slangily
26 Scientist's formulation
29 Prime
32 Puerto ___
34 Winter blanket
35 Do-nothing
36 Fixed course
38 Spanish city where Seneca was born
43 Pricey vodka, for short
44 Produce
46 H, in Hellas
47 Goes on a spending spree
48 Fix up
49 Where kroons are spent
50 Doesn't take a hit
51 Low-aimed headlights
52 Bollywood film costume
53 Camcorder brand
54 Fabricate
55 Crankcase device
57 One sitting on the porch
60 Pyramus's lover, in myth
62 Hunger
63 Actors or athletes
66 "Darn!"
67 Tennis club teacher
68 Stupefied
69 Protective covering
72 Hawaiian band?
76 Fate
77 Natl. Adopt-a-Dog Mo.
78 Hampers
79 "M*A*S*H" setting
83 ___ Stanley Gardner
84 Colonial ___ (insurance firm)
86 Litter contents
89 Banshee sound
90 Zoot suit hats
91 Hyundai model

by Patrick Berry

92 Rulers who inherit their power
93 Flint is a form of it
95 Toxic compound found in cigarette smoke
97 "When Paris sneezes, ___ catches cold"
98 Leafless plants
99 Like planetary orbits
100 Attorney's workload
101 Kipling novel about an orphan boy
102 Musical syllables
103 Vichyssoise vegetables
104 California's Big ___
109 Abbr. on a boiler's gauge
112 Yardbird
113 Air rifle ammo
114 It's sought by conquistadores
115 "That's curious . . ."

ACROSS

1 Mistress of the spirit world?
8 Was an Orly arrival?
14 "The Old Man and the Sea" catch
20 Handles differently?
21 Historic Honolulu palace
22 Beethoven symphony
23 Writer Fleming as a two-year-old?
25 Ibsen's "Hedda ___"
26 Ring count
27 Sweet 16 org.
28 Yevtushenko poem
29 Shark pools?
30 J.F.K. advisory
32 Playground retort
34 Scrubbed
35 Puzzling
36 Scotland?
41 Sprinkling
42 Talk like a baby
43 "Winnie-the-Pooh" baby
44 Estrous
46 Picture on a $5,000 bill
50 Country with a pentagonal flag
54 View
57 Onetime capital of India
58 One lacking bucks?
61 Austin of TV's "Knots Landing"
62 Actress Meyers
63 Game sometimes called "bucking the tiger"
64 French entree
65 Unwelcome twist
67 Far from loaded
69 Burdensome bird
73 Prepares for a Masters?
74 Lose track?
76 It may need a big jacket
77 Cartoonist Addams
79 Wasted
80 Frost lines
81 Bar owner's job on "The Simpsons"?
85 Prefix with -gon
86 Catalan is its official language
88 Fast ___ Felson, real-life hustler portrayed in "The Hustler"
89 Mister
91 Release
93 With 107-Down, Westerner with an oxymoronic-sounding name buried on Boot Hill
95 Forever and a day
96 Doctor's bag?
98 Guillotine?
103 Heads overseas?
106 Mine transport
108 Flambé
109 Take the course
110 ___ Tzu (dog)
111 Well-armed predator?
114 You can be in it and out of it at the same time
116 Indo-Iranian language
119 John Glenn, e.g.
120 Warning on court testimony?
122 "Star Trek: T.N.G." engineer
123 It was named for the infant Jesus
124 Playroom threat
125 One of the Gallo brothers
126 Actress who starred in two Hitchcock films
127 Emergency situation

DOWN

1 Bach bit
2 Listed
3 The Muses, e.g.
4 40, 60, 75 or 100, commonly
5 Chat room initialism
6 Stocking stuffers
7 Treasure
8 Oregon's state tree
9 Desolate
10 Provoke
11 Part of the Illinois/Indiana border
12 Arriving home after curfew
13 "When Schweine fly!"
14 Prefix with millions
15 ___-American
16 Early bird
17 Comedian Tomlin as a bowler?
18 The Pleistocene Epoch, familiarly
19 Shoe specification
24 Door sign
28 Ape's home
31 "One never knows, ___?": Fats Waller
33 Robe fastener
36 Jolly sounds
37 Alley Oop's girlfriend
38 Grendel and Beowulf
39 W. C. Fields affirmative
40 Special request at a shoe store
42 9/11 Commission subj.
45 Nolan Ryan, for most of the 80's
46 The folks
47 Mutually approve
48 Course for a Maytag repairman?
49 Mrs. James Joyce
51 Foreshadow
52 Marc Antony's love
53 Jared of "Panic Room"
55 Opening
56 Sheriff's badge in the Old West
59 Nick name?
60 Hustler's hangout?
63 Just so you know
66 Some film ratings
68 Devoted friend of Greek legend
70 Shade of white
71 In the heart of
72 The Beatles' "___ Leaving Home"
75 Old global positioning system
78 Destination in the movie "Dumb and Dumber"
82 Bearcats
83 Coolidge Dam river
84 Rodents, playfully
85 Judo ranking
87 Baseball scorecard letters
90 Certain buck
92 Distinction, slangily
94 Tenuous
96 Second fiddle
97 Bow pro
99 Cartoonist Hollander

by Bob Klahn

100 Pulverized
101 Moss Hart's "Act One," e.g.
102 Biased writing?
103 Kvetch
104 There's simply no end to it
105 Ozone layer, for one
107 See 93-Across
110 Clobbered
112 Launch sites . . . or crash sites
113 Complex part?
115 Tyler who wrote "Breathing Lessons"
117 Storage space
118 Didn't break
120 Mumbled assent
121 Chaney Sr. or Jr.

ACROSS

1 Cab Calloway catchphrase
7 Another time
14 Deep-sea diver's worry
22 Tiger cat
23 Not your normal imports
24 After-tax investment choices
25 Elevators . . .
27 Deferential
28 Bar in court
29 Sounds at doctors' checkups
30 Reduced by
32 Owner of the History Channel
33 Dumb bunny
35 Diet centers . . .
40 N.Y.U., e.g.
43 Harbor tower
44 ___ test, given to newborn babies
45 Plains tribe
46 Anvils . . .
49 Mice and men, e.g.
54 Pop singer Lavigne
55 Media of exchange
57 Stable baby
59 Cut for a column
60 Settle, for one
61 ___ example
63 Short dash
65 Bride, in Bari
66 Caterpillars . . .
70 Guillotines . . .
72 Paris-to-Lyon dir.
73 Study grant named for a senator
74 Outburst from Homer
76 Ottoman governor
77 Overdoes it
78 Very cool, in 50's slang, with "the"
79 Patio grills . . .
81 Two caliphs
82 Like Sartre's "No Exit"
85 Part of the W. Coast
86 Peace, to Pedro
87 Spanish snack
88 Dernier ___
91 Pace cars . . .
94 Nails . . .
97 Brewery fixtures
98 Make like crazy
100 Department that is home to the Parc Astérix amusement park
101 ___ speak
102 Hilarity
103 Embargoes
104 "Ecce homo" utterer
107 Computer acronym
108 Chews out
110 Real estate developers . . .
113 Minotaur's home
116 Utah lilies
117 NASA vehicle
118 Saint, in Portuguese
119 Cattle . . .
124 "La classe de ___" (Degas work)
126 Make disappear
127 Folk tales
128 Singer Anderson of Jethro Tull
129 Ford competitor, although not in autos
133 Hitchcock specialty
136 Freight trains . . .
141 Boarding school crowd
142 First name in popcorn
143 Typical downtown sign
144 Rasta's messiah
145 African pests
146 Runners' aids

DOWN

1 Julia ___, first woman elected to the American Academy of Arts and Letters
2 Cold treats
3 Ding
4 John of pop
5 Place to wear a gown
6 Polo Grounds slugger
7 Longtime Vermont senator
8 ___ of Evil
9 Dress (up)
10 Biblical verb ending
11 Slowing, in music: Abbr.
12 Visual
13 Barbers brush them
14 "To your health!"
15 Burgle
16 Monet's "Vétheuil en ___"
17 Alternative to reflexology
18 Rough rug fiber
19 Heavens: Prefix
20 Shoemakers' strips
21 Opera singer Simon ___
26 A to Z, e.g.
31 ___-mo
34 Center
35 Self-serving slant
36 Lambs: Latin
37 Conducts
38 Cheer at Gillette Stadium
39 It may be raised at a party
40 Equilibrium
41 Inquisition targets
42 "Dulce et decorum est pro patria mori" writer
44 Make up (for)
47 Friends and neighbors
48 Menotti opera character
50 Prints
51 Pass
52 Stocking material
53 Collar inserts
56 Tanning lotion letters
57 Seafood entree
58 "Members ___"
61 Carol starter
62 Highway department supply
64 Nixon friend Bebe
65 Dr. Seuss's green eggs and ham offerer
67 Times to remember
68 Nutrition author Davis
69 Palme ___ (Cannes award)
71 "S.O.S.!"
75 With it, once
78 Fisher-Price's owner
79 Goes on strike, informally
80 Unlikely pageant winner
81 Penlight batteries
82 Science
83 Author Zora ___ Hurston
84 Son of Henry and father of Henry II
85 Scott of "Ocean's Eleven," 2001
87 Last president of South Vietnam
88 Orangish yellow
89 Acne cream ingredient
90 Enthusiastic assent
92 Violent, perhaps
93 Poodle's cry
95 Hauls around
96 Canadian pump name
99 Bruce of old films
103 Prepared to streak
105 Italy's ___ di Garda
106 State categorically
107 Frequent subject of government approval
109 Hauls around
111 Dallas suburb
112 Mil. commander
114 "Thy Neighbor's Wife" author
115 Rock's Brian
116 Says with a raised hand
119 Godfather's utterances

by Paula Gamache

120 Habituate
121 Photographer Adams
122 Soho serving
123 Grain disease
124 French face cards
125 Counting word
128 Asleep, say

130 Mount SW of Messina
131 ___ Belt
132 CPR pros
134 Serbian city, birthplace of Constantine the Great

135 Six, in Siena
137 "___ had it!"
138 Minor carp
139 Noisy rollers
140 250th anniversary of the incorporation of Los Angeles

18 WORD DISPLAY

ACROSS
1 Berates
8 Customary manner of doing things
13 Orbital extremes
20 City near Fort Roberdeau
21 Smooths
22 Live it up
23 Tornado abhorrence?
25 Nice 'n Easy maker
26 "___ Isn't So" (Hall & Oates hit)
27 Merry-go-round music
28 Change, chemically
29 Where a prince might work at a hospital?
37 Sounds of understanding
40 These, in Madrid
41 Thicket
42 Mekong River land
43 Never
45 Swabs
47 Foreign, to an American, briefly
48 Lesson from Jack Nicklaus?
51 Cargo on the ill-fated Edmund Fitzgerald
53 Close
54 Nike competitor
55 Fakes it
56 Plunder
57 Road warnings
59 Met highlights
60 Homily about gymnastics?
66 Dye-yielding shrubs
67 Oozes
68 Ballet move

70 Forsaker of the faith
74 "___ here"
75 "Peter Pan" dog
76 Users of barbells, e.g.
77 Losers on "The Apprentice"?
82 Coin words
83 Brings in
84 Wore
85 Onslaught of cold weather
86 Kind of princess
88 K. T. of country music
90 Cockney residence
91 Place for unhappy diners?
96 Schools for engrs.
97 Greek theaters
98 Represent
102 Recent reputed spy organization scandal
105 Red Cross sales strategy?
109 Like a size 8 blouse vis-à-vis a size 10
110 "It's déjà vu all over again" speaker
111 Capitol feature
112 Anarchists, sometimes
113 Fresh
114 Extreme joy

DOWN
1 Dosage units
2 Inter ___
3 Tiny, informally
4 This makes sense
5 Boston area, with "the"
6 Response: Abbr.
7 Make lace
8 Goes up against
9 Grammy winner Lou

10 Disciple's query
11 Cariou of Broadway
12 Dropped stuff
13 Entry
14 Camelot sight
15 Spinachlike plant
16 Solo
17 Where Lux. is
18 Inner: Prefix
19 French seasoning
24 Spicy stew
28 Tears
30 Fungal spore sacs
31 Numbered rds.
32 Mark Harmon action drama
33 Ninny
34 Babbled
35 Noggin
36 Tough turns
37 Uneasiness
38 Uproars
39 "The beloved physician"
44 More frequently, old-style
45 One of five
46 Makes a mess of
47 "Untrue!"
49 King of music
50 Pizza places
51 Maya Angelou's "And Still ___"
52 Opens up a hole in
55 Self-congratulated
57 Deep-sea fishing aid
58 Some O.K.'s, for short
59 "What ___!" (famed Bette Davis line)
61 Defeated, in a way
62 Boards
63 Cousin of radial
64 Close by
65 Two-seater
69 ___ basque (dance step)

70 Elite
71 Feather, zoologically
72 Gift ___
73 Traffic control
77 Actress Garr
78 They can be caught at the beach
79 Vacation destination
80 Political slant
81 Spies' info
83 Relieves (of)
86 Nourish
87 Dessert, in Dover
88 Sometime in the future
89 Native South African village
92 Related on a mother's side
93 Maker of Zima and Killian's Irish Red
94 Locker room emanations
95 Recon, perhaps
99 Kind of steak
100 Added conditions
101 "Don't go!"
102 Municipal facility: Abbr.
103 The "Rocky" film with Mr. T
104 In the past
105 Kids' ammo
106 Grazing area
107 Anger
108 Assn.

by Mike Torch

ACROSS

1 Picks up
6 Sea lettuce, e.g.
10 Wide open
15 15-Down rival, once
19 Taxing time
20 Attends
21 They're towed away
22 See 98-Across
23 Footwear eaten by an animal?
26 Tumults
27 Page
28 Instant
29 General ___ chicken
31 Old-time welcome
32 Clue that helped convict a movie snack thief?
38 Wretched
39 Get all lovey-dovey
40 Police car maneuver, slangily
41 Cell, e.g.
42 Like the ans. to this clue
43 One in a six-pack
44 N.Y.S.E. and Nasdaq, e.g.
46 Like some fishing hooks
48 Stubborn person getting on another's nerves?
53 Black
54 ___ weight
55 Built
56 Weed
59 Went after
61 Shot up
62 Rub the wrong way
63 Home to some Mongolian nomads
64 Thug whose books aren't selling?
68 Dust Bowl refugee
69 Mitsubishi competitor
70 Vandals
71 Famed Georgia football coach Vince
72 Sparkle
73 Tuna salad ingredient
74 River isles
75 Thick
76 Nicholson negotiating with Stiller and Affleck?
81 Less than explanatory parental explanation
84 Bowls over
85 H.S. class
86 Call from a meadow
87 Cousin of a cobra
88 It must be in the genes
89 B. A. Baracas portrayer on TV
90 Starting to get blue?
92 Supreme rulers blow up a major hardware store?
98 With 22-Across, movie hero of 1977
99 Hot
100 Mortar mixer
101 Acute
102 Twin sister of Ares
104 Cousins of a disheveled wading bird?
111 Going ___
112 Spots on a graph
113 One of the Waughs
114 Priest's urging
115 "Only Time" singer
116 Annual parade honoree, for short
117 Point
118 Sound at the front of East Hampton

DOWN

1 Buddy of the Clintons, e.g.
2 Apple had one in 1980: Abbr.
3 Funky do
4 Called
5 Due for a drop-off?
6 "Like that matters"
7 Actor Cariou
8 Bugs
9 Leftovers at a barbecue
10 Hedge fund whiz, for short
11 "Whaddaya know"
12 What two palms up may indicate
13 Hoop star's entourage
14 Prevent
15 Traditional Olympics powerhouse
16 Sugary quaff
17 Eastern European
18 Like some provocatively colored lips
24 Pencil holder
25 System start-up?
30 William Styron title heroine
32 Kind of support
33 "This should get you started . . ."
34 Unelite, in London
35 Eccentric
36 Singer/radio host John
37 "___ Lap" (1983 film)
38 Did nothing
43 They don't provide outlets
44 Stuck
45 Be acquainted with Vanna?
46 Diplomat Boutros Boutros-___
47 Tear-jerkers often have one
49 Try
50 Biblical shepherd
51 Shepherd's concern
52 Radiates
56 It has six holes
57 Peter and the Wolf's "duck"
58 Like some sums
59 Horse sound
60 Long walk
61 Andrea Doria's domain
62 Wash out
63 Write (for)
65 Columnist Mike
66 ___ Chris Steak House (restaurant chain)
67 Saturn and Mercury, for two
73 House keepers
74 Negative campaign feature
75 Water, perhaps
76 Be in harmony
77 Billionth: Prefix
78 Intruder's deterrent, maybe
79 Chaps
80 Starr of song
81 "Count me in"
82 Arid
83 Extra
88 Dusty floor cleaner
89 Breakfast cereal
90 Ungodlike

by Joe DiPietro

91 Must pay
93 Station house figures
94 Jump for joy
95 Ship over there?
96 Show agreement with
97 Pint-sized, downsized

103 Irish ___
105 Elhi org.
106 Mil. transport
107 Knockout of knockouts
108 ___-Tiki
109 Beethoven's "Minuet ___"
110 Once

ACROSS

1 "Exodus" hero
4 Film director Petri
8 "Pow!"
12 Chicago's ___ Aquarium
17 Novel by Toni Morrison
19 Coquette
20 View from Mauna Kea
21 Frighten away
22 Winning it is a sweet victory
25 Many an archaeological site
26 Lock, stock and barrel
27 Overdoes it
28 Eats at home
29 Goes over again
31 River in Irkutsk
32 Meddle
33 Big name in ice cream
34 Cheapskate
36 Latin case
40 Lo-___
41 TV show since 1/6/75
43 Treasury
45 Imported wheels
48 D.C. bigwig
49 "À votre ___!"
50 Signature piece?
51 Emulated a cat burglar
53 West Indies isle
55 Deflected
59 Gradually decline
61 Car wash sight
62 Stern who saved Carnegie Hall
64 Whopper
65 Music producer Brian
66 Add light, or not (and do this 13 more times to solve this puzzle)
69 Ocean State sch.
70 Put down, on the street
71 Gushes forth: Var.
72 Owns
73 Criminal
75 Not in the middle
77 Something's brewing here
80 Accompanies to the airport
81 Film buff's cable choice
82 Nut tree
84 Never, to Mozart
86 Followers: Suffix
87 Sweeping
90 Concealable weapon
93 Prefix with friendly
94 1960's TV western
95 Lowermost ship deck
96 Abbr. in a personal ad
99 Like some student housing
102 Subject of a May tribute
104 License
106 Bad state to be in
107 Security holder
110 Bacteriologist's study
111 Sound of a willow in the wind
112 End-of-meal serving
114 More beloved
115 Make up for
116 Needlepoint shop purchase
117 One of two bath towels
118 Popular mixer maker
119 Commuter map points: Abbr.
120 Some 20th-century art
121 Aug. clock setting

DOWN

1 Have big plans (to)
2 Like an imploded soufflé
3 "Well, here goes . . ."
4 Personifies
5 Lucy of "Ally McBeal"
6 Regarding, to counsel
7 Deafening silence, e.g.
8 "Bummer!"
9 Word just before a snap
10 Orders at McSorley's
11 Skylight?
12 Barely enough
13 More strapping
14 Elimination
15 Judge
16 Quality of cooking
18 Spiky plant
21 Resoluteness
23 Hospital danger
24 ___ choy (Chinese vegetable)
28 Intentional loss, in boxing
30 Trapshooting
35 Where gringos live
37 "___ cost to you"
38 King in 1922 news
39 Follower of Paul?
41 Use a towel
42 Show Me State river
43 Pieces of cake
44 How Elvis albums are rereleased
45 Followed, as advice
46 Pertaining to element 92
47 Boot out
50 Statue of Liberty attraction
52 "I'm not making this up!"
54 Skeptics' remarks
55 Corpulent
56 Dodges
57 Most hopeless
58 Little-used clubs
60 How many magazine articles are written
62 "As ___ saying . . ."
63 "Yes sir!," south of the border
67 Land on the other side of the Atl.
68 Figures in Iranian history
74 "No, mein Herr"
76 Badger
77 Shepherd
78 Commerce department staffers
79 "The Da Vinci Code," e.g.
82 High jump need
83 Collie's charge
85 "I" trouble
87 "Portrait of a Musician" artist, familiarly
88 Earns over time
89 Loudly enjoys, as a joke
90 Freshness
91 Hit one out of the park
92 Raised
94 Siren
96 Reacted to a heartthrob
97 Works of artist Max
98 Least restricted

by Elizabeth C. Gorski

ACROSS

1 Long narrative poem
7 Outlaw Kelly
10 Uses a ring, maybe
17 Camp Pendleton group
19 Summer treats
21 Brand of sports drink
22 Long time that just flies by?
24 An Easter egg hunt may have one
25 Long bones
26 Nickname of a boxer who converted to Islam?
28 Board member: Abbr.
29 3 for 2 and 4: Abbr.
30 A camera may be set on this
31 Matter to the jury
32 Mao's grp.
33 Wing, say
36 Supermarket checkout action
39 It gets in the groove
42 Bee product?
47 Befalls
50 Enjoys a hammock
51 Slip into
52 Whom bouncers might bounce
53 Law firm aide, for short
54 Not just approximately
55 Conventioneers' place
57 Duo that might review films based on arcade games?

62 In a workable manner
67 Most fibrous
68 Like some siblings
69 Water color
70 Ticks off
71 What King Arthur's men would like to have seen more of along the way?
73 Offensive basketball position
75 Where a haircut may end
76 Claim of a sort
77 ___ for the long haul
81 Don't chug
82 Stage after pupation
84 Monte ___
86 "Therefore, I have proven the existence of jalapeños!"?
90 With 40-Down, a 1975 horror novel
91 Some crockery
92 Director's second try
96 1940's spy grp.
97 Sound made with outstretched neck
99 Rings of islands
101 O.A.S. member: Abbr.
102 Sitarist Shankar
104 Grizzlies who give great interviews?
108 Movie with a posse
110 Photographer's setting
112 Possible response to "My boss is leaving and I hate his replacement"?

114 Fitting into a joint
115 Phrase usually before a colon
116 1972 U.S. Open champion
117 Stew
118 Cartoonist Avery
119 Got behind, with "for"

DOWN

1 Printer's unit
2 Pope of 1963–78
3 Rubber gaskets
4 Printer's unit
5 Speed-skating gold medalist Karin
6 Common Market letters
7 Angina treatment, for short
8 O.A.S. member: Abbr.
9 "Citizen Ruth" actress, 1996
10 Senators' wear
11 "Trainspotting" star Bremner
12 Short-finned ___
13 Uncommon delivery
14 It's used with some frequency
15 Singer Brickell
16 Where scenes are seen
18 Title with a number, perhaps
20 Heroine of TV's "Alias," for short
21 Cut back
23 Kook
27 Brunch buffet items
30 Father-and-daughter fighters
32 Small brain size
34 Places for fish
35 Forest sticker
36 Part of a heartbeat

37 Cool ___
38 Stubborn one
39 Where God sent Jonah
40 See 90-Across
41 Officer with a half-inch stripe: Abbr.
43 Stepped
44 Substantiate
45 Outhouse issue
46 Simple bunk
47 Part of "The Alphabet Song"
48 Italian-born explorer of the New World
49 Blintz relative
54 Destructive stuff
55 Grass and such
56 Disbeliever's cry
58 Sub
59 Hockey stat
60 Mag. staff
61 Grabs some chow?
63 Put a stop to
64 King Louis XII's birthplace
65 "Network" director, 1976
66 Kind of question
69 Sault ___ Marie
71 Letter before resh
72 Each
74 Trader ___
77 Test results, sometimes
78 United Feature Synd. partner
79 Warm assent
80 Joan Collins's villain on "Batman"
82 U.N. agcy.
83 With, in Wiesbaden
84 Non-dean's list grades
85 Reading and the like: Abbr.

by Trip Payne

87 Chanted sounds
88 Device with a scroll wheel
89 Con junction
93 Surpass in gluttony
94 Ominous-sounding phrase
95 Put down roots?
97 Reims's department
98 Universal donor blood type, for short
99 Skirtight material
100 Tomfool finish
102 Hindu avatar
103 Fat as ___
104 Classroom handout
105 E.P.A. pollution meas.
106 Batter's ploy
107 The Auld Sod
108 "In that range"
109 About
111 Plane heading?
113 Onetime Mideast union: Abbr.

ACROSS

1 White-collar position
6 Big guy
10 "Did you ___?!"
14 Moo goo gai pan pan
17 Sonata movements
18 Not the most reliable set of wheels
20 Little-known
22 It surrounds the Isle of Man
23 "New Look" pioneer
24 Eastern way
25 Half-German/half-Indian film hero
27 Cymbal in a drum kit
31 3-D figures
32 "I hope to see London once ___ I die": "Henry IV, Part 2"
33 Cognizance
34 Carnégte's cronies
36 Comment made after jumping in a pool, maybe
38 State strongly
41 Faultfinders
44 Throaty sound
46 Eye sockets
48 Certain ID check
49 Cross shape
50 Obstructor of congress?
54 ___ Sunday, the fourth Sunday in Lent
55 Farm pitcher
56 "The Time Machine" race
57 Agatha and Dahlia, in P. G. Wodehouse books
58 What this puzzle's circled spaces represent
64 Subject of a Michelangelo sculpture
67 Westminster area
68 L. L. Bean competitor
72 Made fun of, in a way
73 Ring duo
77 Hairstyling need
78 2000 Elton John/Tim Rice musical
79 Fluoroscope inventor
81 Traditional Christmas Eve meal in Germany
82 Drink served in a tall glass
84 Hoof handlers
86 Rtes.
90 Startled cry
91 Reuters competitor
93 Refresher
95 Casino fixture
101 Hunter slain by Artemis
102 Gillette brand
103 "What ___ care?"
104 Five or ten, say
105 Unsuccessful, as a mission
110 Bear in mind
111 Appropriate
112 Blubberless marine mammals
113 Leftmost digital watch no.
114 Recycle bin fillers
115 Tap sites
116 Boon to Scottish tourism

DOWN

1 Fuddy-duddy
2 1988 De Niro thriller
3 Under a false name, briefly
4 G
5 Sleeping sickness carriers
6 Sports ___
7 Cereal grass
8 Schindler's business partner in "Schindler's List"
9 Sonatas, e.g.
10 Like some mushrooms
11 Florida's ___ Beach
12 "Hostel" director ___ Roth
13 1950 film that retells the same events four times
15 Mountain nymph
16 "Beauty is truth, truth beauty" writer
18 Potsherds
19 Passed (away)
21 "What nonsense!"
26 Intersected
28 Grp. involved in "the Troubles"
29 Flavor lender
30 Ludicrous
31 M.I.T.'s ___ School of Management
35 Ending with defer or refer
36 "Goldberg Variations" composer
37 Daughter of Uranus
38 Count
40 Super-duper
42 Big
43 Appeals to
45 Out of sorts
47 The place of one's fodder?
48 Does a run
51 Snakes with vestigial limbs
52 Escort's offering
53 Lettuce type
54 Country
57 "Son of ___!"
59 It serves many courses: Abbr.
60 Juicer
61 Former Hong Kong leader Tung ___ Hwa
62 Lacking sense
63 One of the Bobbsey Twins
64 Star followers
65 Group that includes the U.A.E.
66 Picks
69 Girder with flanges
70 It may come with a gift
73 Render unavailable
74 First of all
75 Molière comedy, with "The"
76 Became an item
80 Brother of Ham and Japheth
83 Honored alumni, usually
85 Rest cure destination
87 Bugs that live in trees
88 Actress Merkel

by Patrick Berry

89 Ancient Turkish dynasty founder
92 Mini-maps
93 Whistle wearer
94 Garden spot
96 Shabby treatment
97 Soirees
98 Pillbox quantities
99 ___ ware (Japanese porcelain)
100 Clipped
102 Hot room, colloquially
106 Gilbert & Sullivan princess
107 Carry with effort
108 Collection agcy.?
109 Took in

ACROSS

1 Codger
5 Mischief maker of myth
9 1945 news, in headlines
14 "Amerika" author
19 Part of the Dept. of Labor
20 Option for heads
21 Indian queen
22 It begins "Sing, goddess, the wrath of Peleus' son . . ."
23 Seasonal salutation
25 "Jeopardy!" phrase
27 Start of quote
29 Column of boxes on a questionnaire
30 Failing grades
31 Shipboard cries
32 Nursery cry
35 Column of boxes on a questionnaire
38 Of a heart chamber
42 New at the beach, maybe
43 Part 2 of quote
49 Very wide spec.
50 Command to a dog
51 -like
52 Geometry figure?
53 Of a certain hydrocarbon group
54 Crew alternative
57 Bombay-born dancer Juliet
59 Lao-tzu follower
62 "The Return of the Jedi" girl
64 Latin 101 verb
65 Montgomery of jazz

68 Part 3 of quote
73 Originally
74 Carry
75 Drug drop, maybe
76 Goolagong of tennis
77 Sight for sore eyes?
79 Capital of Meurthe-et-Moselle, France
82 Trials
83 Like some cats
86 __ minimum
88 Langston Hughes poem
90 __ the finish
91 Part 4 of quote
96 Zero
97 Shark, e.g.
98 Postpaid encl.
99 Suffix with lact-
100 Cup holder
102 Alternative to gov or edu
104 Related maternally
108 End of quote
115 Time to grow rice
117 Pictorial
119 Kind of acid
120 Dock site
121 Tongue site
122 Slick
123 Actress Graff
124 Goes a mile a minute
125 Cache contents
126 Fill

DOWN

1 Shipping option, for short
2 Words on a medicine bottle
3 Opposite of hog
4 Closet contents of a 21-Across
5 Trysts
6 Admits, with "up"
7 Acquaintances

8 Very impressed
9 Ray, Klee and Millais
10 Thai money
11 "That's __ haven't heard!"
12 Willfully tightening the screws, say
13 Calcutta native
14 Wellington natives
15 Architect William van __
16 Computer protection
17 Chiang __-shek
18 Pop-ups, e.g.
24 Pad user
26 Slippery
28 Miles away
33 Jai __
34 Drove
36 1999 Ron Howard comedy
37 Nine inches
39 Robert, for one
40 Police dept. employee
41 Guru habitat
42 Purple shade
43 Colorful wrap
44 Fictional donkey
45 Oliver's love in "As You Like It"
46 "__ the Needle" (1981 movie)
47 Like some acoustic music
48 Composer Mahler
49 Stationery brand
55 Something to pop
56 Nobel-winning economist Lawrence
58 Medical suffix
60 Rodney Dangerfield's "I don't get no respect," e.g.

61 Like the arrangement of gems in some bracelets
63 "The Shelters of Stone" heroine
65 A Ryder
66 The Supreme Court, e.g.
67 View for Shakespeare?
69 Eur. land
70 Undo
71 One of the Gandhis
72 "Holy cow!"
77 Grabber's cry
78 People: Prefix
80 Cig. purchases
81 Film character who says "Do, or do not. There is no 'try' "
83 Fifth-century year
84 2003 A.L. M.V.P., to fans
85 Go-getter
87 1977 double-platinum Steely Dan album
89 Checks out
92 Exclamation at the end of a trip
93 Résumé parts
94 __ Mix
95 Actress Zellweger
100 Utah's __ Canyon
101 Literary inits.
103 Bright circle?
105 Bushes rarely seen nowadays
106 Leg part
107 Glorify
109 "Come __!"
110 Fall off
111 Madonna's "La __ Bonita"
112 No bystander

by Ashish Vengsarkar

113 Physicist with an element named after him
114 ___ Penh
115 Diamond stat.
116 MSN competitor
118 Burn cause

ACROSS

1 Voyaging
5 Hitchhiker
10 Percentage
15 Somewhat
19 Writes quickly
21 Plaque, e.g.
22 Volcanic formation
23 Show a Woody Allen feature?
25 Heart
26 Mangy mutt
27 Medical research org.
28 Not a substitute
29 Thomas Paine, for one
30 Magazine supply
32 Certain spawner
34 Quick trip
35 Bryologists' study
36 What ageists do?
41 Sad
44 One side in a debate
45 Kung __ chicken
48 Off the mark
49 Razzes
53 Ties up
55 3.26 light-years
57 Abandon the Centennial State?
59 Sound from a hot tub
60 Yellow flag
61 Env. science
62 Night school subj.
65 Not-so-Big Apple?
72 Lead-in for long
73 Abbr. on an envelope
75 Words of concession
76 Airline abbr.
78 Cut an awful demo?
84 Sot's state
88 Saw
89 Feel extreme discouragement
91 Sports page news
92 Show featuring many alumni of L.A.'s Groundlings comedy troupe
93 Mineral residue
95 Made multiple
97 Drink at a Kyoto reunion?
101 Certain Arab
104 Each
105 Book before Phil.
106 Make a mad dash
110 On the range, say
111 Summertime quaffs
114 Like about half the world's pop.
116 God, in Roma
117 Insipid
118 What a hypnotist might do for help?
121 Construction financed by a hedge fund?
122 Eastern European
123 Happens
124 Tavern selections
125 To the point
126 Köln or Nürnberg
127 Like a spent campfire

DOWN

1 Org. for pound watchers?
2 Flu fighter
3 Vast, in verse
4 Descriptive wd.
5 Most spicy
6 Wrapped up
7 Monk's title
8 Greek vowels
9 Best Musical of 1996
10 Experts, slangily
11 Babe or fox
12 Alternative to a dish
13 Big laugh
14 West end?
15 Public __
16 Czar in a Mussorgsky opera
17 Busy
18 Transcripts
20 Capitol Hill abbr.
24 Biblical verb
29 Crunchy chip
31 The Pearl of the Black Sea
33 Like ears
35 Traveler's stop
37 It runs down the leg
38 Peter Fonda title role
39 Actor Beatty and others
40 Completely
41 Baby's resting spot
42 G.P.'s grp.
43 45-Down in Russian
45 43-Down in English
46 Fire
47 "__ Mio"
50 One-pointers
51 First name in courtroom drama
52 Stay up nights
54 Charlemagne's realm: Abbr.
56 A.L. or N.L. Central city
58 Ejaculate
62 Tombstone brothers
63 Place for an outboard motor
64 Maj.'s superior
66 Just a bite
67 Suffix with form
68 Mary in the White House
69 Longtime Ferrara family name
70 Places for forks: Abbr.
71 Where something may be brewing
74 Mo. with topaz as its birthstone
77 Precisionist
79 Automaker's bane
80 Donald Duck, e.g.
81 Stove or washer: Abbr.
82 How you may know something
83 All-American name
85 La __, Bolivia
86 Ben Jonson wrote one to himself
87 Like Twizzlers, usually
90 Hospital hook up
94 Unknown element
96 Emily Dickinson's home
97 Bidding card game
98 Cultural entertainment
99 Spin
100 Candid
101 Kind of queen
102 Acoustic
103 Cup, maybe
107 Best and Ferber
108 Common aspiration
109 Grier of the gridiron
111 Memo starter
112 Makes a move
113 Politician's goal
115 Star athlete, briefly
118 Outer: Prefix
119 Reggae relative
120 In the manner of

by Timothy Powell

ACROSS

1 Wide-eyed
6 "Help wanted"
9 Bass productions
13 Big name
in cards
18 Kind of spray
19 Investment mgr.'s
subject
20 Exasperated
cry in a 1950's
sitcom
21 "Wake up!"
22 Gold gathering
dust?
25 Shish-kebab need
26 Tested in
a fitting room
27 Lower oneself
28 It has wings but
doesn't fly
29 On Soc. Sec.
30 Deportment on
the Discovery?
32 One having a
ball at the circus?
35 "Don't make
such ___!"
37 Prefix with phobia
38 Hi-___
39 Rear ends,
slangily
41 One slightly
higher in a tree
44 Very, very
soft, in music
46 Supersized
marathon?
50 Attacked, in
a way
54 Summer cooler
55 Not agin
56 Target
57 Hit musical
with the song
"Razzle Dazzle"
59 Kind of badge
61 Mix
62 Spread dirt
63 What Edmund
Hillary had?

68 Advertising
"spokesman"
since 1916
71 Oscar ___ Hoya
72 Strepitous
76 Model
77 1945 Robert
Mitchum war film
79 Datebook abbr.
81 Old home
loan org.
82 Shorthand taker
83 "Let's try
e-tailing!"?
87 Dress (up)
89 Snoopy
90 Lets go
91 Trouble
94 Place for a stream
96 Like some buggy
drivers
98 Sudoku and
others
99 Pre-trial blunder?
104 "Concentration"
pronoun
106 Struck out
107 Turn red, maybe
108 She may be
off her rocker
112 Outdid in
113 Neigh?
115 Diner
116 Really digging
117 It may be inflated
118 Bait
119 Comics canine
120 Role for 45-Down
in "Angels in
America"
121 Spotted
122 Some hook shapes

DOWN

1 Acad.
2 Product that
comes as a
cream or wax
3 City ESE of Turin
4 Ignominious end
5 Pass over

6 Ink
7 Venus or Mars
8 Allies in
the Gulf war
9 "___ lost!"
10 Dramatist
Pirandello who
wrote "Six
Characters in
Search of an
Author"
11 Low-budget prefix
12 Dict. listing
13 Ruthless attitude
14 Thalassographer's
study
15 Tankard material
16 State capital
since 1889
17 Pressure
21 Only key Irving
Berlin composed in
23 What a lover
of kitsch has
24 Marked down
28 HBO competitor
30 Deliberate
31 Turkey club?
32 Split
33 ___ Cologne
34 Li'l Broadway
role for Peter
Palmer
36 Longtime
baseball union
head
Donald ___
40 Strong out
of the gate
41 Hershey bar
42 Diminutive suffix
43 Little louse
45 See 120-Across
47 ___ fide (in bad
faith)
48 Sundial hour
49 Ones getting
base pay?: Abbr.
51 High fiber?
52 Sensitive
subject, to some

53 Strauss's "___
und Verklärung"
58 Philosopher
Chu ___
60 Words from
a backpedaler
61 12-time
baseball All-Star,
1934–45
62 Fed. property
overseer
64 Game with a
seven-card draw
65 Trevor who
directed "Cats"
66 Low hand
67 First Hebrew
letter: Var.
68 AWOL chasers
69 Backstabber
70 Opposite of post-
73 Red leader?
74 Drew back
75 Eastwood's
"Rawhide" role
77 It was "really
lookin' fine" in
a 1964 pop hit
78 "___ for
Innocent" (Sue
Grafton novel)
79 Dos follower
80 In the sky, maybe
84 "Dedicated to
the ___ Love"
85 Russian poet
___ Mandelstam
86 Transgressions
88 High spirits
91 Building blocks
92 Put down
93 Sleep inducer
95 Part of a U.K.
business name
96 On the calm side
97 Playful creatures
100 Playful creature
101 Home of the
Black Bears
102 Last inning,
usually

by Patrick Blindauer

103 Secretly watch
105 Refuse
108 Wax
109 Turns down
110 Brood
111 Army members?
113 Quick shot?
114 Crg. for drivers

ACROSS

1 Where to stick a pick
5 Stay-at-home dad
10 Volunteer's words
14 Spanish eyes
18 Seller of Kenmore appliances
20 Belly button type
21 Well-known
22 Chianti or Orvieto
23 Horoscope Writer
25 Hostlers
27 ___ kwon do
28 "Two eggs over easy," e.g.
29 Look
30 Illegal lighting?
31 Hardly a hipster
33 Puzzle Editor
37 Rainbow component
38 Fifth word of the Gettysburg Address
39 Bakery offering
40 The son on "Sanford and Son"
42 Foreign Affairs Editor
46 "Jurassic Park" terror, for short
48 Soldiers of Saruman, in Tolkien
49 Connecticut collegian
50 Go over again, in a way
52 Like a prima ballerina
54 Nickname for Dartmouth
58 Peak in Thessaly
61 Pince-___
62 Washington city on Puget Sound

63 "Handyman's Corner" Columnist
67 Survivor
68 Sicilian seaport
69 Debonair
73 Obituary Writer
75 Start eating
76 Clear (of)
77 Survive
78 Dogs that rarely bark
79 Lettuce
81 Sparkle
85 A as in Amiens
86 Coin in Cancún
87 Nero's love
90 Book Reviewer
94 Some are blessed
96 Opposite of kick
98 One way to go
99 It may be run up
100 Travel Editor
102 Fruit with a pit
106 Like the stone that slew Goliath
108 It's just over a foot
109 Cockpit need
111 Isaac Asimov mystery "Murder at the ___"
112 Lost one?
114 Weather Page Editor
117 Shamu, for one
118 Bounder
119 News in sports
120 Traditional Sunday fare
121 Oom-___ (tuba sounds)
122 Something that's struck
123 Alternative to stamp
124 Cinematic beekeeper

DOWN

1 Send an invitation for
2 Untamed
3 Like the crown of the Statue of Liberty
4 Places for M.D.'s and R.N.'s
5 Antiquated
6 Any of TV's Clampetts
7 Turkey's highest point
8 Quaker State, e.g.
9 Tillis who sang "I Ain't Never"
10 Viewable
11 Party professional
12 Maytag acquisition of 2001
13 Colo. neighbor
14 [continued on the other side]
15 High School Sports Reporter
16 Perfume quantity
17 14-liners
19 Butt of jokes
24 Element whose name comes from Greek for "inactive"
26 Holy man
29 Non-PC?
32 Away's partner
34 "Good shot!"
35 Present time in France?
36 A year before the Battle of Hastings
39 Fats Domino's "I've ___ Around"
41 Velvety cotton fabric
42 Physicist with a unit named after him
43 Ticking
44 Star in Orion

45 ___ à manger (ready to eat, in France)
47 Morales of "N.Y.P.D. Blue"
51 "M" star
53 Hire
55 Area between posts
56 Change, as part of a computer program
57 Accusatory phrase
59 British actress Sylvia
60 "No seats left"
63 Pantry stock
64 Put on cloud nine
65 Race
66 Spanish cubist Juan
68 Org. whose members' lies are discussed on TV
70 Twain's ___ Joe
71 "Goosebumps" author R. L. ___
72 Canadian lout
74 Light
75 See
76 Gardening Columnist
78 The N.B.A.'s Elvin Hayes, to fans
79 First Irish P.M.
80 Ski wear
82 Hurl everywhere
83 Number's target?
84 Person living along a large stream, informally
86 Litter site
88 Lover of Eurydice, in myth
89 Gold watch recipient, maybe
91 Animal with a flexible snout
92 Turmoil

by Maxwell H. D. Johnson Jr.

93 King, in Portugal
95 Air Force noncom: Abbr.
97 Shell game
101 Schoolyard retort
102 Chicago's ___ Planetarium
103 Lock site
104 Scale-busting
105 Discrimination
107 Peeples and Vardalos
110 White House worker
113 Dadaist Jean
114 NCR product
115 Ante-
116 Slip in a pot

ACROSS

1 Trumps
6 Frame part
10 Thrill
14 Slaves
19 Ring around the collar?
20 Copycat
21 Tones
22 Like some monuments at night
23 Dear old dad the comedic foil always told me to __
26 Châteauneuf-du-Pape locale
27 This may shock you
28 Scottish turndowns
29 German crowd?
30 Whine
31 Tower, often
34 The first place
35 "Quit dreaming"
36 Peace, in Russia
37 Common connections
39 Period
41 Supermarket chain with the slogan "Hometown Proud"
42 Dear old dad the umpire always told me to __
47 Termite clearer?
49 Oxlike antelope
50 Windflowers
52 [That punch hurt!]
53 Brooklyn-born rapper
54 The Seven Dwarfs, by profession
56 Tropical ornamental
61 Blaster
62 Hatha and others
63 Hick
64 Horse/donkey cross
65 Extend, as a line
67 Clinch, with "up"
68 In
70 Traffic director
71 W.W. II aircraft
74 One making a pit stop, maybe
76 New Test. book
77 Hollywood setting
79 Like some sects
80 Bygone polit. cause
81 The Maurice Podoloff Trophy is awarded to its M.V.P.
82 "Green Acres" co-star
84 Tony winner Uta
86 Learn about through books
90 Dear old dad the builder always told me to __
92 Commuting options
93 Impala, e.g.
95 Booster grp.?
96 Fairness-in-hiring abbr.
97 Marine bioluminescence
99 Stay in line
101 Honeyed pastry
105 This clue has two of them (for short)
106 Eats
107 Big name in faucets
109 Wallace who wrote "Ben-Hur"
110 Habituate
111 Dear old dad the sharpshooter always taught me to __
115 They're easy to catch
116 Support, with "up"
117 Jackie Robinson's alma mater
118 An emirate
119 Panda hangouts
120 Itches
121 Turn off
122 Economize

DOWN

1 More lowdown
2 Woman's name that sounds like two consecutive French letters
3 Sell outside the stadium
4 Great deal
5 Regular: Abbr.
6 Modern name for old Cipango
7 Place for icons
8 Queens subject?
9 "It's a cold one!"
10 Bilbo's home
11 City NW of Crater Lake
12 Old pop
13 Reason to reset the clocks: Abbr.
14 Dear old dad the cosmetic surgeon always told me to __
15 Wealthy biblical land
16 "Fantastic!"
17 Extraction
18 Out of this world
24 Pacify
25 Supplements
30 Pie chart part
32 A sultanate
33 Dear old dad the C.E.O. always told me to __
34 Coated Dutch exports
35 Geometry suffix
37 Problem in bed
38 Braves, but not Indians, briefly
40 Out
42 Prime
43 South American cowboy
44 Hunting times, for kids
45 Three Gorges Dam site
46 Fund, as a museum
48 From south of the Mediterranean
51 Cry at the sight of 107-Down
55 Marker
57 Spider-Man foe
58 Busy
59 Lip curler
60 Aid for the blind
63 Thumbs-up
66 __ behold
67 "'Tis a pity"
69 Island chain
72 Alexander's wife in "Uncle Vanya"
73 Gun on the street?
74 Keeler and Dee
75 Hello or goodbye
78 Wowed ones
79 Procter & Gamble soap
83 Of yore
85 Baseless?
86 1967 #1 hit whose title is spelled out in the lyric
87 Noted Roosevelt
88 Generally
89 Words of praise
91 Was serious, with "it"
94 PC protection brand
98 __-lance
100 Removes from the schedule
101 Joy of daytime TV
102 Out

by Ben and Mark Tausig

103 One with a strict diet
104 At all
106 People's 1999 Sexiest Man Alive
107 See 51-Down
108 Look like a creep
111 Person with intelligence
112 Yukon or Xterra
113 60's grp.
114 Word repeated before a hike

ACROSS

1 Day-___
4 Hat trick trio
9 Envelope opener
14 Racket
17 Race
18 Greenwich Village resident of a hit 1980's sitcom
19 Low clouds
20 Ponte Vecchio's river
21 Enzyme suffix
22 Pastel shade
23 Jeweled pieces
24 Hand holder
25 "The Sound of Music" role
28 Channel bought by TV Guide in 1999
30 Many new corp. hires
31 Flock member
32 Stout relatives
33 Comparison shoppers
34 Capital of Pas-de-Calais
36 Lab vessel
37 Prefight ritual
38 Fixing up a house in Britain
42 See 7-Down
43 "No problems here"
44 Wear
46 Not the most maneuverable ship
49 Endorse
53 Series of shocks?
54 Come across as
55 Epoch 50 million years ago
58 Month after Shevat
59 Toothpaste tube abbr.
60 They're out of reach

61 National flower of Mexico
62 Home of golf's Blue Monster
64 Asian country in which English is an official language
68 Puts (away)
69 Clothed
71 Too smooth
72 2002 champion at 62-Across
74 Da-dah, da-dah, da-dah, poetically speaking
75 Cocktail with 108-Down
76 Cold spot
77 ___ were
78 Overthrows first, e.g.
79 "Love is my ___ . . .": Shak.
80 Lose badly
82 Lei Day greetings
84 Become active
87 Ones with guns put away
92 Shut (up)
93 Heroic verse
94 Bouncing off the walls
95 Noisy censure
96 In the past
97 Fox dialect
100 Dealer in futures?
101 Chemical "twin"
102 Former western English county
105 Prep exam, for short
106 Capital city captured by Mussolini's forces in 1939
109 Heads-up
110 Edible South American tuber
111 Mark of a ruler
112 Toughens

113 Item often stored upside-down
114 Pro ___
115 "Ixnay"
116 Set, as a price
117 Lady love?
118 Help-wanteds, e.g.

DOWN

1 What this clue ain't got?
2 Former Buick
3 Kind of pitch
4 Inaugural ball, e.g.
5 It may be stuck in a bar
6 Sanction
7 With 42-Across, an NPR host
8 Part that's broken off
9 Leaflet appendage
10 Tourist hazards
11 ___ candy (pop music)
12 ___ loss
13 Like some highly collectible paper money
14 Quick deposit receiver
15 Successively
16 Jottings
19 Year-round camp
20 Don of "Cocoon"
26 Golfer ___ Aoki
27 Monsoonal
29 Truck stop stoppers
33 Tree in a Christmas song
35 Reagan program inits.
36 It has two jaws
37 Maine radio station whose call letters spell a pronoun

39 Rachel's baby on "Friends"
40 Phoned-in info
41 Tropical porch
44 Like land not drained
45 Baja bread
47 One that makes one
48 Wild things
49 Noted German spa
50 Hebrew title for God
51 Arizona football V.I.P.
52 Reuben ingredient
54 Musical exercise
56 Intl. assn. created in 1948
57 Make sore
60 Like a tightrope walker
63 Herd hangout
65 Breakfast place
66 Fix, as a golf green
67 Root of diplomacy
70 "Laugh-in" host
73 Yds. rushing, e.g.
76 Golf course feature
77 Melmac alien et al.
81 No-goodnik
82 Up to, in poetry
83 ___ orch.
85 Friendliness
86 Caen confidante
87 "Lakmé" and "Lulu"
88 Alternative to plastic
89 The tiniest amount
90 Like some ears
91 Begs (for)
92 Company that makes the Skyhawk
93 Smoothed
95 Use, as one's savings
96 Tony-winning actor Denis

by Jim Page

97 Kind of panel
98 Combat zone
99 Info holder
103 Not fancy
104 One foot forward
107 ___ panic
108 See 75-Across

ACROSS

1 Some radio dispatches, for short
5 Album feature
10 ___ Popular
15 Small handful
19 "George of the Jungle" elephant
20 Historic symbol whose shape can be found hidden in this completed puzzle
22 ___'acte
23 Southern side?
24 Made better
25 French noodle product?
26 Shot by a doctor
28 1776–1876: Abbr.
29 Guitarlike Japanese instruments
31 Better set
32 Hypodermics
34 Alexander Hamilton's place, informally
35 It's filled with bills
36 Allegro ___ (music direction)
38 Grps.
40 Prefix with dermis
41 Lateral lead-in
42 Takes power away from
46 Henpeck
47 Bard's nightfall
48 Shavings
51 TV canine
52 Old washing machine feature
56 34th U.S. pres.
57 Opposite of blow up
59 "I beg to differ!"
61 Neat
63 Stage elevator
64 Bighearted one
65 Out
66 Ones making amphibious landings?
68 They go all out at beauty shops
69 Center of Florida?
72 Coulter who wrote "Godless: The Church of Liberalism"
73 Mention
77 Kind of I.R.A.
78 Broadcasts
81 Big bird
82 U.S. atty. gen. in 1962
83 In a Weird Al Yankovic song, he "looks like a Muppet, but he's wrinkled and green"
84 Get-up-and-go
85 Certain fungus
86 Book before James: Abbr.
87 "Cool" amount
88 Saturate, in dialect
89 "Sweet as apple cider" girl
90 Cheesehead
91 Ballantine, e.g.
92 First group of invitees
95 "Consider it done!"
98 More fit
100 Moving away from the sides
102 German auto pioneer Gottlieb
103 Carpentry supplies
104 Like Saturn
105 Skin cleanser component
106 In the middle of
107 Not dis
110 Whirler
112 Comedy shtick
113 Twisty turn
116 Within reach
121 Savory French appetizers
125 "Tell me about it"
126 Much-photographed White House area
127 Accent
128 Misses the wake-up call

DOWN

1 Like many T's and P's
2 Emergency calling plan
3 Image that appears with the 20-Across on an old half dollar
4 Go over the limit?
5 Groups that run
6 Olympic officials
7 Still snoring
8 Actor Gibson
9 Like a Rolls-Royce
10 Talking Heads co-founder David
11 Legal org.
12 Pulls in
13 Baseballers' wear
14 Graybeards
15 Houdini's real name
16 Longtime setting for 20-Across
17 Things needed around dictators
18 High reputes
21 Ornament that may be worn with sandals
27 Org. with operations
30 Pulls
32 Original ___
33 Hang
37 Mozart's birthplace: Abbr.
39 From Phila. to Miami
43 Hard stuff
44 Repeated phrase in Martin Luther King Jr.'s "I Have a Dream" speech
45 Like a juggernaut
48 Elapse
49 Polished off
50 Fraudulent contestant
53 Welcome, as the new year
54 Green: Prefix
55 Check over
58 Hat, slangily
59 Top-secret grp.
60 Sounds of woe
62 It often gets glossed over
66 Airport area
67 Previously recorded
70 Dish prepared in a skillet
71 Rutabagas, e.g.
74 Starr and others
75 Japanese noodle product
76 Temple with curved roofs
78 Put forward
79 Muslim leader
80 Call
93 Series
94 Rocks
96 June honorees
97 Author Deighton
98 Direct contact
99 Routine
101 Domestic Old World birds
103 Creme-filled chocolate treats
107 Talking point?
108 I.R.A. part: Abbr.
109 "There's gold in them ___ hills!"

by Elizabeth C. Gorski

111 Oil producer
112 Afrikaner
113 Earth, to Mahler
114 Flight segment
115 Payroll dept. ID's
117 Follower of
    Benedict?
118 Pastoral cry

119 P.O. box item
120 Comics shriek
121 Granada gold
122 Natl. Novel
    Writing mo.
123 British verb
    ending
124 It may follow you

ACROSS

1 Makes sticky
7 Old Spanish gold
14 Plato dubbed her "the tenth Muse"
20 Turkey's highest peak
21 Buddy
22 Served the drinks
23 It means "strained" in drink names
24 Author of "The Fall of the Horse of Usher"?
26 Mad cap?
28 Dudgeon
29 "Dinner and a Movie" airer
30 Prefix with friendly
31 Caring grp.
32 Coal byproduct
33 Hard slog
35 Arthur and others
36 It may be legally beaten
37 Accomplish flawlessly
39 Essential part
40 American representative to France during the Revolutionary War
41 Love hate?
46 Iron man?
49 If things go well
50 Cry with a pompom
51 What golf pencils lack
54 Brand of craft knives
55 Cubes
59 Unable to make "Ocean's Thirteen," maybe?
62 Actress Olin
63 Break down
64 Professionals' earnings
65 From scratch
68 Exotic means of suicide
69 Brewed beverages
71 Organ that can perform martial arts moves?
78 Writing set?
81 Alprazolam, more familiarly
82 Femme fatale, often
83 Progressive ___
84 Quick-change artists?
86 1983 Nicholas Gage book
87 Ex-wife's refrain?
93 Products with earbuds
94 2004 spinoff show
95 Lip-puckering
96 Long ride?
99 Recording device
100 Blue
101 All for
104 "___ dien," motto of the Prince of Wales
105 Specialist M.D.
106 Reason to retire
107 Monstrous bird of myth
108 How a diaper is removed?
111 Cry to a lunch sandwich before it's eaten?
115 Set off
116 Arctic natives
117 "Eureka!"
118 "Is this a ___ which I see before me": Macbeth
119 Salary after deductions
120 Sequoias and Siennas
121 Whiles away

DOWN

1 Angel
2 Beethoven's Third
3 Hurry on horseback
4 River through Kazakhstan
5 Jotted down
6 Alien
7 Three-sided blade
8 Mubarak's predecessor
9 Company with the motto "A Business of Caring"
10 Old carrier name
11 Have the gumption
12 ___ roll
13 Roman Helios
14 Catalyst
15 Top-notch
16 Spot early on?
17 Able to change shape
18 Unwanted plant in farmyards
19 Spacecraft orbiting Mars
25 Mislead and then some
27 Hook worm
33 Pan coating
34 Off-color
35 Hebrew for "house of God"
38 Wahine accessory
39 Very, to Verdi
40 Horror movie figure, informally
41 British bludgeon
42 Year that Spenser's "The Faerie Queene" was published
43 Set of rings?
44 Food item that can be soft or hard
45 Historic Swiss canton
46 Prepare to give what you received?
47 Brooks Robinson, for 23 years
48 Secure tightly, with "down"
52 Lament
53 Chooses to leave
55 Units of force
56 Late wake-up call?
57 Seemingly not there
58 Ancient manuscripts
60 Black layer found in Morbier cheese
61 Put dishes away
66 Stretch (out)
67 Pull ahead yet further
70 Small suit
72 Left
73 Actress Bates
74 Ending with sever or suffer
75 ___ avis
76 It'll turn you around
77 In a proper manner
79 Shaw's "___ and the Man"
80 Research center
84 On-the-water front
85 Wildean quality
87 Drug taken mostly by kids
88 Inferior imitator
89 Pack up and go
90 Deplane dramatically
91 Common street name
92 Nero Wolfe's obsession
96 Not harmful
97 Together
98 They're rounded up in a roundup
100 Punk

by Patrick Berry

101 Utah County seat
102 Big name in reference books
103 ___ vincit amor
107 Nino who composed the music for "The Godfather"
108 Scold severely

109 Feedbag's fill
110 "Splendor in the Grass" writer
112 Currency of Laos
113 It may come straight from the horse's mouth
114 "Now the truth comes out!"

ACROSS

1 Pelvic
6 P.M. times
10 Fast feline
14 They don't do Windows, as a rule
19 Sheryl Crow's "All I ___ Do"
20 Goggle
21 City south of Moscow
22 Lollygag
23 EVIL BRAT IN THERE
26 Muchachas: Abbr.
27 Part of the refrain before "hey hey hey" in a 1969 #1 song
28 ___ League
29 Absorbed
30 CANNY OLDER AUTHOR
34 Notches, usually
38 Honk
39 Frown
40 School for King's Scholars
41 Not manual
42 Signs
44 Passers, briefly
47 TO APPEAR ON ELBA, NON?
52 Diminutive suffix
53 Nevada county
54 Sharper
55 P.O. items
56 1940's–50's All-Star Johnny
57 Old cars with 389 engines
58 Secretary of state before Shultz
59 Diet doctor
61 EAGER TO USE LYRICAL MOLD
68 Benedict XV's successor
69 Vault
70 Narc tail?

71 Playfully roguish
72 Jason ___, longtime Denver Bronco
73 Touch
76 Recipe instruction
79 Sci-fi drug
80 SEEN ALIVE? SORRY, PAL!
84 Co. founded by Perot
85 Old-fashioned contraction
86 Good buddy
87 Abbey area
88 Like some Fr. nouns
89 God whose wife had hair of finely spun gold
90 Storyteller's challenge
93 EVER THE CRISP HERO
98 Taos sight
99 Picnic hamperer
100 "Clever thinking"
105 Esther of "Good Times"
106 I VALUE NICER ROLE
109 Affaire
110 Some wings
111 B'way showing
112 Part of a platform
113 Carryalls
114 Dying words?
115 It's usually slanted
116 Pete ___, 1970's–80's General Motors chief

DOWN

1 "Bingo!"
2 Source of basalt
3 ___ uproar
4 Tolstoy heroine
5 Short break
6 Operatives

7 Al ___ (Mideast group)
8 Philosopher Mo-___
9 Sun. talk
10 Herculean literary character?
11 Concentrated, in a way
12 Peach ___
13 Cask contents
14 "I give up"
15 St. Stephen, in the Bible
16 Soviet cooperative
17 One doing heavy lifting
18 Meth.
24 Hopper
25 Nocturnal animal: Var.
29 Start of a refusal
31 Part of an instrument measuring fluid pressure
32 Kind of blade
33 Pirates and Cards
34 Kind of diagram in logic
35 Dog command
36 Word before and after "against"
37 "Wheel of Fortune" buy
41 Industrious one
42 Some nerve
43 Pulitzer-winning critic Jefferson
44 Dennis of "The Alamo"
45 Hip-hop jewelry, in short
46 Pick up
48 Glove material
49 Potentially dangerous strain
50 Boot
51 Winged
56 Their tips turn up

57 Wax rhapsodic
58 Short flight
59 Race of Norse gods
60 Group of three
61 Rush
62 Was on
63 Goos
64 Texas hold 'em announcement
65 Catalytic converter?
66 Temple tender
67 Flight maneuver
72 Boot
73 Pergola
74 Baseball Hall-of-Famer Bobby
75 Dad's namesake: Abbr.
76 "Kubla Khan" river
77 First name in 50's TV
78 Salon supplies
80 Amazon.com and others
81 Stop from running, maybe
82 One-seeded fruit, botanically
83 Parked oneself
88 1959 #1 hit by the Fleetwoods
89 Craving
90 Start a drive
91 Like Ford's logo
92 Garment size
93 1980's–90's New York governor
94 Spartan serf
95 Toothbrush handle?
96 1945 Physics Nobelist Wolfgang ___
97 Madrid month
98 Something to fall on
101 Composer Charles

by Ashish Vengsarkar

102 Force
103 Clown shoe width
104 Culture
106 August person
107 "Wait Wait . . . Don't Tell Me!" network
108 Bus. driver?

ACROSS

1 Corp. honcho
5 Some Filipinos
10 Starter's need
13 TV alien
17 Storyteller of Samos
19 Virtuous sort
20 Duration of many a TV show
23 Wine that causes incoherent talk?
25 Vietnamese city painted in soothing colors?
26 Pseudopod formers
27 Capital on the Mississippi
29 "Missed it!"
30 Literary governess
32 Girl's name that's a Texas county seat
33 Second word of many limericks
34 What a dummy!
37 French priest born in early July?
41 Worry, it's said
45 Calif. hub
46 Not quite right?
48 Mint hardware
49 Fillet
51 Poppy derivative
53 W.W. II-era enlistee
55 They're trident-shaped
57 Dries, in a way
58 Popular British society magazine
59 Steamed
61 Authorize
63 Life of ___
64 Monologist of note
65 Start of Montana's motto
66 Source of iron

67 Defeats regularly, in sports lingo
69 Cracker spread that's a little sparse on top?
74 Shook down
75 Game with matchsticks
76 Yearbook sect.
77 Brownie, e.g.
78 ___' Pea
80 Dasher, to Dancer
83 Gave in
84 Haberdashery item
87 Put out
88 It melts in your mouth
90 Journal add-on?
91 Attire
92 Bungled, with "up"
94 Common order, with "the"
96 Bit of sports news
98 Foreign exchange option
99 Kind of engr.
100 Discontinued investigative series?
103 Chanson de ___
105 Some choristers
107 Spot in a Manilow tune
108 Ad headline
110 Centers of squares, maybe
113 Brute
116 Deli offering
120 Expert in ornamental fabrics?
122 Rate at which a personnel manager works?
124 Orchard starter
125 Cream
126 "Not my problem!"
127 1940's first lady

128 Rehabilitated, in a way
129 Boxer-turned-actor
130 Ring

DOWN

1 Jumper, briefly
2 Enlarge, in a way
3 Salinger dedicatee
4 Lamenting one
5 Common Internet letters
6 Bireme gear
7 Sidesplitter
8 With no guarantees
9 Was of use to
10 Make it big
11 ___ corda (music marking)
12 Trojan War sage
13 Like pure gold
14 Dept. of Labor div.
15 Romp
16 Place for a pad
18 After-school arrangements
21 Punished, in a way, in the Bible
22 Fair-hiring org.
24 U.S. ally since '48
28 Green
31 Old five-franc coin
34 Place on the schedule
35 Auto parts giant
36 Trick shot that knocks the balls off a French pool table?
38 Freely
39 Drew nigh
40 Old "public diplomacy" org.
42 Enthusiastic cheering section at a bullfight?
43 Unbroken

44 Just back from vacation, say
47 They do the thinking
50 River whose delta is Cape Tortosa
52 [sigh]
54 "Please?"
56 St. Andrews golf club member
60 Pacific kingdom
62 Like a cardinal
67 Promptly
68 Peace Nobelist called a "messenger to mankind"
70 Concerning
71 "Had enough?"
72 Lively tempo
73 Catkin bearers
74 Kind of blast
76 J. M. Barrie pirate
79 Flute, e.g.
81 Sweet after-dinner drinks
82 Additionally
83 "You've got to be kidding!"
85 Lend support to
86 ___ Coty, predecessor of Charles de Gaulle
89 Simple, pretty songs
93 Grandparents, often
95 No longer good
97 He hoped to succeed H.S.T.
101 Authorized to travel
102 Actress Anderson
104 Fishing gear with fine mesh wire
106 Garage job
109 Enzyme suffix
110 Simple headstone
111 Put on record, but not actually on a record

by Fred Piscop

112 Intensifies,
    with "up"
114 Clarifying phrase
115 Rink leap
117 Sleek, for short
118 Jazzman Saunders
119 Tranquil scene
121 Suffix with front
123 Apology starter

ACROSS

1 Carousel contents
5 Life may be spent here
11 Ones whose work isn't picking up
16 Flightless birds
21 Nabisco brand
22 Against
23 Country/rock singer Steve
24 "Anybody home?"
25 Start of a comment by 3- and 126-Down
28 Oil holder, maybe
29 Wig wearer
30 "It's ___ to the finish"
31 Overhead bin, e.g.
33 Dearie
34 Kia model
36 Yellow or gray
37 Popped
38 1914 battle line
39 Comment, part 2
46 Brim
47 La-la lead-in
48 Trike rider
49 Some racehorses
50 Puffed up
54 Library Lovers Mo.
55 Natural pump outlet
57 Former U.N. chief U ___
58 Comment, part 3
61 Proctor's call
63 Cabinet dept.
64 "So ___ to offend . . ."
65 Phone book abbr.
66 Where many Sargents hang, with "the"
68 When repeated, an old TV sign-off
70 Spanish pronoun
71 Drink sometimes flavored with cinnamon
72 Whiz
74 Dirt in a dump truck, maybe

76 Isle of Mull neighbor
78 "The Torch in ___" (Elias Canetti memoir)
79 & 81 Landmark 1972 album by 3- and 126-Down
83 Actress Van Devere
87 TV series featuring the war god Ares
89 D-Day transports: Abbr.
91 Very narrow, in a way
92 Football Hall-of-Famer Herber
93 Dated
96 Russian assembly
98 Spanish eyes
100 Damone of song
102 Land on Lake Chad
103 Swear
105 Lexicographer's study
107 Comment, part 4
110 Sloughs
112 Cape in the Holy See
114 Colorful moths
115 Piña ___ (drinks)
116 Monetary unit of Panama
118 Where the Snake River snakes: Abbr.
119 Constellation near Cancer
120 Put out
121 Comment, part 5
125 Seventh-century year
129 Opera singer Mitchell of "Porgy and Bess"
130 Strand material
131 Afrique du ___
132 Had in view
133 Most dear
136 Ken and Lena of Hollywood
138 Belt and hose, e.g.
141 "I'm ___ here!"

142 End of the comment
145 Kind of call
146 Publication that clicks with readers?
147 Helping hands
148 A Sinatra
149 Some Romanovs
150 Honey bunch?
151 Entertain, as a child at bedtime
152 Real lulu

DOWN

1 Base for the old British East India Company
2 Indo-Europeans
3 With 126-Down, a noted humorist
4 Not so pleasant
5 Some hallucinogens, for short
6 Really clobber
7 Temporary
8 Recipe direction
9 Places for R.N.'s
10 Bubkes
11 Waste
12 Judge in 1990's news
13 Kill ___ killed
14 R.&B. singer Cantrell
15 Establishes
16 Electrical resistor
17 Subject of many a sad ballad
18 Couturière Schiaparelli
19 Something to break or shake, in phrase
20 Unduplicated
26 Up to, in ads
27 Slangy commercial suffix
32 Activate, as a switch
35 String group, maybe

37 Put oneself where one shouldn't
39 "Beam ___ . . ."
40 "___ no?"
41 Ride around
42 Order
43 "The Family Circus" cartoonist
44 Cousins of ospreys
45 Minute Maid Park player
46 Barely got along
50 One begins "The Lord is my light and my salvation"
51 Anthem start
52 Con game
53 Favoring bigger government, say
54 Kind of conservative
55 Bit of tomfoolery
56 With full force
59 Circus trainee
60 Butterfingers
62 Brian of early Roxy Music
67 Cinders of old comics
69 Straighten
73 Station along Route 66
75 Basis of a biblical miracle
77 Exuberant cry in Mexico
79 Now you see it, now you don't
80 NW Missouri city, informally
82 Cry one's head off
84 Opening for a coin?
85 Tuscany cathedral city
86 Ranch stock
88 Wrench's target
90 Sequel title starter
93 Latin dance
94 Feathered, say
95 Tulsa daily, with "the"

by Victor Fleming and Bonnie L. Gentry

97 Show up
99 Trash pads?
101 Drink that's stirred
104 On-site supervisor?
106 Concocted
108 Night calls
109 What's expected
111 Midwest harvest

113 Noncellular phone
117 Wall St. figures
119 Lists
120 Led astray
122 Flexible reply
123 Plays
   peacemaker for
124 Bantu language

125 Not hearing
126 See 3-Down
127 Chant
128 Battle cry
132 Radar fig.
133 Toll
134 Baseball Hall-of-
   Famer Aparicio

135 Not this or that,
   in Spain
136 Medical suffix
137 Shoot up
139 Acerb
140 Italian bone
143 ___ dye
144 Golfer Michelle

ACROSS

1 See 131-Across
4 Root holders
10 End of "Lohengrin"
16 Minor player
19 Manning the quarterback
20 Good to go
21 Perfume bottle
22 Itinerary info: Abbr.
23 Yo-yo
24 Demonstration against a Miss America pageant?
26 Riddle-me-___
27 One making calls from home
29 Off one's feed
30 Tourist's aid
31 Fingerprint feature
33 Multiplying rapidly?
38 Legendary elephant eaters
40 Sinuous swimmer
41 It maddens MADD
42 Italian innkeeper
43 Loose rope fiber used as caulking
45 Ruckus
47 Shoebox letters
50 Grant-giving grp.
51 Collection of publications about historical advances?
58 Rush violently
59 Interstice
60 Northern Ireland politician Paisley and others
61 Dog it
63 Follower of Shakespeare?
65 Matter of aesthetics
66 Honored Fr. woman
67 Fab Four forename

68 One who accidentally blurts out "I did it!"?
75 De ___
76 Do-do connector
77 In excelsis ___
78 Perp prosecutors
79 ___ B'rith
80 Is indisposed
81 Use as a resource
82 Nobel-winning poet Heaney
87 Nose-picking and belching in the White House?
92 L.A.P.D. part
93 Work for eds.
94 Untilled tract
95 Coil inventor
96 Where people travel between poles?
100 "Little Birds" author
103 Twisted letter
105 Person who's not straight
106 Competitor's dedication to hard training?
111 Shaded spots
112 Carnation or rose
113 Gray spray
114 Come back again
117 Bird ___
118 Item to be checked on a census form?
123 Bit for an accelerator
124 Considerably
125 Taking prescription drugs, informally
126 Put something on
127 Ki ___ (Korea's legendary founder)
128 Antigua-to-Barbados dir.

129 What to see in a Chevrolet, in old ads
130 Got as a result
131 With 1-Across, an agreeable guy

DOWN

1 Course offerer
2 '06 class member, e.g.
3 Hairsplitter
4 One born on a kibbutz
5 "Splitting Heirs" actor
6 Patterned after
7 Tiger Stadium's sch.
8 Minor, at law
9 Like some hair
10 Recipient of much intl. aid
11 Opposite of tiptoe
12 Turkic language
13 Fruity frozen treat
14 Cyclades island
15 Unwelcome visitor
16 Healthful exercise, informally
17 Home of the John Day Fossil Beds National Monument
18 "The Quiet American" author
25 Bulldoze
28 Dig
32 4-Downs, e.g.
34 Really run
35 "Jenny" co-star, 1970
36 Feudal estate
37 Canines to beware of
38 "Zuckerman Unbound" novelist

39 Locale of Interstate H1
44 Teatro alla Scala locale
46 Players for prayers
48 Like some sees
49 Sister of Thalia
52 Contorted
53 Sometime sale site
54 Decided one would
55 Continuously
56 Male issue
57 Starchy foodstuff
62 In place of
64 With great strength
67 Take as an affront
68 Flyboys' hdqrs.
69 Pow!
70 Leave a mark on
71 Drain of color
72 Faith of fakirs
73 V.I.P. at V.P.I., say
74 Burkina ___
80 Stubborn sorts
83 Penguin variety
84 Nashville nickname
85 Where Lew Alcindor played
86 Critic's award
88 Touchy subject
89 Fails to be
90 Garlic relative
91 Whodunit title word
96 Gibes
97 Down Under denizens
98 Have covered
99 In
101 "___ robbed!"
102 More prone to pry
104 Flash light?
107 Pot-___ (French meat-and-vegetables dish)
108 Must have
109 Lyon is its capital
110 Under a spell

by Mark Feldman

115 Watering aid
116 Some till fill
119 Abbr. after Sen. Judd Gregg's name
120 Nine-digit ID issuer
121 Org. that publishes American Hunter
122 Knock

ACROSS

1 Pitch in
7 Sight near an igloo
11 Show utter disrespect to
17 Something in France
19 Plastic surgeon's target
22 *Discount brokerage formed in 1996
23 *Site of a famous drawing?
24 Scorch
25 My dear man
26 Run the show
28 Ratio phrase
29 Hardly raining?
32 *Writer who coined the word "booboisie"
35 Wane
38 Fee follower
39 Biological rings
40 Satellite counterpart
41 *Deceased writer whose work was the basis for a hit 2005 film
44 Kiss, in "Harry Potter"
45 Former Span. money
48 Something a bride may have
50 Newsman Potter and others
52 Doll
54 Old man of the sea, to Homer
55 Pop
57 How 265-pound football Hall-of-Famer Larry Little was named?
59 Legal hearing
60 Bonus

61 1939 Best Picture nominee banned in the Soviet Union
63 Year Chaucer died
65 *Kids' cookie makers, informally
68 Folk duo ___ & Sylvia
69 Johnnycake
72 Porcelain piece
73 Alpine sight
76 Some takeout
77 Spy, at times
79 Damned doctor
82 First two words of "Waltzing Matilda"
83 Building contractor's study
84 These provide relief
85 ___ Kosh B'Gosh
86 Language whose name means "army"
89 *1970's–80's TV villain
92 Knick rival
93 French West Indies isle, informally
95 Bit of a comic
96 Peter the Great's co-czar
98 *It was retired in 2005
101 Chestnut
103 Make ___ for it
104 Capital of Belarus
107 As well
108 Daily ___, "Spider-Man" newspaper
113 *QB who was the 1963 Player of the Year
116 *World order
119 Dumps
120 "Mission: Impossible" types

121 Skip
122 Seven ___
123 Treat as a villain

DOWN

1 Its logo is four rings
2 Iced, with "up"
3 Waste
4 *Measure of brightness
5 Attorney's advice
6 Breviloquent
7 Peewee
8 Record producer ___ Adler
9 Latin 101 verb
10 Regard
11 Barefoot
12 "Gotta catch 'em all!" sloganeer
13 Its logo is five rings: Abbr.
14 How Holmes beat Ali in '80
15 How chicken à la king may be served
16 Scandinavian language, to natives
17 Milk purchases: Abbr.
18 In the main
20 Fill up
21 University of North Carolina
27 Prot., for example
30 Some college staff
31 Tree that's a symbol of sorrow
33 "Don't Bring Me Down" grp., 1979
34 Pesters
35 Continental abbr.
36 *It provided tires for Lindbergh's Spirit of St. Louis
37 Good relations
39 "Just ___!"
40 French Dadaist

42 Ones getting coll. counseling, maybe
43 Harry Bailly, in "The Canterbury Tales"
45 *Not for everyone
46 ___ blue streak
47 Kind of race
49 Go with
51 Setting for part of Kerouac's "On the Road"
53 Kind of symbol
55 Precipitate
56 What Indiana once pursued
57 River to the Danube
58 "A seductive liar": George W. Ball
60 Grp. with balls and strikes
62 Ending with cash
63 Singer Marilyn
64 Film executive Harry and others
66 #26 of 26
67 Fall behind
70 Brussels-to-Amsterdam dir.
71 Nice ones
74 Neighbor of Rom.
75 Lab safety org.?
78 Hot and heavy, e.g.: Abbr.
79 Crosswords, say
80 The Runnin' Rebels, for short
81 Mach 1 passer
83 Like Larry of the Three Stooges, surprisingly
84 Healthy amount
87 Football positions: Abbr.
88 Pioneering German auto
90 ___ boost
91 Barbara on the cover of 15 TV Guides
93 "Apollo 13" actor

by Derrick Niederman

94 Symbol of perfection
97 *Beetles
98 Lee of the old Milwaukee Braves
99 Look inside
100 Quiet, now
102 Truth, old-style
105 Figure (out)
106 Common arthroscopy site
109 Mountain West Conference team
110 Actress Gershon
111 1990's Senate majority leader
112 Nav. designation
114 Zenith
115 Singing syllable
117 Zenith rival
118 Chou En-___

ACROSS

1 Pop group with a hit Broadway musical
5 "Dido and Aeneas," for an early English example
10 Three-time Masters winner
15 Smack
19 Pasteleria offering
20 Had
21 Challenger's quest
22 Agitated, after "in"
23 Affectionate aquarium denizen?
25 Opposed to getting more angry?
27 Changes a mansard
28 Popular women's fragrance
30 Force in the Trojan War
31 French department
32 Glyceride, e.g.
33 Hatched
34 Monty Python member
37 Two-time L.P.G.A. Championship winner Laura
39 Grime fighter
40 Dark suit
42 Hub of a wheel
43 Grade enhancer
44 Does one's part
45 "Invasion of the Body Snatchers" invaders?
49 Trombonist Winding
52 Tiny amount
53 Preceder of Peter in a phonetic alphabet
54 Ear flap?
55 Listing
57 Less taxing
60 They're all that matter
62 A little flat?
63 At a slow pace
65 Evening thing
66 Sub
67 Wannabe surfers
68 Pluvial
69 Cot on wheels
70 "There's ___ for that"
71 Rhine feeder
72 Peach or beech
73 Panama, e.g.
76 "Miss Pym Disposes" author, 1946
77 Lettuce in the spring?
81 It's long in fashion
82 Actress Long and others
83 Beef cut
84 Discharged
86 Stink
90 It might raise a stink
92 ___-length
93 Ranchero wraps
94 Sine or cosine
95 Author of "Chaim Lederer's Return"
97 One offering compensation, maybe
98 Fit
99 Calm
102 Very scared insect?
104 Tainted tapioca?
107 Start of the Order of the Garter's motto
108 Bring down
109 Not done as well?
110 Switch attachment?
111 Puts on
112 Beat
113 Sty sound
114 Home, informally

DOWN

1 Patriots' grp.
2 Memory, sometimes
3 Invited
4 Sci-fi figures
5 Concert hall
6 Made pants?
7 Certain Prot.
8 Low-___
9 Stuff on tape
10 Union members
11 Number in C.B. lingo
12 Suffix with novel
13 Iran's Ayatollah ___ Khamenei
14 Actor William of "My Three Sons"
15 Desperado
16 Newscast segment
17 Sowing machine
18 Cremona product, for short
24 TV's Michaels
26 Stretch
29 Part of many a Civil War statue
32 Get out of
33 Blockhead
34 It's administered in H.S.
35 Capital whose Parliament house is called Fale Fono
36 The best time to elope?
38 Choice words
39 First or economy
41 Loot
43 Feather in one's cap
46 Hypnotist's directive
47 Deceiving
48 Old Nick
49 Young warmonger?
50 Others, in the Forum
51 Pour ___
56 Lyricist's need
58 Faithful servant in "As You Like It"
59 Lesser cut, usually
60 Not native
61 It fades in the fall
62 Play up
63 Pointer's reference
64 Primo
65 Oenone's husband, in myth
66 Like a defendant in court
68 Police car feature
69 Purplish
71 "So long"
72 Beat
74 Bit of skating practice
75 Marigraph activator
78 Take in too little
79 Rub the wrong way
80 Cubans' locations
81 Cousin of a herring
85 Went back and forth
86 Kind of acting
87 Near
88 Tour de France cyclist Floyd
89 Newspaper piece
90 Like Captain Kidd
91 Modern-day rhymer
93 Olympic skater Cohen
94 Awaken
96 End of many a race
98 Way up
99 ___-Asiatic

by Richard Silvestri

ACROSS

1 Not generic fashion
6 Hurry
11 Complaints
16 Soldier's fare, for short
19 Accustom
20 Appropriate
21 Full-length
22 Anthem contraction
23 Parent's admonishment
26 Records that are easily broken
27 Greets
28 Catchers
29 Drink with a three-leaf logo
31 Water source
32 26-Across, e.g.
35 Disorder
36 Landon of 1930's politics
39 1986 Pulitzer-winning novel set in a cattle drive
43 Computer-animated hit film of 1998
44 Vein holder
46 "In principio ___ Verbum"
47 Hot, in Vegas
49 Delta hub
52 They're hooked
55 Satisfy
58 Paul Theroux novel made into a Harrison Ford film, with "The"
60 Hebrew name meaning "Hill of spring"
62 Biased
63 Solid South, once
65 Thus far
66 "___ my case"
69 Cheering loudly
71 Snap, e.g.
76 ___-free
78 Dangerous place
84 Painting and printing, e.g.
86 1982 #1 hit with the lyric "living in perfect harmony"
89 Nixon commerce secretary Maurice
90 Dickens boy
92 Certain book addendum
93 Zip
95 Rossetti's "___ Ancilla Domini"
97 ___ II, first man-made object to reach the moon
98 Baker's stock
100 Sign of affection
105 Form W-9 datum: Abbr.
106 Initial progress
108 Response to "am not"
109 Canon camera
111 Black ice, e.g.
112 About
114 Goes for the bells and whistles
119 Suffix with infant
120 TV announcer's exhortation
124 U.S.S.R. successor
125 Reds, once
126 Host of TV's "In Search Of . . ."
127 New Mexico county
128 Salon job
129 Candymaker Harry
130 Sends to Hades
131 Spring

DOWN

1 Gifts of greeting
2 One-two connector
3 Water mark?
4 Young's partner in accounting
5 Devastating
6 Un plus sept
7 Invite to one's home
8 Lyon who played Lolita
9 Word of encouragement
10 Gabriel Fahrenheit or Anders Celsius
11 Actor Young of the "Rocky" films
12 Specialist M.D.'s
13 Prefix with system
14 Causing more laughs
15 Strengthen
16 Soft rock?
17 Evangelist's cry
18 Imitation
24 Slimming procedure, briefly
25 One of two rivers forming the Ubangi
30 Personal, often
33 180-year-old in Genesis
34 Avoid
35 "Halt!"
36 Something to remember
37 Reveal
38 Two-timing
40 More trim
41 Adulterate
42 Minn. neighbor
45 Common Web site content
48 Olympics city after St. Moritz
50 Rapa ___ (Easter Island)
51 More trim
53 Pat
54 Puerto Rico, e.g.
56 Paramedic's need
57 Seth and Abel's mother
59 Pablo Neruda's "___ to Common Things"
61 Online brokerage since 1993
64 ___ Nostra
67 Curtain raiser?
68 Mug in a pub
70 Founder of the American Shakers
71 Duplicates, briefly
72 Bran material
73 Marmalade ingredient
74 Home of Carthage College
75 Superlative suffix
77 Little squirt
79 "Kid-tested, mother-approved" cereal
80 It can't be good
81 Part of a magical incantation
82 Smooths
83 Ronan ___, "God Bless America" singer at Yankee Stadium
85 Didn't lie?
87 Flower girl, sometimes
88 Some pool sites
91 Bookkeeper's mailing: Abbr.
94 Through
96 Salad morsel
98 Law school class
99 One interested in net savings?
101 Grp. founded in Washington on 4/4/1949
102 Pulverized
103 Creator of Genesis

by Seth A. Abel

104 Somewhat
107 Where a person might get into a habit
110 "___ say . . ."
112 Bill producers
113 Site for sore eyes?
115 Sci. class

116 Lord in France
117 Net
118 Part of a piggy bank
121 Originally
122 Kind of operation
123 "Let me think about that . . ."

ACROSS

1 Thwacked but good
7 Come to one's senses
13 Trial case
20 Needing crackers, say
21 Spotted cat
22 More than tanned
23 Is acquainted with a quartet of wildebeests?
25 Consummate skill
26 Have coming
27 Poetic contraction
28 Religious sch.
30 Clears for liftoff
31 What is that in Mexico?
33 Community character
36 Drill one more time
38 Early run?
40 Booby-trapped nudist resort?
43 Soul buddy?
46 Skin ___
48 Cornmeal creation
49 Like 60% of people
51 Prudent time to get to the airport
54 ___ Dinh Diem of Vietnam
55 Old guy, slangily
56 Young guy, slangily
57 Subject of some gossip
61 Busy
62 Poet ___ García Lorca
65 Had plenty
66 "Once in Love With ___"
69 Vegetarians' supermarket protests?

73 "Um" cousins
74 Sulking more
76 One who's fallen
78 Home of the world's second-oldest written constitution, after America's
79 Make it big
82 Traveling
86 Old Olds models
87 Record producer Brian
88 Belief in disbelief
91 Contractions
92 Outskirts of the outskirts
96 Italian, e.g.
97 ___-wolf
98 Transported a couple of Porta-Potties?
101 C.S.I. evidence
102 Zoom in on
105 Sought morays
106 Foolish talk
108 "Fanny Hill," supposedly
110 Hockey's Tikkanen
112 Fifth and Mad.
114 Skip it
117 City on the Smoky Hill River
119 Rose raised by a sardonic gardener?
123 Less considered
124 Title heroine of a hit 2001 French film
125 Diplomat Harriman
126 Emotional
127 Busybodies
128 Towers above

DOWN

1 Expressway
2 Trollope's "Lady ___"
3 Place for strikes or strokes
4 Dots on a map
5 Salon workers, for short?
6 Nimble
7 Pointed
8 Main threat?
9 Calc. prerequisite
10 Blood sharers
11 Old French coins
12 Results of piercing pain?
13 1972 treaty subj.
14 Available on the stock exchange
15 "And they went ___ in a Sieve": Edward Lear
16 Robin Williams-esque
17 Eastern European guy who loves both sexes?
18 Word turned into its own opposite by putting a T in front
19 Big name in ice cream
24 Shy person?
29 Candy billed as "The Freshmaker"
32 Heed
34 She was famously married 3/20/69 at the Rock of Gibraltar
35 Initials for two Belushis
37 Bagged leaves
38 Horizontal, perhaps
39 Oktoberfest serving
41 "Exodus" hero

42 Word on a wall, in the Bible
44 Vulture, e.g.
45 Beginnings
47 Symbol on the front of some bars
49 Halt
50 Mideast capital
52 Campaign dirty trick
53 Trumpeter on the "Kill Bill" soundtrack
55 "___ go!"
58 Sis, e.g.
59 Horned Frogs' sch.
60 Kind of pain
63 Key of "The James Bond Theme"
64 List for St. Peter
65 Fidgety
66 Horrifies
67 Cabbage
68 Christmas quilters' haze?
70 Number cruncher, for short
71 Ad follow-up?
72 "Wait ___!"
75 Poi source
77 Individually
79 One-spot
80 En route
81 Oval-shaped loaf
83 Alternative energy source
84 Speller's phrase
85 Community ctr.
89 Prefix with realist
90 Teeny, slangily
92 Manhattan, for one: Abbr.
93 Follower of Manhattan
94 Milk source
95 Convalescent sites
98 Noble partner
99 Current resisters
100 Had too much

by Lee Glickstein and Ben Tausig

103 "The Prince of Tides" co-star
104 Certain 60's protest
107 Bouquet
108 When repeated, a dolphinfish
109 Abba of Israel
111 French weapon

113 Calif. force
115 Ill-gotten gains
116 Mound stats
118 Poetic preposition
120 Long
121 Place for a toothpick
122 Postgrad field

ACROSS

1 Major-league team with the most season losses, 120, in the 20th century
5 Fills positions for
11 A mouse moves over it
14 "Get __!"
17 Former enemy capital
18 Kind of wrestling
19 House painting attire, maybe
22 Electrolysis particle
23 Whining from execs?
25 Be slightly turned on?
27 "Son of Frankenstein" role
28 Mint family plant
29 Rock guitarist Barrett
30 Flight
32 Pens and needles
35 "Summer of Sam" director
36 Day __
39 Laid up
41 "Yikes!"
42 Fashionable gun?
47 Lose resilience
49 Ringside shout
50 Regard
52 Cheesy snack
53 Engineering project begun in 1898
55 Usher to, as a table
57 Princess of Power
58 Money in the bag, maybe
59 "Well, this pays the rent"
61 Bug
62 Whit
63 Deletes

66 "Then join you with them, like __ of steel": Shak.
67 Assistants at a Kate Spade factory?
71 Valle del Bove locale
72 __ Park, N.J.
74 NASA vehicle
75 Part of a winning combination
76 Irish-born actress McKenna
78 Washer setting
80 Like James Brown's music
82 Snoops
83 Someone sexy
85 60 shares, e.g.
87 Cordial
88 The Wildcats of the N.C.A.A.
89 New England hockey hero
90 Unit amount of sunlight seen?
92 Knotted up
94 Central
96 Suffix with Ecuador
97 Accident
100 Missouri city, briefly
102 Flit (about)
103 Equi- equivalent
106 Motivated
109 As recently as
111 Reunion no-shows?
115 Hemlock?
118 Go blading
119 Literary orphan
120 Swimming
121 Glacial ice formation
122 Three of a kind, in poker parlance
123 Suffix with bass

124 Scenic vistas, briefly
125 African antelope

DOWN

1 Stick
2 Isolate
3 Play garden produce like a horn?
4 New York's Mount __ Hospital
5 No-no's opposite?
6 Letter-shaped fastener
7 Mine entrances
8 In a proper manner
9 Braved
10 High-hatter
11 Beer can feature
12 __ right
13 W.W. II event
14 Shaggy sponsor of a sort?
15 Lodge
16 N.Y.C. arena
17 "The Laughing Cavalier" artist
20 Sprightly dances
21 Brief online message
24 A. A. for children
26 Place trailers are in
31 Wires
33 __ land
34 Footnote word
37 Grenade part
38 Santa __ (hot winds)
39 To whom "We'll always have Paris" was spoken
40 Time for crowing
43 Key with three sharps: Abbr.
44 Separation
45 "Voilà!"
46 Examination of an English royal house?

48 Phazyme alternative
50 Raison __
51 Relieving knee pain?
53 Uninteresting
54 Cat's sniffer?
55 Kingdom of Broadway
56 Beat
60 Long jumper
62 Inconstant
64 Prevent from making a hit?
65 Gets some color
68 Wreck site
69 Supermarket chain
70 Nurse
73 Able to see right through
77 "Say as he says, __ shall never go": "The Taming of the Shrew"
79 Gang land
80 Farm young
81 Old
83 "Gilligan's Island" dwellings
84 Attending to a task
86 F.D.R. plan
90 They meet in the middle
91 __-European
93 "Go, and catch a falling star" poet
95 City connected to Philadelphia by the Benjamin Franklin Bridge
98 Where kites may be found
99 Canon competitor
101 Sommer in the cinema
103 Ishmael's half-brother
104 Rap relative

by Joe DiPietro

105 Ready to be drawn
107 "One Good Cop" actress
108 Tiny time period: Abbr.
110 Jerk
112 ID's with two hyphens
113 It may be given from father to son
114 PC screens
115 Station personalities
116 Actress ___ Dawn Chong
117 Back again

ACROSS

1 Outstanding football player
7 Keep after further changes
13 Indian-related
19 Letter-shaped tesserae
20 Little sucker
21 He wrote "Even the worthy Homer sometimes nods"
22 Store I most like to shop at?
24 Ready for publication
25 Comic Auerbach
26 2600, 5200 and 7800, gamewise
27 Photo ___
29 Site of July 1944 fighting
30 Jack who hosted the 1950's game show "Dotto"
32 Mouse catcher, in Madrid
34 Actress Aniston, to friends
36 Missing from 22-Across
37 Melee in a Dumpster?
42 Fix up, as old floors
45 "Too bad"
46 1957 hit for the Bobbettes
47 Combine
48 Hang around
51 Missing from 119-Across
52 ___ Corner, Va. (Washington suburb)
53 N.R.C. forerunner
54 What you will
55 Cabbie's call
57 Worked (up)
58 Missing from 73-Down

59 Clothing retailer beginning in 1969
60 Flipper?
62 Most calm
65 Discounted by
66 Rouses
68 Seasonal beverage
69 Perennial best-seller subjects
71 Medieval chest
74 Dr. Egon ___ ("Ghostbusters" role)
77 Imagine
81 Signals
83 Missing from 13-Down
84 Busy travel day, typically
86 East German secret police
87 Baseball Hall-of-Famer Al
88 Actress Gardner
89 Glacial ridges
91 Missing from 61-Down
92 Where Zaragoza is
93 Blue Stater, more likely than not
94 Pioneering weather satellite
95 Federico of Clinton's cabinet
96 Novel
98 Place to wash clothes in old Rome?
100 U.S. News or YM
102 Gold units: Abbr.
103 Vater's boy
105 Memorable 1966 hurricane
106 "I Ain't Marching Anymore" singer
108 Cry of surprise
110 Overflowed
113 Arab capital

117 Senator's locale
119 Droid in an oil container?
122 Looked like Groucho
123 Some T-shirt designs
124 Arose
125 Pitcher's quote
126 Cops' weapons
127 Tone deafness

DOWN

1 Soprano Gluck
2 Astronomical meas.
3 Good news on a gloomy day, e.g.
4 Objections
5 Exhibit
6 Baja bruin
7 Missing from 37-Across
8 Forces
9 Apelike
10 Starbuck's order?
11 Dictionary abbr.
12 Prefix with -derm
13 A particular bit of typography?
14 Casting need
15 It's usually blue, green or brown
16 Certain eligibility requirement for Little League?
17 Amtrak service
18 Deceived
20 Where Kofi Annan received an M.B.A.
23 Finely honed
28 Attire with pics of sheep, maybe
31 ___ Martin (cognac)
33 Source of spices for old traders
35 Charlie Chan player on TV

37 Soaks
38 Thrown for ___
39 Super Bowl XXXVII winner, for short
40 Sheet of ice
41 Leanings
43 Go over
44 Communications orbiter
47 Get by
49 Pilots' info
50 Sales crew
52 Bolt holder
56 "Maybe this is fate"
58 "Be ___" ("Help me out")
61 Heeds humorist George?
63 Memory trace
64 Across
67 Jon with the 1992 hit "Just Another Day"
70 "___ of the D'Urbervilles"
71 "Lonely Boy" singer
72 Crowd sound
73 What you hear on a Chris Rock recording?
75 Faux "buttons"
76 Hoist again, as a sail
78 Whiz
79 Not abstaining
80 Type measures
82 Actress Aimée
85 Missing from 16-Down
89 Expiate
90 Airer of many games
95 Founder of Lima
97 Show to a seat, informally
98 1992 Elton John hit
99 Postgame productions

by Brendan Emmett Quigley

100 Cabbage
101 Functioned
104 Four Holy Roman emperors
107 Missing from 98-Across
109 Passing mention?
111 Range: Abbr.
112 Quizzical sounds

114 OPEC member
115 Italian artist Guido
116 Saint from Kiev
118 Dripping
120 Mouths, zoologically
121 Org. receiving royalties for "God Bless America"

41 ALL-KNOWING

ACROSS

1 With 126-Across, author of the quip starting at 27-Across
6 Kind of race
10 "Come Back, Little Sheba" playwright
14 Modern home of the 10-Down
18 Product sold with a bag
20 "Hop ___!"
21 Tyros
23 Bill Clinton memoir
24 Nasty sort
25 Effecting a release
26 Blue
27 Start of a quip from Court and Society Review, 1887
30 V.I.P.
32 Literature Nobelist Morrison
33 What "Lucy in the Sky With Diamonds" may or may not be about
34 Quip, part 2
38 Edit
44 "An Affair to Remember" star, 1957
45 Berlioz's "Les nuits d'___"
46 Man of mystery
47 Layered
48 Project completion?
49 King Minos, for one
52 Site for Franklin Roosevelt
54 Matter of debate
55 Pageant prize
57 Quip, part 3
60 "It's about time!"
62 Lucre

63 Energizer or Duracell option
64 Low-value wad
65 Quip, part 4
70 "The Thief of Bagdad" actor, 1940
73 Ramallah grp.
74 Mystique
75 W.W. II wolf pack
79 Quip, part 5
83 "Rubber Duckie" singer of children's TV
84 See 112-Down
85 Winter pear
86 Brynhild's beloved
90 Granting grp.
91 It can be found in a tree
93 Cry with eyes lit up
95 4×4
96 Cold war winner
97 Huge, to Hugo
98 Quip, part 6
102 Lao-___
104 Dutch export
105 Dia's opposite
106 End of the quip
113 Try to win, in a way
116 Like a Swiss Army knife
117 One of a sailing trio
118 Time competitor, informally
120 Used a crowbar on, maybe
121 Election day: Abbr.
122 Fish that may someday spawn
123 Call after a hammer is hit
124 Agrippina's slayer
125 Prize since 1949
126 See 1-Across

DOWN

1 ___ law
2 Nutritious bean
3 Breakfast in a box
4 Flying start?
5 Common ink purchase
6 Tittle
7 It's read word for word
8 Fun house item
9 "Revolution From Within" author
10 Old inhabitant of 14-Across
11 With every hair in place
12 Ones dressed in black
13 F.D.A.-banned supplement
14 Match player?
15 Dramatic rebuke
16 Scout leader?
17 S O S responder: Abbr.
19 Satisfied subscriber, apparently
22 Part of a manger scene
28 Stem
29 Poet with the longtime NPR program "A Word in Your Ear"
31 Pencil holder, sometimes
34 Muscular watchdog
35 Sparked anew
36 "But on the other hand . . ."
37 Early sixth-century year
39 Put out
40 Stain
41 Actor Williams of "Happy Days"
42 Revolution, for one

43 Hammock supports
47 Sic on
49 Bills, e.g.
50 Exactly, after "to"
51 Court plea, briefly
53 Anne of comedy
56 Bygone Crayola color
58 Black piano key
59 Pearl City setting
61 Imbibe
62 Brigham Young University site
66 "Let's ___ There" (1980's NBC slogan)
67 Dim responses
68 ". . . ___ saw Elba"
69 Retired
70 Tired
71 Mark Twain/Bret Harte play
72 Game of chance
76 "Black Beauty" author
77 Link with
78 ___ Tranquillity
80 Offer that seems too good to be true, probably
81 Birthright seller
82 Lug
87 Floor (it)
88 Knoxville sch.
89 Get back on track
92 Begin something, in slang
94 Just firm enough
96 Lofty degree
98 It's a test
99 Element that quickly oxidizes in air
100 Artist with the 2002 #1 hit "Lose Yourself"
101 Winter fishing tool

by Mark Diehl and Kevin McCann

ACROSS

1 Mitsubishi S.U.V.
8 Knocked their socks off
15 Earth
20 Wake-up call, e.g.
21 It may be said after kissing the tips of one's fingers
22 Healing plants
23 What the peddler owes?
25 B-ball
26 Bust ___
27 Construction material in King Solomon's temple
28 National rival
30 Driver's aid
31 Maker of the first walkie-talkie
34 "All My ___ Live in Texas" (1987 #1 country hit)
36 Berate
38 Lt.'s subordinate
39 Top Tatar's tattler?
44 Jellied dishes in England
45 Place for a father-to-be: Abbr.
46 First name in gossip
47 Passes
49 Squad leaders: Abbr.
52 Way to the top
54 Shirt tag info
56 Not knowing what to do
59 "You're ___!" (Archie Bunker comment)
60 Advice for an understaffed yachtsman?
63 ___ seul (solo dance)
64 Change for a fin
66 Net alternative
67 Close pitches
69 Kind of acid
70 Unable to get loose
74 Site of a 1797 Napoleon victory
75 Cause of some spots
77 Screwball
78 Apple holder, maybe
80 St. Martin, e.g.
81 Result of whipping?
85 Architect William Van ___
86 Simmons competitor
88 Suffix with flex
89 Cartoonist who drew the Shmoo
90 Mimics
91 Some hotel visits
93 Summer coolers
95 Clamor
96 Spanish for "are"
98 Best-selling baseball equipment?
102 Sec
105 Neverland
107 Common street name
108 At no charge
110 Classic New Yorker cartoonist ___ Irvin
111 100 centimes
114 ___ set (group of tools)
117 Early Beatles, affectionately
118 "The Goat, or Who is Sylvia?" writer
120 Packer fan's angry cry after an interception?
124 Massey of "Rosalie"
125 Slimmest election margin
126 Cupidity
127 Cake part
128 Balcony's edge
129 Gifts

DOWN

1 ___ Defarge of "A Tale of Two Cities"
2 Hells Canyon locale
3 "Quit your excuses"
4 All, in music
5 That, to Tadeo
6 Call
7 Ouija, e.g.
8 Blue dye
9 Dancing girl in "The Return of the Jedi"
10 "The ground ___ she trod": Milton
11 Urban carriers
12 Patterned fabric
13 Operation Exodus participant
14 "Every ___ king"
15 Literally, "big water"
16 Grp. with the 1977 platinum album "Out of the Blue"
17 Hoboes by nature?
18 Anti-Prohibitionist's cause
19 Ledger column
24 Burn
29 Repetitive sort
32 Delivery lines: Abbr.
33 Law man?
35 Unknown
37 Riga native
40 Show horse
41 Ring figure
42 Ox-eyed queen of myth
43 Means to ___
45 Fla. vacation spot
48 Black currant flavor in wines
49 Bush activities
50 Skeletal support in a sponge
51 Muppet seller's gender guideline?
52 Lao-___
53 1940's first lady
55 Woeful words
57 Flashback caption
58 Transfers
60 Cry made with one's arm behind one's back
61 Less than right?
62 Real-life boxing champ who appeared in "Rocky II"
65 Lubrication channel
68 VCR insert
71 Bottom-of-letter abbr.
72 Panpharmacon
73 Insomnia cause
76 O'Connor successor
79 Alley ___
82 Recipe abbr.
83 Fast server?
84 Island that's part of 90-Down: Abbr.
87 Big fat mouth
90 See 84-Down: Abbr.
92 Clash (with)
94 Floor wiper
95 Elevs.
96 Overseas train service
97 ___ Artois, beer from Belgium
99 "Mr. Belvedere" co-star
100 Hit man
101 Pawed

by Ashish Vengsarkar

102 Attract
103 Blue-pencil
104 Impatient agreement
106 Start to a bit of bad news
109 Blaze
112 Opposite of under
113 Kid watcher
115 Suffix with electro-
116 Sarcastic comment
119 Little Rock-to-Memphis dir.
121 Seductive Longoria
122 New Deal inits.
123 Chess champion Mikhail

MISSING LINKS

ACROSS
1 Fooling (around)
8 Open, in a way
13 7, on modern phones
17 Alternatively
21 "Way to go!"
22 Weeping daughter of Tantalus
23 Perfectly, after "to"
24 Must have
25 White ___ House
27 Moved to and fro
29 Adds to the pot, say
30 Each
31 "The Sound of Music" name
33 Hunting canine
34 Intermittently, after "off"
35 Small spray
37 Muse of mimicry
39 Singer Mann
40 Big name in faucets
41 N.L. East team, on scoreboards
42 Double ___ play
45 Sun. talks
46 Loop loopers
47 Streamlined
49 Some E.M.S. cases
50 Address
52 U.S. 1, for one: Abbr
53 Ultrapatriot
55 Ole Miss rival
56 Postgrad degs.
59 Orange ___ Bowl
66 Sign of love . . . or rejection
68 Heavenly hunter
69 Bruin
70 One given "unto us," in Isaiah
71 Sundae topper
72 Spur (on)
73 Defeater of R.M.N.

74 Latin twinklers
75 Monocle part
76 Easter ___ bunny
85 Airline rarity, increasingly
86 Had a lame-duck session, say
87 Part missing from a vest
88 Poet laureate before Southey
89 Fails to
91 Attending to the matter
92 Too, in Toulouse
95 Skater Slutskaya
97 Had
98 e ___ Bay
101 Comprehend
102 Answer to the riddle "The higher it goes, the less you hear it"
104 Stand
105 Early third-century year
106 Alternatives
108 Engine part
109 Nada
111 F.B.I. facility
114 Thickening agent
117 New ___ Latin
120 Head's opposite
121 Only: Fr.
122 Fanatical
124 Fab Four name
125 Whacks
127 Part of MGM
128 Tropical fruits
130 Like many benefit tournaments
132 Computer file suffix
133 University in Greenville, S.C.
134 Like the 1915 San Francisco Mint $50 gold coin
136 Flag ___ Day
139 Exhausted
140 Seconds

141 Words after "put an" or "see no"
142 Fit for consumption
143 Time long past
144 Cornerstone abbr.
145 "The Exorcist" actor, with "von"
146 :-) :-) :-)

DOWN
1 It's tied up in knots
2 Tractor powerer, maybe
3 Progress
4 Printemps, par exemple
5 Norwegian playwright
6 Relatives of AND's and OR's in Boolean logic
7 High school class
8 Big name in auto racing
9 Kind of acid
10 Where streets meet: Abbr.
11 Support
12 Noblewoman
13 Contents of some patches
14 i ___ Pod
15 Gas station abbr.
16 Darns
17 Body ___ language
18 Lentil or bean
19 Petitioner
20 Whirlpools
26 Big ___ time
28 Bond rating
32 MGM motto opener
35 Start of many Québec place names
36 Former Patriots QB Steve
38 Mountain nymph
41 Pub offerings
43 Something carbon monoxide lacks

44 Rep.'s opposite
47 Render speechless
48 German canal name
51 Nut in mixed nuts
52 Varig destination
54 Hush-hush govt. org.
56 Abdominal pouches
57 Down's opposite: Abbr.
58 Blue shade
59 Average guys
60 Spur (on)
61 Bone connector
62 Take into custody
63 Beauty queen's wear
64 "The Thin Man" pooch
65 Actress Martin, star of TV's "National Velvet"
67 Tape, say
71 Dollar, slangily
73 Shock
74 It's the law
77 Suffix with Congo
78 Bit of beachwear
79 Setting for part of "King Henry VI, Part 2"
80 Mideast bigwig
81 Himalayan sighting
82 Hindu titles
83 Harmony
84 Furniture wood
89 Follow relentlessly
90 Show a deficit
92 Reproducing without fertilization
93 Letters at sea
94 1956 trouble spot
95 Desire
96 Goal for a D.H.
98 Trivial Pursuit edition
99 Kind of tide
100 Latin "behold!"

by Derrick Niederman

103 Former CBS military show
106 Buck ___ eye
107 In a tangle
108 Chianti containers
110 Part of L.A.
111 "Go away!"
112 With respect to hearing
113 Light-headed people?
114 Fleet of ships
115 Bola user
116 One who suspends an action, at law
118 Leandro's love, in a Mancinelli opera
119 Urban renewal target
121 Soap format
123 Hammarskjöld of the U.N.
126 U-shaped river bend
127 Civvies
129 A portion
131 When repeated, a top five hit of 1968 or 1987
133 Deception
135 Turndowns
137 Like 9 or 5
138 Former defense secretary Aspin

ACROSS

1 Slanted
7 Silly smile
13 "Le Rhinocéros" playwright
20 Protracted prayer
21 Relative of a rhododendron
22 Start of a hole
23 Job for a ballroom dance instructor?
25 Refuse to help in the garden?
26 Is in the Vatican
27 Sing ___ Daily, major Hong Kong newspaper
28 Altar in the sky
29 "Nonsense!"
31 Internet message
32 Discovery accompaniers
34 Job for a lingerie salesclerk?
38 Popeye, for one
39 Divine
41 Jimjams
42 Sainted pope called "the Great"
43 No. of People, say
44 Start of Idaho's motto
45 Anatomical enclosure
47 Banks on
50 Vegetable with sushi
52 Officer who may not be in uniform
55 Elects
56 Bus. runners
59 Job for a coffee shop employee?
64 Base approval
66 Shrinks' org.
67 Modern music genre
68 Blocks
70 Mucho
71 Mass. summer setting
72 "Family ___"
74 Decorate, as a 54-Down
75 It rolls on a Rolls
77 127-Down grp.
78 PC user's shortcut
80 Fearsome weapon
83 Martinmas's mo.
84 Grind
85 Miscellany
87 Job for a high school teacher?
90 Diamond of note
91 Bite
93 Suffix with super
94 Info at SFO
95 "Forget it"
98 Sermon subject
100 Man chaser?
103 Fix
105 "___ take arms . . ."
106 Queen of the fairies
109 Rosencrantz or Guildenstern, in "Hamlet"
112 Least bit
113 Job for an architect?
116 Roughly
117 Yawning
119 What a keeper may keep
120 Poetic ending with how
121 Idled
123 The Divine, to da Vinci
124 "With All Disrespect" essayist
126 Job for a business tycoon?
130 Supremely spooky
131 Skirts
132 Putter's near-miss
133 Jilts
134 Mixture of many spices, in Indian cookery
135 Ties a no-frills knot?

DOWN

1 Green
2 It has a tip for a ballerina
3 Rama and Krishna, e.g.
4 Was up
5 Quick approval: Abbr.
6 Appetite whetter
7 Baseball's Maglie
8 "The Compleat Angler" author Walton
9 Siege site of 1936–39
10 Flexible
11 Extra-wide spec
12 Farriers' tools
13 Most eager to go
14 Antipoverty agcy.
15 Moriarty, to Holmes
16 X Games airer
17 Job for a film photographer?
18 Multi-Emmy-winning NBC sportscaster
19 Bewhiskered animals
24 Subject heading for strategizers
30 In a tizzy
33 Party prep
35 Worrisome mechanical sound
36 Prime meridian std.
37 Kids' jumping game
40 Absolutely fabulous
46 Italian sweetheart
48 Farm measures
49 "___ Excited" (Pointer Sisters hit)
51 "This one's ___"
53 More cordlike
54 See 74-Across
57 Flub
58 Development sites
59 Subordinate deity, in classical myth
60 Modernize
61 Job for a dating service counselor?
62 Ascend
63 "You can't get out this way"
65 Lift
69 Harmony
73 Where some major arteries go
76 Medea, for one
79 Move, in Realtor-speak
81 Box
82 Certain specialty docs
86 See 108-Down
88 Competitor of State Farm
89 Handled
92 Disgraces
96 Hobbyist with toy trains, e.g.
97 J.F.K. debater in 1960
99 Chinese restaurant sign
101 Help from on high
102 What's left
103 Steamy, maybe
104 "Hear, hear!"
107 Early NASA rockets
108 With 86-Down, popular serial comic strip beginning in 1940
110 Functional

by Norma Johnson & Nancy Salomon

ACROSS

1 How sale goods may be sold
8 Hardy bulbs
13 Hockey game starter, often
20 Contract
21 Even if, briefly
22 Humbled
23 Ann Landers, e.g.
24 Further shorten, maybe
25 Fooled around
26 Dirty coat
27 Hollywood stars, e.g.
29 Hang loose
31 Swim routine
32 Chaps
33 Henna and others
34 Helgenberger of "C.S.I."
38 Heroine of a Gershwin opera
39 Horse course
41 Swing around
45 Praise from a choir
47 "Here ___"
49 "Holy mackerel!" and others
51 Utilizes fully
53 Where to find an eBay listing
54 It's often left hanging
55 ___ Brazzi, star of "South Pacific"
56 Harvester ___
57 Personae non ___
60 Cur
61 Conforming to
65 Sympathetic
66 Hands down
67 Williams with a crown, once
74 Hits hard
75 Mr. Big, e.g.
76 High points
77 Suffix with Ecuador

78 Bilingual Muppet
81 Legendary
85 Soldier's accessory of old
86 Actress Gardner
87 Precisely
88 Hymn pronoun
89 Small racer
90 Honks off, so to speak
91 B. D. ___ of Broadway's "M. Butterfly"
92 Staff note
94 Henley who wrote "Crimes of the Heart"
95 Hopper
99 Irish revolutionary Robert
100 Had dinner at home
102 Natty sorts
106 Vulnerable to fire
108 Product label abbr.
110 Teases
112 Kind of family
113 Masonry, for one
114 Sho ws
115 Hands out, as homework
116 Some HDTV's
117 Haifa money

DOWN

1 Hieroglyphic figures
2 Huxtable boy, on "The Cosby Show"
3 Florence is on it
4 Trap contents
5 Some ducts carry them
6 Highway behemoth
7 Heavy hitters

8 "Haven't Got Time for the Pain" singer, 1974
9 Like non-oyster months
10 Some score notations, for short
11 Leafy green
12 "Thanks, pal"
13 Ancient
14 Soft-soap
15 Leather sticker
16 Carter of sitcomdom
17 Part of a score
18 Heavy
19 Interjects
28 Heave-hos
30 Go after, as a rebound
34 Hepburn, Garbo and Gable employer, once
35 Huntsville's home: Abbr.
36 Seoul soldier
37 Rocky Mountains line
38 Tip of Manhattan
40 Very expensive contest prizes?
41 Hera, to Persephone
42 Drug once available under the commercial name Delysid
43 Emma player in "The Avengers"
44 Fancy name appendage
46 Hebrew of old
48 Diamond cutter?
49 Series terminal
50 Macho way to fight
52 Old atlas abbr.

57 Former high-tech co.
58 "Citizen X" star, 1995
59 Response: Abbr.
62 Cousin ___ of "The Addams Family"
63 Name separator
64 Dept. store stuff
67 Ad ___ (how tariffs may be assessed)
68 Homes, for some
69 Norse goddess of fate
70 Heckler's missile
71 "I ___ bad moon rising"
72 Hand cleaners at the dinner table
73 Phoenician fertility deity
78 Bit of sch. writing
79 "How exciting!"
80 Halmstad's locale: Abbr.
82 "How was ___ know?"
83 Place for a duck
84 Hosp. readout
93 County with the White Sands National Monument
94 Blue
95 Howe who wrote "Pride's Crossing"
96 Weight
97 Hyperbola parts
98 "Hallucinogenic Toreador" artist
99 New York cardinal
101 First name in a dictionary
102 Hall-of-Fame catcher Carlton
103 Plains native

by Harvey Estes

104 Apostle who wrote "Ye see how large a letter I have written"

105 Heathrow sights, once

107 Photog's image

109 Spank

111 Heavy-duty cleanser

ACROSS

1 Modern wall hanging
5 Military letters
9 Kind of case in grammar: Abbr.
12 Fruit of a flower
19 Place
20 Water carrier
21 Shetland turndown
22 Nail polish remover
23 Cheery fellow in the neighborhood?
26 One for the books
27 "You got that right!"
28 Slowly ascended
30 Class clown, e.g.
31 More furtive
32 Actress Kelly
33 Empties (of)
35 Bit of tax planning, for short
36 Excellent portrayal of a Gary Cooper role?
39 Hitch
40 Brainy
45 Work periods
46 Fireplace
47 Social breakdown
48 Turkish title
49 Answer men
50 "Let me repeat . . ."
51 Tattoo an anonymous source?
56 Dried coconut meat
57 Charlotte ___
58 "Holy mackerel!"
59 Night spot
60 Clears
61 Something to "call me" per an old song . . . or a hint to this puzzle's theme

65 Tin Man's malady
68 Let up
70 Turn red or yellow, say
71 Impermissible
72 Flat storage site
73 "The A-Team" actor on the cover of GQ?
76 Lines on a staff
77 Presenter of a likeness?
78 Start of a Latin conjugation
79 Minnesota college
80 Match
81 "Enough!"
84 Gemstone quality
86 Running in circles?
87 Father's song about a 79-Down character?
89 Bard's "before"
90 Pull (in)
91 "It's Too Late Now" autobiographer
92 All in ___ work
97 Mountain climber, e.g.
99 Saint whose feast day is December 25
102 1969 hit by the Who
103 Nuts
105 Get a bald advertising icon out of the slammer?
107 In pieces
108 Father figures
109 Cover girl Heidi
110 Razor name
111 AOL alternative
112 Sheffield-to-London dir.
113 Big name in games
114 Outdoor wedding rental

DOWN

1 Returnees from Mecca
2 Not laugh-out-loud funny, perhaps
3 Place for a programme
4 Dance in France
5 "This is right ___ alley"
6 Mediterranean isl.
7 Keep from overheating, in a way
8 Rococo
9 Recipe amount
10 Starr of the N.F.L.
11 Bach's "___, Joy of Man's Desiring"
12 Campus figs.
13 Candles in a menorah, e.g.
14 They may go under the arms
15 Response to a backstabber
16 Putting up a guy in the bath?
17 Among other things
18 Aristocracies
24 "Babi ___" (Yevtushenko poem)
25 They may make you sick
29 Kind of income
32 Extinct flightless bird
34 Security needs
36 Test before further studies, for short
37 Geom. line
38 Many a NASA employee: Abbr.
39 Showy bloom
40 Stone heap
41 Come after
42 Honored a monocled man at the Friars Club?

43 Diplomats
44 Wait
46 Game player's gleeful cry
49 View by computed tomography
51 Noted polar explorer
52 Charles, for one
53 Natural bristles
54 Wyo. neighbor
55 John on a farm
59 Angled
61 Attention-getting cry
62 Open ___ . . .
63 Typing test stat.
64 Election closer?
66 RC's, e.g.
67 Fashion plates, in British lingo
69 Low part of a high top
71 Place for a béret
72 Havana's home
73 Column material
74 "Typee" sequel
75 Idiotic
77 Pitcher
79 See 87-Across: Abbr.
81 Turn red or yellow, say
82 Dunk
83 Singer Lopez
84 Achieve through trickery
85 ___ St.-Louis, Paris
87 Mabel who sang "Fly Me to the Moon"
88 Lighthouse signals
90 Aptly named author Charles
92 Film buff's channel
93 Key of Prokofiev's Piano Concerto No. 1

by Elizabeth C. Gorski

94 Mountain ridge
95 Pine
96 Overseas assembly
98 Mozart's __ Symphony (No. 36)
100 Mail letters
101 College application nos.
102 "Joy of Cooking" author Rombauer
104 Sign of success
106 Kisser

ACROSS

1 Whizzes
5 "Well done!"
9 It can give you a pointer
16 Some sports cars
19 Response to many a punch line
20 Domain
21 Fitness
22 Directional suffix
23 "Ah like to ___ with diffr'nt huntin' spots"
25 "Don't let the man stand outside, ___!"
26 Royale automaker
27 Most overcome
28 Rose and Fountain
29 Persistent critic
31 Forward
32 Is under the weather
34 Typo
36 Writing surface, in old Rome
38 Many Forbes readers have them
40 Sound units
41 Encyclopedia offering
44 "___ is gettin' a bit tight on mah finger"
46 Gulf port
48 Took some chips, maybe
51 Bleach
53 Goddess with the gift of life
57 Jeans man
58 Cancel
59 Brogue or twang
61 Darrow of "King Kong"
62 Ancient Asia Minor region
65 Distance around
67 Supporter of arms, for short

68 "___ tard of this bad weather"
71 "Let's hep preserve our natur'l ___"
73 Bill's partner
74 Takes a powder
75 Harass
76 Capital of Romania
77 Oahu attire
79 Classic suit
81 It's above the tonsil
85 Basic French verb
86 Left alone
89 "On the Road" writer
90 Many bucks
92 "___ pa? He feelin' better?"
94 Show that's launched many film careers: Abbr.
95 1994 Peace Nobelist
98 Ratón chaser
100 Member of a ladies' club
102 End of a race
104 Onetime World Cup star
105 Become flabby
110 Crescent-shaped
111 Title words before "Music" and "You Knocking"
114 "It doesn't matter"
116 "Disgusting!"
117 "___ drink Pepsi, but ah'll have a Coke few don't mind"
119 "The waitress will be heah soon. I ___"
120 The Divine, to da Vinci
121 Hubble telescope subjects
122 Recommend
123 Chemical endings

124 Mateo or Diego, e.g.
125 Gorge crosser
126 I-80 and U.S. 10, e.g.
127 Come clean, with "up"

DOWN

1 Newsgroup messages
2 Indian coin
3 Drink, so to speak
4 Archeological bit
5 Get specific
6 Perfume source
7 Horseman?
8 Fill the bill?
9 Gives up the fight
10 Life preserver?
11 Pittance
12 Ionized gas
13 Glasses may improve it
14 Rouses
15 Transmission site
16 "Ma momma's from Virginny, and ma daddy's from ___"
17 "The Power and the Glory" novelist
18 Pig patter
24 Good comedian
28 Relative of the banana
30 Like a break-in at a burglar's house
33 Tennis's Nastase
35 "The wolf"/"the door" connector
37 Like some reading lamps
38 Elementary particle
39 Caviar fish
41 Texts for eds.
42 Army member
43 "I'm gonna use mah new ___ to cut the grass"

45 Actress Lollobrigida
47 Departure
49 Water-to-wine site
50 Literally, "skill"
52 One of the Kramdens
54 "___ up, why dontcha grab me a beer?"
55 About
56 RR stops
60 Temper
63 "Waiting for Lefty" playwright
64 "Piece of cake"
66 Fussy film director
68 Capstone
69 Landslide
70 Give the slip
71 Title for Jesus, with "the"
72 City near Virginia City
75 One of the "Little Women"
78 Sawbones
80 Cubemaker Rubik
82 Runs down
83 Singer Janis
84 Seventh-century date
87 Proof part
88 Like some citizenships
91 Contest player
93 Late golf champion Payne
95 Bridge signals
96 She played Cher in "Clueless"
97 "Ken I have ___ 'stead of the sausage?"
99 Bad blood
101 Post-It
103 Word with ear or peace

by Greg Staples

104 Check word
106 Typographical flourish
107 Woolly
108 Shriners' headwear: Var.
109 Lock
112 Old-fashioned police cry
113 Airline to Ben-Gurion
115 Extremely successful
118 U.K. award
119 It might bite

ACROSS

1 Pilgrims to Mecca
7 More than a cause
14 Enjoyed a soak
20 Protozoan
21 Having a few buttons missing
22 Fighting
23 Start of a verse
26 Quake
27 Mauna ___
28 Fairy tale meanie
29 Pupil's place
30 Newsmaker of 2/20/62
32 Mystery writer Josephine
33 Kind of whale
37 Not even-tempered
38 "Out, dagnabbit!"
39 "Passion According to St. John" composer
43 Like new
44 Game in which the 13 spades are laid faceup
45 Buck's love
46 Tortosa's river
47 More of the verse
54 To boot
55 Cries of discovery
56 Prom needs
57 Johnson's vaudeville partner
58 Secretary of War, 1940–45
60 Hunk
62 Thorny
63 Loose
65 Old holder of writing fluid
67 Loud
70 Epoch in which mammals became dominant
72 New York tribe
76 Actor Reeves
77 Either of two O.T. books
78 Site of the forges of Vulcan
79 River inlet
80 More of the verse
85 Rain check?
86 Suffix with Christ
87 Nosegay
88 Gr. 1–6
89 "A one ___ two . . ."
90 Before, once
91 Yellow shade
93 Nita of "Blood and Sand," 1922
94 The works
95 Chili accompanier
96 Blackbird
98 Kind of dame
101 Table scrap
102 Helped in a heist
106 End of the verse
111 "Mysterious" locale
112 Strips
113 They're seen at court bashes
114 Aware of, slangily
115 Girl of barbershop quartets
116 It's flashy

DOWN

1 "Left!"
2 Writer Kingsley
3 "How ___ the little busy bee . . ."
4 King in II Kings
5 Footnote word
6 Yellowish-red
7 Driver who talks
8 Hightailed it
9 Burma's first P.M.
10 Moved easily
11 In Shakespeare, the star in "The star is fall'n"
12 Israeli leader with an eyepatch
13 Conductor ___-Pekka Salonen
14 Planned for, in a way
15 Wroth
16 Actual
17 Sartre's "___ Clos"
18 Extensions
19 Batiking need
24 Opposite of 1-Down
25 Department store department
30 Blood's partner
31 Nut
33 Jimmy of "N.Y.P.D. Blue"
34 Red or white wine
35 Ballade conclusion
36 Map abbr.
37 Dallas team, informally
38 Solidarity's birthplace
39 "Coronation of the Virgin" painter
40 Humiliate
41 Town ___
42 Like rhinos
44 James Bond woman in "Thunderball"
48 Patent medicine, e.g.
49 Gunwale pin
50 Everyone has one
51 ___-law
52 Razorbacks
53 Actual
59 The old folks
60 Ancient market
61 Designer's job
62 Pretty, to Burns
64 Sharpen again
66 How some arguments are conducted
67 Dog with a long, curled tail
68 Satirist Brendan
69 Nixon's first Defense Secretary
71 Tip
73 Part of a fire safety program
74 Felt bad
75 Game ragout
77 Prague's ___ University
78 Start of North Carolina's motto
81 Bows before
82 "Wheel of Fortune" choice
83 Mud, say
84 Indeed
91 Leatherneck
92 Tricky
93 Birdbrain
94 Concerning
95 Like many wartime messages
96 Medicine's ___ system
97 Red-spotted creatures
98 Halliwell, formerly of the Spice Girls
99 Baseball stats
100 Sheltered
102 Addie's husband in "As I Lay Dying"
103 "___ she blows!"
104 Architect Saarinen
105 Humdrum
106 Salaam
107 Writer LeShan
108 Infamous Amin
109 Cognizance
110 Wind dir.

by Frances Hansen

ACROSS

1 Eagle org.
4 Chuck alternative
8 Whiplike?
13 Surly
18 Make fun of
19 Truck stop entree
20 "___ Was a Lady" (1932 song)
21 Go back to the drawing board
23 What an Italian wheeler-dealer wants?
26 Completely
27 Instruments used by the Beatles
28 Popeye's rival
29 Snappy comebacks
30 1954–77 alliance
31 Highest point in Italy?
34 Shoe specification
35 Passionate
37 Shakespearean prince
38 Dumfries denial
39 1974 title role for Dustin Hoffman
41 When Georges burns
42 Golden Horde member
44 "___ bien"
45 Midwest Indian
46 Barton and Bow
48 Filled Indian pastry
51 Do boring work
54 Outfit
57 Wedding wear
58 Like some terminals: Abbr.
59 One of the Simpsons
60 Off the street
61 Sorry sinner
63 Baton Rouge sch.
64 Kitchen gadget
65 1984 Jeff Bridges film
66 Sea off Sicily
69 It's charged
70 Peter Jennings or Shania Twain, by birth
72 Neanderthal man, for one
73 Exile site of 1814
75 Scratch the surface of
76 Atlas abbr.
77 With the mouth wide open
78 Parliament prize
79 E'erlasting
81 Dress down
82 Staff associate?
84 Dress fancily, with "out"
85 Distinguished
86 Diploma word
89 Billiard table cloth
91 "___ time"
92 Cutesy add-on
93 Fifties revival group
96 Some sports score notations
97 Italy's leading auto manufacturer?
101 Part of a joint
102 Presided over
104 On the double
105 Hit the road
106 At the tail
107 No particular place in Italy?
110 Make hard to read
111 Shearer of "The Red Shoes"
112 G.P.A. spoilers
113 Athletic supporter?
114 Struck out
115 Gray
116 Bygone era
117 Job listings, e.g.

DOWN

1 Number two wood
2 Full of wisdom
3 Provoke
4 Styx ferryman
5 Millinery
6 Olive kin
7 Yemen, in biblical times
8 Like Iran's government before the Ayatollah
9 Barbie's maker
10 "Later"
11 Carnival locale
12 Jack's inferior
13 One of the L.A. Rams' Fearsome Foursome
14 Lake cabins, often
15 As far as
16 Top and bottom of an Italian room?
17 Make stout
22 Hardly unconcerned: Var.
24 Stuff
25 AAA
29 A.A.A. suggestion
31 Closed in on
32 One in numismatics
33 Expose
36 Accommodations on an Italian ship?
40 British blueblood
43 Feather bed?
44 Greatest possible
46 Checked item
47 Bob's cousin
48 Daily occurrence
49 Tom, to the piper
50 Italian medical man?
52 Pounce upon
53 ___ Thursday
54 Big 12 team nickname
55 King of music
56 Italian Thanksgiving serving?
57 Lachrymal
61 K-12 grp.
62 Browning work?
65 Fugue feature
67 Fail to mention
68 Opening time, maybe
71 N.B.A. Hall-of-Famer Holman
72 Hound
74 The gamut
77 Thou
80 Parks of civil rights fame
81 Pin
83 Lower in quality
85 Escaped
86 Choral composition
87 Squeaky, maybe
88 Symbols of authority
89 Bowling game
90 Within reach
91 Like Bach's "Magnificat"
92 Warhol works
94 Army command
95 Spruce
98 Joined a conger line?
99 The Beatles inspired it
100 Full of cattails
103 Object of devotion
105 Cold draft
107 North Sea feeder
108 Name in Cambodian history
109 Old Olds

by Richard Silvestri

50 STARTING OVER?

ACROSS

1 One of a study group?
7 Strengthen
13 Checked for heat
20 Potential tennis opponent?
21 Can't take
22 It may be represented by a tree
23 Chevy Chase and others
24 Like a 54-Across
25 Like standard music notation
26 Somme time
27 Start of an idle question
30 Lip
32 Can't take
33 Old lamp fill
34 "My Friend Flicka" author
37 Key material
39 Face of time?
43 Question, part 2
49 Gathering point
50 Beethoven's Opus 20, e.g.
51 Washed away
52 Finger board?
53 "King ___" (1950–65 comic strip)
54 Boot part
56 Athenian H
59 Prospector's dreams
60 Cold development
62 "Apollo 13" subject
64 Knighted dancer ___ Dolin
66 Pilothouse abbr.
67 & 69 Asker of the question
71 Push-up aid?
74 Muff
75 Actor Andrews
77 Psychophar-macologist's prescription
79 Donnybrook
82 Wasn't off one's rocker
84 Nodding one, sometimes
86 ___ mundi
87 Cloudiness
88 Propeller holder, perhaps
90 1954–76 national capital
92 Helps with a con job?
93 Question, part 3
96 Nordstrom rival
97 Work time
98 Like a 117-Across
99 Bow
100 They're heard when Brits take off
103 Sound from a pen
107 End of the question
116 Soccer ___
117 Encircling ring of light
118 Like AB negative, of all major blood types
119 It was defeated in 1588
121 Reedlike
122 Pilot
123 Unsubstantial
124 Service providers?
125 Time-___
126 Superlatively slick

DOWN

1 Loafer's lack
2 "West Side Story" girl
3 Memory units
4 King of France
5 From the top
6 Musician John
7 "King of Hearts" star
8 Up
9 Cheese place
10 Preoperative delivery, once
11 Start of a break-in
12 Helen's mother
13 Smooth
14 How baroque architecture is ornamented
15 Digging, so to speak
16 A-line line
17 Intoxicating Polynesian quaff
18 Major Hoople's outburst, in old comics
19 Take-out order?
28 They may be lent
29 Twelve
31 Infatuated with
35 Get a move on
36 Masters
37 ___ lamb
38 Dwell
39 Botherer
40 One way to serve coffee
41 Plot, perhaps
42 Big name in chips
43 Autocrats
44 Toast beginner
45 Archilochus work
46 It doesn't sting
47 Hero of medieval romances
48 They might get drunk in the summer
49 His "4" was retired
55 It's good to meet them
57 Red ___ (Japanese food fish)
58 Vantage point
61 North American dogwoods
63 Shade provider
65 Unliquidated?
68 "Tuning in the U.S.A." broadcaster: Abbr.
70 68-Down's medium
71 "You are correct!"
72 Talk a blue streak
73 It may precede other things
74 Some are lean
76 In ___ way
78 Head set?
79 Corp. recruits
80 Portoferraio's place
81 Vichyssoise ingredient
83 Schussboomer's transport
85 Took away (from)
89 Accident-assessing areas, briefly
91 Wonderment
93 Dispute subjects, perhaps
94 Beekeeper's exclamation?
95 "Now ___ you . . ."
97 Greeter
100 Spelling and Amos
101 Skip ___
102 Focus of some tests
104 Effigy
105 Meeting points
106 It's headquartered in Troy, Mich.
107 Stinger
108 Molokai show
109 Vultures were sacred to him
110 Carnival sight
111 Winged one in Wonderland
112 Latin I word
113 Collapsed
114 Highland toppers
115 Oblast on the Oka
120 What "5" can mean

by Elizabeth C. Gorski

ACROSS

1 Lets up
7 Rosé alternative
13 Rogue
18 Rossini setting, in España
20 Ancient galley
21 Funnies format feature
22 Start of a verse
24 Where matches are booked
25 Done, for Donne
26 Embedded, in a way
27 1969 Series winners
29 Arab League member
30 Conical-toothed tool
32 Verse, part 2
36 Bargain hunters look for them
39 Nero's title: Abbr.
40 Inveigled
41 Most reliable
45 Start of a recipe direction
48 Place to hibernate
49 Verse, part 3
53 Clayey deposit
56 1951 N.L. Rookie of the Year
57 Suffix with tyranno-
58 Big number, slangily
59 Cal. page header
61 Skydived
64 Verse, part 4
70 Like some sculptures
72 Shine, in commercial names
73 Titillates
74 Verse, part 5
79 Becomes less high, with "up"
80 Indeed

81 Sch. founded by Thomas Jefferson
82 Drone, e.g.
84 Capital of Moravia
85 King Mongkut's realm
88 Verse, part 6
93 Noted Turner
95 Stocking shade
96 Table with a map
97 Metal marble
101 Long-jawed fish
103 Actress Kelly of "Chaplin"
106 Verse, part 7
112 Collars
114 Vexed
115 Prefix with phobia
116 They may compete with boxers
119 Prompt
120 Ace, maybe
122 End of the verse
126 1996 Madonna musical
127 Cricket teams, e.g.
128 Rushed at
129 The Haggadah's read here
130 Bar food
131 Way out

DOWN

1 Nancy, the first woman in Parliament
2 Take off the top
3 Reluctant
4 Hall-of-Fame pitcher Keefe
5 Big South Conference college
6 Pivot around
7 Telephone part
8 A fleur
9 Sphygmo-manometer's place

10 French cathedral city
11 Roast host
12 Grow grinders
13 Where one might take off on a vacation?
14 Early American colony
15 Feeble
16 Gun wielder, say
17 Did some shaving
19 Kind of D.A.
20 "America" pronoun
23 Old verb ending
28 Smooth, in a way
31 Medium for announcements
33 He played Yuri in "Doctor Zhivago"
34 Salon creation
35 Check
37 Director Jean-___ Godard
38 Málaga Mrs.
42 Capt.'s aide
43 Attempt
44 Bull's head?
46 Like some errors
47 SEATO part
49 Hula dancers
50 Daewoo competitor
51 Shorthand system inventor
52 Island north of Montecristo
54 Parents, e.g.
55 Lake of Four Forest Cantons
56 "Home to Harlem" novelist Claude
60 Bas-relief medium
62 W.W. II action locale
63 Morse code click
65 Grp. that sang "Do Ya"
66 Sentences
67 Abbr. in ages

68 Sticky stuff
69 Applied well, as sunscreen
71 Great Lakes fish
75 Level
76 Prego rival
77 Mort from Montreal
78 "Waiting for the Robert ___"
83 Fraction of a joule
86 Personal account
87 ___ fides (bad faith)
89 Sharp quality
90 Squad
91 Special person
92 Musician Brian
94 Brown of Talk magazine
97 Pinches
98 Flourish
99 It moves in a wink
100 Emulates Rembrandt
102 Spring cheepers
104 Unbranched flower cluster
105 Corrupt practices
107 Happy-go-lucky song part
108 Shack
109 Treat for Rover
110 Entreaty for Rover
111 Congers and kin
113 Origins
117 Gala
118 Portmanteau pollution mixture
121 Besmirch
123 "The Loco-Motion" singer Little ___
124 Was a bellwether
125 Are all wet

by Cathy Millhauser

ACROSS

1 Telephone user
7 Obeyed "Down in front!"
10 Everybody
13 Clean the last bit
18 Not straight up
19 A "man that is not passion's slave," in Shakespeare
21 Home of Kansas Wesleyan University
22 Antic
23 Energize
24 Roswell visitors?
25 Cry from Homer Simpson
26 System of measuring cereal by weight?
28 When repeated, an island NW of Tahiti
29 Down
30 ___ while
31 Cracker Jack surprise
32 Big name in real estate
33 Where diners use dinars
34 Prison library's contents?
38 Baseball fig.
39 Stared off into space
41 Sticky stuff
42 Place for a pad
43 Reeve role
44 Family's coat of arms, say
47 In a group of
49 Not yet actualized
52 Ordinary worker
53 Mayan ruin site
57 Grayish
58 Columbus's birthplace
59 Ship salvager's aid
60 Actress Thurman
61 Forbidding
62 Unhip cabbie with passenger?
65 OS/2 company
66 Play bumper-cars
67 "There's ___ In My Soup" (Peter Sellers comedy)
68 Frighten
69 "My ___!"
70 Sit in the bleachers
72 Overhauled
73 Himalayan kingdom
75 Impressionist
76 More sullen
78 Reagan Cabinet member
79 Original Stoic
81 Swiss snowfield
82 Garment industry innovator
87 Line in a voting booth: Abbr.
88 Complain at restaurants?
92 Popular paperback publisher
93 Common desk items
94 Kind of tracks
95 Lobster eggs
96 ___ Xing (street sign)
97 Propeller-head
98 The Merry Men in Sherwood Forest?
103 Hospital V.I.P.'s
104 Took to the stump
105 Musical embellishment
106 Family men
109 They're called "transfers" in Britain
110 Condition sometimes treated by hypnosis
111 Pilgrim's goal
112 Perfect places
113 Ringed?
114 LAX monitor info
115 Most like Iago

DOWN

1 Fort Peck, for one
2 First name in dance
3 "The Naked and the Dead" star
4 Island in a Scottish bay?
5 Grp. with standards
6 Business solicitor
7 33-Across, once
8 Top-notch
9 Fictional teen sleuth Belden
10 Diagonally
11 English professor's deg.
12 Leopold's partner in crime
13 Southeast Asian natives
14 Actress Lena
15 Gun with a silencer?
16 Rattle
17 Bible reading
20 Name on a fridge
21 Clip joint?
26 200-milligram unit
27 Straddling
28 Auction action
29 Exhausted
35 Of the breastbone
36 John ___
37 Fenced-off area
40 Cartoon dog
42 Flesh and blood
45 Lycanthrope's catalyst
46 Waterskin
47 Wing-shaped
48 Bébé watcher
49 Hideouts
50 Music org.
51 Mostly-empty spice rack?
52 Pressed one's nose to the glass
54 Surg. study
55 Planetary shadow
56 Irish P.M. ___ de Valera
58 Doggedness
59 Took places
62 One way to explain a coincidence
63 Algae product
64 Pop singer from Nigeria
69 Emotional scene with actor Grant?
71 TV's "___ Sharkey"
72 Evasive answer
73 Greeted a shepherd
74 Part of H.M.S.
77 Miner's quarry
78 Duncan ___
79 Numbers on letters
80 Went back on stage
81 Laplander, maybe
83 Watch words?
84 Be situated above
85 Goes downhill
86 Objective
88 Potters' needs
89 Flip comment?
90 Chevalier
91 Cheapen
99 Hall-of-Famer Coveleski
100 Performer who fills the club

by Patrick D. Berry

101 Tarpeian Rock's location
102 Pare, say
106 Preamble to the Constitution?
107 Stanley Cup org.
108 Primed

ACROSS

1 See above
7 Refuse
12 Less cool
19 Three-time hockey M.V.P.
20 End product
22 Artist known for his street scenes of Paris
23 Actor getting bad press?
25 Destroy a person
26 Light opening?
27 Gymnast's perch
28 Barely beat
30 Actress who's cold?
34 Karate schools
38 Scriptures volume
41 Suffix added to large numbers
42 Son, sometimes
44 They may be picked out
45 Actress with punishing roles?
49 Sack
50 Tool points
51 Begin liking
52 Grampuses
53 "The __ the limit!"
54 Seconds
55 Article in Der Spiegel
56 Fan sound
57 Slip-up
58 [Boo-hoo!]
59 "Min and Bill" Oscar winner
64 Manilow song setting
65 State-of-the-art
66 Actor who plays terrorists?
69 Trans World Dome player
72 A pluviometer measures it
74 Come before
75 __ breve
76 Go around
78 Tiny particle: Abbr.
80 It comes in sticks
81 Hitter of 660 career home runs
82 Start of a selection process
83 Mrs. Dithers, in the comics
84 Pull out
87 Word processing command
88 Telephone __
89 Actress famous for boxing?
91 Read the U.P.C.
92 Dead accurate
94 Hideaway
95 Equals
96 Baby food
97 Actress in a dressing room?
102 One may be silent
104 St. Paul's architect
105 Grp. with holes in its organization
108 Sri Lanka's capital
111 Actress with the keys to a city?
116 Patron saint of shoemakers
117 Impeach
118 Gelcap alternative
119 Do-nothing's state
120 June of "The Dolly Sisters"
121 Says scornfully

DOWN

1 Fünf und drei
2 Miss Marple's discovery
3 Eastern royal
4 His #4 was retired
5 Big step up from the bleachers
6 Gave a darn?
7 It may be organized
8 Roaster, perhaps
9 "What would you like to know?"
10 Suffix with hand or fist
11 Strips blubber
12 Urbanite's vacation spot
13 Langston Hughes poem
14 More dignified
15 Ford failures
16 France's Belle-__
17 "Boola Boola" singer
18 Ex-Yankee Guidry
21 The Hambletonian, e.g.
24 Heyerdahl craft
29 Lady of Spain
30 Jackson and James
31 Its business is growing
32 Laughfest
33 Words after "yes"
35 Actor with a special way of talking?
36 Initials, maybe
37 Common thing
38 Bunco artist
39 Firebird
40 Actress who does the twist?
43 Julio, e.g.
45 It had the earliest parliament on the European continent
46 They're sometimes split
47 Textile trademark
48 Like some love affairs
53 Forest runner
57 Archaic attention-getters
60 Aquanaut's base
61 Dict. listing
62 "Saving Private Ryan" craft: Abbr.
63 Tampa-to-Orlando dir.
64 Some liqueurs
66 Punster
67 British surgeon Sir James
68 Chopin piece
70 Three-time placer in the 1978 Triple Crown
71 "Free" people
73 Station closing?
75 Comedian, e.g.
76 Framed
77 Actor Reeves
78 Feldspar variety
79 Fremont National Forest site
83 Midwest city, on scoreboards
84 Mark for life
85 Assam silkworm
86 Screwballer Hubbell
89 Sound system components
90 Unearthly
93 Peace of mind
95 Scribe
98 Gulf of Finland feeder
99 Registration datum
100 Dernier __
101 "Endymion" writer
103 Power stats
105 "Here Is Your War" author
106 One on the move
107 Stratagems
108 Early third-century date

by Lloyd E. Pollet

109 First or second,
 e g.: Abbr.
110 Capp diminutive
112 Color TV pioneer
113 Informal British
 address
114 Sussex suffix
115 Tac's dad

ACROSS

1 Wild place?
5 Here, elsewhere
8 Zimbabwe's capital
14 Plow puller
18 Doozy
19 Narrow margin of victory
21 They may come from Qom
22 Big Indian
23 Dull routine
24 "Good Stykeeping" award?
27 Garlicky dish
29 Princess of Nintendo games
30 Three-time Wimbledon winner
31 Report from a Pamplona beer bash?
37 Relative of a mandolin
38 Some are wicked
39 Financial backer
42 Simps' syllables
46 Shoot for
47 Humped ox
51 Gem symbolizing the soul
53 Kind of jacket
54 Biblical particle?
56 Fumbles for words
57 Popular analgesic
59 "___ boy!"
60 Set free
61 Chew the rag
62 Burst into laughter
64 Franklin and Jefferson, for two
65 Understudies for a star of "The Piano"?
70 Nickers?
73 Bring back to life, in a way
74 Whup

77 Oppenheimer development
78 Elhi orgs.
82 Timex competitor
83 Kachina doll carver
84 Containers of gourmet ice cream?
86 Application blank info
87 Scottish ___
89 Souvenir buys
90 Coarse-grained
91 Fast time?
93 Symbol of authority
94 Pizzeria order
95 Not up
97 Feeling ill, simply put?
107 Divert
109 Silly
110 Regulars' requests
111 Uneasy feeling regarding have-nots?
117 Thumbs-down reactions
118 Complex division
119 The Sandwich Islands, today
120 Georgia Senator until 1997
121 Yellowfin, e.g.
122 The King of Egypt sings in it
123 91-Across ender
124 Véronique, e.g.: Abbr.
125 Cut down

DOWN

1 Defeat
2 Methuselah's father
3 Stiff hairs
4 Terrified ones
5 Be firm
6 Rimsky-Korsakov's "Le ___ d'Or"

7 Maker of the Amigo S.U.V.
8 Poet Doolittle
9 Thundering
10 The "so few" of 1940: Abbr.
11 It makes men mean
12 Shred
13 Second sight
14 Lucky strike
15 Like some roofs
16 Cracked open
17 Oast filler
20 Extra-wide
25 Unser Jr. and Sr.
26 McCarthy's quarry
28 Comedian Poundstone
32 Logician's abbr.
33 "Middlemarch" author
34 Priests
35 City named for an Indian tribe
36 Classified listings: Abbr.
39 Far from ruddy
40 March Madness org.
41 Stare, like a tourist
43 Oscar-winning actress Miyoshi
44 Sanctuary
45 Frère's sibling
46 Singer DiFranco
47 Pueblo builders
48 Diner sign
49 Jolly old chap
50 Instruments from 119-Across
52 Root beer brand
55 Express doubt about
58 Rock's Reed
62 Sauce style
63 Kind of dispenser
64 Clear, in a way
65 Apples, e.g.

66 Townie
67 Pol's concern
68 "Barnaby Jones" actor
69 Numeral in a Uris title
70 Slew
71 Anne Nichols hero
72 Stop listening, with "out"
74 Related
75 Eat like ___
76 "Great shot!"
78 Romeo's rival
79 Wrist-radio wearer
80 Befuddled
81 Onetime lottery org.
83 Recruits, in a way
85 Troy Aikman's alma mater
88 Encourages
92 Espied, to Tweety
94 Appear
96 "The ___ Identity" (Ludlum novel)
97 Actor Dennis
98 Former court org.
99 "Socrate" composer
100 Biblical land of riches
101 Never, in Nuremberg
102 Nascar broadcaster
103 Big bills
104 "Le Bestiaire" artist Dufy
105 "Uncle Vanya" woman
106 Blue-book filler
107 Light hue
108 Certain bond, for short
112 Any ship
113 Regulatory org. since 1958
114 Injection reactions, maybe
115 Maze runner
116 Where Windsor is: Abbr.

by Brendan Emmett Quigley

55 TWIN STATES

ACROSS

1 Scampi ingredients
7 Pent up
12 Wire-haired terrier of film
16 Soften up
20 More than budding
21 Down East town
22 Axis/Allies conflict: Abbr.
23 Take out
24 They never need to be renewed
27 Kind of situation
28 "You got that right!"
29 Opposing
31 Plundered, old-style
35 Jet
36 Confucian path
38 Bit of energy
39 Pharmaceutical giant
45 All __ Airways
50 Bicyclist's choices
51 Haemoglobin deficiency
52 Uncreative
53 Unrefined
54 Series continuation
57 Poet Sexton
59 Thou
60 Walter Reuther's org.
61 Suffix with cannon
62 Cable staple
65 They're coated with red wax
68 Inadvisable action
70 Spanish wave
71 One may be a favorite
72 Thick-plumed songbird
73 London landmark
77 Ladies of Versailles: Abbr.
79 Doesn't keep
80 "The Old Wives' Tale" playwright

81 One may be taken to the cleaners
83 Actress Graff
85 "Zuckerman Unbound" novelist
88 Relieves
90 1991 Midler/ Allen comedy
95 Yamaguchi's rival at Albertville
96 Literary Inits.
97 Korea's Roh __ Woo
99 Seat of McLennan County, Texas
100 Invest
101 Kelly classic
106 "Black utopia" of 1920
107 It may be recombinant
108 Sending to the canvas
109 One available for future reference?
110 Traveled in tandem?
112 Remove the dirt from?
114 Wife of King Mark of Cornwall
116 Flaw
118 They have a glow about them
119 More apothegmatic
120 Look like
124 Roadside jumpers: Abbr.
126 "La-la" lead-in
127 Ages
128 Hebrew for "delight"
129 "L'Isle joyeuse" composer
136 Tracy's pair
138 Beleaguering brother
139 Question from one who doesn't get it
146 Perfidies
147 Women's rights pioneer

148 R. J. Reynolds brand
149 Aiea apparel
150 Perturb
151 Turner and others
152 Like Henry VIII
153 Procure

DOWN

1 Compadre
2 Diamond letters
3 Furry fellow of 80's TV
4 Job experience?
5 "Don't look at me!"
6 "__ People" (Le Carré best seller)
7 Begins airing
8 Hammer in oil
9 Elapse
10 Chemical ending
11 L'Age __
12 Dr. Seuss's "Horton Hears __"
13 Go through channels?
14 Home of the brave?: Var.
15 Laon's department
16 Enterprise counselor Deanna
17 "Foul Play" star
18 Message on a tag-sale tag
19 Didn't stop
23 Occupying oneself with
25 "Melodies and Memories" autobiographer
26 Length and width
30 Bouquet __
31 Firefighter, at times
32 Where many Goyas hang
33 Add to the dossier
34 Scrabble draws
36 Bar need
37 Vigorously
40 Joseph Smith's denom.

41 One kept in the bag?
42 Menotti hero
43 When many people punch in
44 Indian of the Sacramento River valley
46 Lustrous velvet
47 Frequently exhibiting
48 Steal a march on
49 Atomic experiments
54 Game show lineup
55 Like an idol
56 Flat rate
58 Eponym of an old auto
63 "Really!"
64 See 143-Down
66 "Happy Days" fellow
67 Bankruptcy follow-up
69 Raised-eyebrow remarks
74 It was once divided
75 Where to have a cabin
76 Anita Brookner's "Hotel du __"
78 Goof
79 Staff differently
82 Houston-to-Dallas dir.
84 __ Valley, San Francisco
85 Take the chance
86 Of no use
87 More chic
89 Writer Shelby
91 Hereditary title
92 Teed off
93 Crescent moon
94 Attacks, in a way
96 Targets of criminal probes
98 Unpaid debt
102 Lions' prey
103 "Sunny" singer Bobby
104 Less emotional

by Frank Longo

105 St. Gregory's
residence
111 Bearded
revolutionary
112 Embargo
113 Small suckers
115 Kind of secret
117 Robbins and others
118 Riviera resort

121 Ho polloi
122 Look good on
123 Nursery supply
125 Early adders
129 High-hatter?
130 It may be
found in a cone
131 Iraqi V.I.P.
Tariq ___

132 Ubangi feeder
133 Eskimo
transport
134 Wallop
135 Fast Atl.
crossers, once
136 Eye
137 Short end
140 Equi-

141 Pick up
142 It's heard
before a snap
143 With 64-Down,
1964 Beatles
tune
144 Rapa ___
(Easter Island)
145 Starter's need

56 CO_2

ACROSS

1 Action film sequence
6 TV monitor?
9 Kind of car
13 Twist
18 Until, in Tijuana
19 Solid backing
21 Sauce
22 Suggestions
23 Deep red garnet
24 Not skimpy
25 One who wants the crème de mint?
27 Steak, e.g.
29 Relations
30 Bewail
31 He's a doll
32 Tilts
33 Simple sack
34 Failures
37 Basted
38 Macaroni shape
41 Pro___
42 Very smart
44 Professional suffix
47 Sound of thunder
48 Where a suit may be pressed
51 Large-print edition of the Bible, e.g.
53 Do-nothing
55 Pulls down
56 The T in M.T.M.
57 Brezhnev, to Khrushchev
58 Yacht centers
60 Veneer
61 Slicker
62 Subject of environmentalist study
63 Pass out
64 Plantations' stations
66 "___ stirreth up strifes": Proverbs
67 Heavy
70 Some clarinets
71 Street clearer
72 Greenish blue
73 Nostril wrinkler
74 Ice pack?
77 Love symbol
78 "Go on . . ."
79 Fit
80 Bounce
81 Operative
82 Tricksters
84 Passes on principle
87 Do a takeoff on
88 Brownie topper
91 Department in Provence
92 ". . . sat down beside ___"
93 Actor Vigoda
96 Where U.P.S. is headquartered
98 Visitor from the sticks
102 Furniture ensemble
103 Didn't flare
105 Crime scene evidence
106 Gardener's gadget
107 Hoosier neighbor
108 Plains Indian
109 Ships
110 Major finale?
111 Pepper, for one
112 More reliable

DOWN

1 Peeper
2 Tonkin Delta capital
3 Like a fly reel
4 Phaser setting
5 Suffer embarrassment
6 Parking lot sign
7 Occurred
8 Loon
9 Fallen apart
10 Slammer
11 Poet's time of day
12 Stag party?
13 Boxer's sparring partner, at times
14 School without dorms
15 Subject of sailors' knowledge
16 Big splash
17 Stimulates
19 Heavy blow
20 Prepares for a hand
26 No longer hot
28 Button in Bond's car
33 Avoiding a clash
34 Dolt
35 Blyth of "Mildred Pierce"
36 Looked down on
37 Participants in 32-Across
38 Sweeping
39 Follower of the news?
40 Birds fly back and forth in it
41 Fool mistake
43 Barbarous brutes
45 Diamond ___
46 Counterfeit cops?
48 Hands over
49 "Give me your answer"
50 "Educating Rita" star
52 A little work
54 Burrows
56 Running figure
58 Committed a hockey infraction
59 Tenochtitlán resident
60 Bat eyelashes
63 Detour
64 Chairman of note
65 Two-time Emmy winner as best actor in a comedy
66 Rise
68 Barge ___
69 Jay's home
71 Sounds of unhappiness
72 Anagram of 71-Down
74 French royal name, 987–1328
75 Wake attendees
76 Expensive gift
81 Opportune
83 They go for the gold
85 Undergo natural selection
86 Hit 70's sitcom
87 Truman's nuclear agcy.
88 Bags of diamonds
89 Liszt's "La Campanella," e.g.
90 Set straight
92 Noted park name
93 One of 3.5 billion
94 Pig out
95 Computer command
97 "___ forgive our debtors"
98 Western weapon
99 H.S. subject
100 Let out
101 Major animal?
104 Bit of repartee

by Harvey Estes and Nancy Salomon

ACROSS

1 Half of a 1955 merger: Abbr.
4 Florida footballer
9 "Zip-___-Doo-Dah"
13 Mallow family plant
17 Strive
18 Horror film director George
19 Like relaxed-fit jeans
21 Conch shell effect
22 VIOLENCE ON THE ICE GETS OUT OF HAND!
26 Some Iroquois
27 Burdens
28 Releases
29 Great bargain
30 Shoe strengthener
31 Does something appealing?
32 Ending with Smurf or Rock
35 Dormmate
38 Word on the Great Seal
42 CONCERT ENDS WITH DISH ON FAN'S HEAD!
48 Partially
49 "The Sound of Music" song
50 Hibernia
51 Do in
52 Half-and-half half
54 Dudley Do-Right's beloved
55 ___ Tan (cigar brand)
56 Paesano's land
57 Clueless
59 Ref. room offering
61 Chapeau's perch
63 INSURGENT'S PARKA IS GUNFIRE CASUALTY!
71 Michigan college
72 Blue shade

73 Section of Queens
74 Five-iron, once
78 Year in the life of Constantine
81 Figures on Pharaohs' headdresses
83 Afoam
84 Basket material
85 Symbol on a phone button
86 Works with measures
88 Back-to-sch. times
89 OPERATING PHYSICIAN HAS TROUBLE WITH STATIC CLING!
93 Squid squirts
94 Back-baring top
95 Autocrat
96 Church center
97 Juanita's "those"
100 Not upright
105 Dancing man in "Dancing Lady"
109 Zealous
111 Don't mind
113 ONE PART OF EMPLOYEE RETURNS TO JOB!
116 As old as ___
117 Postembryonic
118 With class
119 A.A.A. recommendation
120 Bank take-back
121 Campaigner's stand
122 Kind of mail
123 Teakettle sound

DOWN

1 One of the Three Musketeers
2 Attack locale
3 French school
4 "Tauromaquia" artist
5 Rockers' equipment

6 Part of A.T.&T.: Abbr.
7 Electioneer
8 Shade of blue
9 A lot, maybe
10 First of two related lists
11 German resort
12 Overflowing
13 Lunchbox treat
14 Brown and Williamson brand
15 Large number
16 Pounds' sounds
18 Colorful partridge
20 Union member
23 1990's car
24 Prefix with version
25 "The Nanny" network
30 "___ off to see the Wizard"
31 Ancient Sernite
33 Pro ___
34 Window over a door
36 Chit writer
37 Medley
38 ___ cosa (something else): Sp.
39 Kind of time
40 Lucie's father
41 Ready to go in
42 Somewhat, slangily
43 "Er . . . um . . ."
44 Poet/dramatist Larry et al.
45 Country towers
46 One who makes a bundle
47 Checks to make sure
48 Fraud
53 Heavy sweaters
56 Oft-misused contraction
58 Something underfoot?
60 Criticize, slangily

62 Catholic Reformation writer
64 Feeling
65 Animal with striped legs
66 1997 boxer of the ear?
67 Extinguish
68 Corinthian, for one
69 Gossamer
70 Those opposed
74 ___ operandi (ways of working)
75 ". . . unto us ___ is given"
76 Like some Jokes
77 "___ a Rebel" (1962 Crystals hit)
79 Four-striper: Abbr.
80 Rock's Mötley ___
82 Gnats, rats, etc.
85 Drooled
87 Married mujer: Abbr.
90 Zhivago portrayer
91 Ragú alternative
92 Lush, in a way
96 Biomed. research agency
98 Lord's workers
99 Alan of "Havana"
101 Throw, as a grenade
102 Certain girders
103 Sunnites and Shiites, e.g.
104 Wee ones
105 At a distance
106 Pro or con
107 Kisser
108 Shots, for short
109 Morales of "La Bamba"
110 Hand-held holers
111 Vier preceder
112 "___ show you!"
114 Posting at SFO or LAX
115 Old Spanish queen

by Cathy Millhauser

ACROSS

1 Doesn't stop cold turkey
10 Chooses
13 First call?
17 Hesitant
23 No longer painful
24 Like a chandelier
26 Kind
27 It may pick up in the afternoon
28 Like most bottles
29 Turn out
30 Hear
31 Fished in crevices
32 Performer of complicated operations
34 Toulouse time
35 ___ Day
37 Pertaining to church taxes, old-style
38 See 83-Across
40 Ground for a claim
43 Unbalanced
47 Testify
49 Tighten
51 Cavern
52 Utter
54 Descendant of Muhammad the Prophet
55 Spread out
58 Like some traditions
60 Mount Vernon, e.g.
62 Treasured instrument
64 Dwight Eisenhower's mother's name
65 With judgment
67 Flushed
69 Windy City rail system, briefly
70 Noted Russian shrine
73 Isn't cautious (with)
76 "Buy" or "sell," say
77 Word in Kansas' motto
79 Like
80 Hopper
81 Mathematician Hein
82 Legalistic adjective
83 With 38-Across, popular entertainment
85 5.5-point type sizes
87 View
90 "Description of the World" writer
92 Connected
93 Mescaline source
94 Kind of vaccine
95 Work on
96 With the bow, in music
97 Shade of green
98 Year the Roman writer Persius died
100 Fictional lawyer
101 Tell-tale weapon?
106 Reason for coyness, maybe
110 Exercise
112 Liaison
113 Subject of Project Blue Book
114 Put on the shelf
116 Kid
117 Blatherskite
118 Early game score
120 Milking area
121 Nut
124 "Ah'm ___ it!"
125 New Jersey ___
126 Bridge comment
130 Childish doings?
132 Earthquake aftermaths
134 Isolate
136 Duplicate
137 More subtle
138 Crayola shade
140 Verse style
143 Debussy subject
146 Shows level-headedness
153 Feuding
154 Can
155 "An Old-Fashioned Girl" author, 1870
156 Entertaining thoughts
157 Cooks
159 Top
160 Fertilizer ingredients
161 Like most paparazzi
162 Volleyball player
163 Wraps up, so to speak
164 TV drama settings
165 Place for verbal expression

DOWN

1 Soupçon
2 Whistle, maybe
3 Old-time entertainer
4 "Chicago" lyricist Fred
5 Goes back over
6 Shooter's supply
7 1887 La Scala premiere
8 Hats with tassels: Var.
9 "The Godfather, Part II" character
10 Tough luck, in Britain
11 Medicare cutback proponents?
12 Hit hard
13 "Immediately!"
14 Up
15 Bringing down
16 Crane
17 John Huston's film-directing debut
18 Opposite of smooth
19 Big bird: Var.
20 Chapter
21 "A Loss of Roses" playwright
22 Fantail, for one
25 "It ___" ("Who's there?" response)
33 Cry before disaster
36 Colorado natives
39 Kind of valve
41 Onetime military engineer for Cesare Borgia
42 Seat of Humboldt County, Calif.
44 Examine thoroughly
45 Starve
46 Gave birth to whelps
47 Buyouts, e.g.
48 Actor M. ___ Walsh
49 Log carrier
50 Show fear
53 Kids
56 Was moved by
57 Take over
59 Lily, in Lille
61 The Euphrates crosses it: Abbr.
63 Site of a black hole
66 Web site?
67 Capitalist's concern
68 It's tied at the back
71 Manet, at times
72 Fundamental
74 "Symphonie espagnole" composer
75 Tangy ethnic food
78 One of the Channel Islands
83 Group with Grammy's 1982 Record of the Year
84 Word with sing or string
86 Mailing to a casting director
87 They don't take turns
88 Some canines
89 Nonsense
90 Wing, say
91 Model
92 Upstairs, in Uruguay
93 Igneous rock far beneath the earth's surface
94 Dear people?
96 Intermission ender, maybe
99 Part of a football play diagram
100 Like some bedsheet corners, in Britain
102 Bind, as grass stalks
103 Setting of many Stephen King novels
104 Instrument lens
105 Detaches, in a way
107 Printing amount
108 Poet's eye
109 Rupture

by David J. Kahn

111 Fliers with wedge-shaped tails
115 Sad feeling
119 Six-time Rose Bowl winner, for short
122 Billion years
123 Major fishing area in the Pacific Rim
127 Blows away, so to speak
128 1979 Duvall title role
129 ___ month (moon phase recurrence)
131 Roy Orbison classic
133 How complainers complain
135 It can put you to sleep
137 "The French Lieutenant's Woman" author
139 Appalachian feature
141 Apology preceder
142 Alpha, beta, gamma, etc.
144 Top dogs
145 Order to a typographer
146 Family dogs
147 Latin pronoun
148 Macintosh, e.g.
149 Plug
150 Anvil locations
151 ___ stroke
152 Spot
158 Rounder than round

ACROSS

1 Eritrea's capital
7 Heart contraction
14 "The ___ Williams Show" of 1960's TV
18 Bearers of calves
19 Many a Floridian
20 Dressed (up)
21 Alaska denizens
23 Fiasco at the bar?
25 Trial
26 Rural tracts
28 Lecterns
29 Hosts
30 Minimally
32 The Baron, of college basketball
34 Bleaching solution
35 Maximum
36 Direct
38 Jupiter and others
40 "Dream-Land" poet
41 Conscription problem?
43 City or province of Spain
47 Ornamental attire
48 Dick
49 Fire
50 Crepe de Chine, e.g.
52 Actor Erwin
53 "___ fliegende Holländer" (Wagner opera)
55 Part of a classical trio
57 Inexpensive cigar
59 Black
61 A little knight life?
65 Actress Benaderet
66 Desktop problem
68 Unconventional
69 Effective
71 Pop musician Ocasek
72 Tom's fishing gear?
75 Sound units
76 They can be twisted
78 Nerve opening?
79 Bubblehead
81 It's bigger than a med.
82 Lighten up?
83 "Le Coq ___"
84 Summit gatherers, for short
86 Locale in the game Clue
88 Lampoons
91 Pop stars turned versifiers?
95 Publisher Ballantine
96 How to give a reprimand
98 ___ nous
99 Unruffled
102 PC component
103 Kid's ball material
105 "Leaving Las Vegas" actress
106 Opening at an opening
107 March
109 River to the Colorado
111 Inuit: Abbr.
112 Little laughter while still on the runway?
115 Suggest
117 Dentist's request
118 Column feature
119 Amazed onlooker, e.g.
120 Vaulted church area
121 Yields
122 Yield

DOWN

1 Opposite of smooth
2 Marksman
3 Did some quick metalwork?
4 Ryan's "Love Story" co-star
5 "Get ___!"
6 Poser
7 S.A.T. takers
8 Shrill cry
9 Cop's contact
10 Do some craftwork
11 Saturnalias
12 Princess who observed the Force
13 Yet, in poems
14 Ancient Incan capital
15 Cooper's tools
16 Sign a new lease
17 Summer quaffs
20 Became faint
22 Fahd, for one
24 Stench
27 Light arrays
31 Fallback position
33 Diving maneuver
35 Very soon after
37 A.C.L.U. concerns: Abbr.
39 Infant's need, for short
42 Oft-framed document
43 ___ Grande, Ariz.
44 Bear, in Bolivia
45 Hypothesis about the origin of bracelets?
46 Property recipient, in law
49 "The Life of the Insects" playwright
51 Poet who wrote "A thing of beauty is a joy for ever"
52 Steinbeck's birthplace
54 Light brown
55 Union locale
56 Cougar, briefly
57 60's–70's hallucinogen
58 Yardarm attachments
59 Jettison
60 Cigar end?
62 Judicious
63 1984 Peace Prize recipient
64 Some deer
67 Replies of confusion
70 Spray alternatives
73 Queue before Q
74 End of a trip
77 Actor Cariou
80 H. Rider Haggard adventure
83 Buggy terrain
84 According to
85 "Buddenbrooks" author
87 Rue Morgue culprit
89 One of the Lennon sisters
90 Filled
91 Show
92 Full of feeling
93 One on a board
94 Pleasure ___
96 Benchwarmers
97 Lozenge
99 Old money
100 Formal jackets
101 Put out
104 Dentist's suggestion
106 City on the Yamuna River
107 So
108 Surveyor's work
110 Architectural pier
113 11-member 19th-century org.
114 MS. preparers
116 Vocal objection

by Rich Norris

ACROSS

1 "Much Ado About Nothing" friar
8 Long Island town with a weather station
13 Diversified
20 Lake of the Four Forest Cantons
21 Queen topper
22 Quite a while back
23 Without change
24 Pianist Claudio
25 To the extent that
26 Chat
27 The
29 Film frame
30 Kin to blackguards and knaves
32 Some coal carriers
33 Opening run
35 Bill passers
36 Boulez's New York Philharmonic successor
37 Psalm ender
42 Pulitzer playwright Akins
43 Carry out
45 "I'm so glad!"
46 Biblical question
47 Overlooked
49 Purple shade
51 Heavy-duty hauler
52 Pretend
53 Gather with difficulty
57 "Batman" sound effect
58 Language of Mexico
61 A castle of Blackbeard overlooks its harbor
63 ["Oh my!"]
66 Russian name meaning "holy"
68 "___ your disposal"
69 Where Davy Crockett was born: Abbr.
70 Ghostlike
75 Word that's an accidental acronym of a Hemingway title
77 Santa Fe-to-Roswell dir.
78 Overwraps
79 Oversight
83 Home with a view
85 Great times
87 Showed off, as biceps
89 Substantial
90 Finish completely, with "up"
93 Juice providers?
95 "___ then I said . . ."
96 Doesn't work
97 Become a member
99 Shot maker
100 Race place
101 Phony
102 Experience
103 Wedded
104 Slips, e.g.
110 Uncomfortable
114 Gourmet sprinkle
115 ". . . ___ in the affairs of men": Shak.
116 Offender
117 Driving force
118 Mission in "The Thin Red Line"
119 Short solo
120 More lathered
121 Downing Street family, 1955–57
122 Is displeased and then some

DOWN

1 One way to fall
2 Stratagem
3 Soufflé ingredient?
4 Fit together
5 Barbaric
6 ___ the finish
7 Kind of shorts
8 "That makes sense"
9 Begets
10 1968 British comedy "Only When I ___"
11 Poker player's declaration
12 Potbellied
13 Get way too thin
14 Stravinsky and others
15 Skillful
16 Morales of "La Bamba"
17 Bust maker
18 Alike: Fr.
19 Two teaspoons, say
28 Itty-bitty bit
31 Car co. bought by Chrysler
33 Blue, in Baja
34 Cut to the ___
35 Can
36 Big drawer?
37 When early-bird specials often end
38 Emergency PC key
39 At risk
40 Transport of song
41 Offers?
43 Sicilian spouter
44 Rear end
48 Zing
50 Be off
51 Beats in a pie contest?
54 Got off
55 Little dog, briefly
56 Pennsylvanie, e.g.
59 "I love you, Juanita"
60 As well
61 Like some transactions
62 Like a rat in ___
63 One of a Christmas trio
64 Appropriate
65 Panoramas
67 Roscoe
71 They rise above sea level
72 Tee follower?
73 Flynn on screen
74 Whom "she saw . . . on a seesaw," in a children's ditty
76 Where to find Aletsch Glacier
80 Our world
81 Cause to go
82 Swirl
84 Short order, for short
86 Mount in 1980 news
87 Clones, e.g.
88 "Who am ___ judge?"
90 Many a dinosaur
91 Doing kitchen duty, to a G.I.
92 Set up
94 Caustic cleanser
98 Preached
100 Sulking
101 Kind of heart or teeth
102 Was sustained by
103 Stan's man
104 Goddess in "Aïda"
105 "Little ___"
106 Spanish appetizer
107 "The Bronx ___ . . ."

by Manny Nosowsky

ACROSS

1 Brute
7 Pregame fixture
13 Joke
20 Embodiment
21 Solar wind source
22 Property receiver
23 I (1946)
26 Reactions to baby pictures
27 Big bang creator
28 Sci-fi extra
29 Cancún kinsman
30 Curlew's cousin
31 Drive gear
34 Chicago's ___ Expressway
36 Anticipatory exclamation
39 "My Mama Done ___ Me"
40 Burning heat
41 1998 report producer
43 It (1961)
47 Misfortunes
51 Charles de Gaulle's birthplace
52 Cell component
53 Capitulate
55 Employ a therapeutic technique
59 Fed. grant giver
62 Red dye no. 1?
63 They may get a licking after dinner
64 From the heart
67 Frostflower
68 Serb, e.g.
71 He (1975)
74 Person with vows
75 More than flinches
77 Features of a face
78 1930 Triple Crown jockey
80 Viola d'___
81 Part of B.C.E.
82 Flivver

85 Movie that Khrushchev watched being filmed
87 Fritter away
91 Kind of sprawl
93 Accordingly
94 They (1951)
100 Cabbage
102 1990 stage and film biography
103 Renowned British runner
104 Marxist?
105 After-bath application
108 Sleep inducer
110 Recycled item
112 Itinerary abbr.
113 Refuse
115 Old Plymouth
117 Itinerary word
120 You (1977)
125 Triumph
126 Does more than see
127 Relative of jujuism
128 Revolution's enemy, maybe
129 Fixes firmly
130 Novelist's need

DOWN

1 Roman-fleuve
2 Testify
3 Distillery items
4 Letters in a long-distance
5 Cartoonist Wilson
6 Recluse
7 With intensity
8 Prohibition
9 National debt unit
10 Dearie
11 Insect study: Abbr.
12 Muslim messiah
13 De Niro's role in "Raging Bull"

14 The Morlocks ate them
15 Beam
16 Confident solver's tool
17 Bind
18 Kerensky's successor
19 Building toy
24 Flavor
25 Remove a slip?
30 We (1945)
32 Slangy suffix
33 Demond's co-star, in 70's TV
35 She (1989)
36 Night stalker
37 It grows on you
38 Mideast peace talks site
42 Kind of welder
44 Yaw
45 "The Beggar's Opera" writer
46 Buttinsky
48 Slow, to Salieri
49 Shroud of Turin material
50 Lewis Carroll animal
54 "Gotcha!"
56 Bike part: Abbr.
57 Baggy
58 Moore co-star
60 Discretion
61 Negotiate, as a loan
64 Successor to the Prophet, in Islam
65 Cry of pain
66 Road houses?
68 Parker's need
69 Missouri town where Truman was born
70 Onward
72 It's a drag to fishermen
73 "___ momento"
76 Part of a Hemingway title

79 Oil container
82 Copy cats?
83 "East of Eden" girl
84 Picnic hamperer
86 York, for one: Abbr.
88 "Comin' ___" (1981 3-D western)
89 Close
90 Air
92 Vocal opposition
95 Without interest
96 Oversight
97 Straight, in a way
98 Laplander, e.g.
99 Corrupt
101 Part of a Hemingway title
105 Proffer bait
106 Fur seal
107 Morning alarm
109 Ship that brought the Statue of Liberty to the United States
111 Join securely
114 This pulls a bit
116 Endorsed
117 Middle of a famous boast
118 ___ a secret
119 Worked up
121 1960's singer Little ___
122 Flight
123 Ballot abbr.
124 Provincetown catch

ACROSS

1 Buñuel collaborator
5 Satan, at first
10 Brought on board
15 Stadium that seats 55,000+
19 Orwell's alma mater
20 Dog or hound
21 Accustom
22 Jacks take them
23 Big boom boxes?
25 Smoking settlements?
27 Forger
28 What dispensaries dispense
30 Suffuse
31 ___ Lingus
33 Stands for
34 Items for those seeking closure
35 Like some candles
39 Cub house
40 Secular
41 Bach wrote over 200 of these
43 1773 jetsam
46 Moscow resident
50 Baseball's Vizquel
51 Strip joint instruction?
55 Like some fears
56 Singer Clark
59 Madonna, originally
60 They're exclusive
61 Sodium or chlorine
63 Insurance co. employee
64 List abridgements
66 Like Life Savers
68 A deliveryman may have one
69 Outstanding
73 Hindu honorific
75 Readies, in a way
80 Car owner's headache
81 Brush
84 First-aid item
85 Sleipnir's master
86 Clucking clairvoyant?
88 Machu Picchu worshipper
89 Drink
91 Flexible fish
92 Toy for indoor play
95 Jumpers, informally
96 Pride
99 Puck stoppers
100 Swinger
103 Michelangelo's marble source
107 Maui's ___ Crater
108 Oriental nursemaids
109 Uses a shortcut
111 94-Down's faith
115 Binary language?
117 F.B.I. director's side of the story?
119 Pole, e.g.
120 Papal court
121 Skater Stojko
122 Cubic Rubik
123 Newcastle's river
124 Bridge guardian
125 Studio stock
126 Ocean

DOWN

1 G.O.P. opposers
2 First half of the files?
3 Burt's ex
4 What many a baby throws?
5 Overpower
6 Convention
7 Classic 1925 Von Stroheim film
8 Undercut
9 Basic amino acid
10 "Start playing!"
11 "Seven ___ blow" (boast in a children's story)
12 Hicks
13 History chapters
14 Christmas time: Abbr.
15 Spare tire eliminator?
16 Seasonings
17 Finish
18 Boobs
24 Kind of radiation, in science fiction
26 Paramecium fringe
29 Happy
32 Like Gen. Schwarzkopf
34 No-goodniks
35 Aim improver
36 Great Pyramids sight
37 Related through a mother
38 Cassette type: Abbr.
40 Black-and-white engraving
42 Break down, in a way
44 Ship's heading
45 Sign to look elsewhere
47 Methane's lack
48 Goya's duchess
49 Noun suffix
52 Dry run
53 Kind of nut
54 Stevenson's "Prince ___"
57 Admit
58 Quotation notation
60 Gregg grad
62 Locks
65 Needle case
67 Pitch-dark
69 Make a splash
70 Fix up
71 Drop a line?
72 Royal records?
73 People in photos, usually
74 Ocasek of the Cars
76 Mealtime prayer result?
77 Site of 1967 fighting
78 Tom or Sam
79 Carillon sounds
82 Letters on a scoreboard
83 Female lobster
86 Novel creation
87 Like certain battery terminals: Abbr.
90 Crow
93 Unnamed litigant
94 Dervish
97 Muster
98 Brooks Robinson, e.g.
100 Biblical verb
101 "Our Town" heroine
102 Heathen
103 Where the Mississippi meets the Ohio
104 Use
105 Kind of gland
106 Get ___ on (hurry)
109 Innuendo
110 Like Darth Maul
112 Capital of Rome
113 Top-notch
114 The L train?
116 Be in a cast
118 Slalom curve

by Greg Staples

ACROSS

1 Stone of some Libras
5 AM selections: Abbr.
9 Tussle
14 Raising a sweat, perhaps
19 Pitch
20 Foot: Prefix
21 Verse from Villon
22 Do some campaign work
23 When to slop in the mud on the farm?
26 Kind of joint
27 Gray, for one
28 Maryland athlete, for short
29 Almost purée
31 "___ dreaming?"
32 Like some apartments
33 Council of ___ (1409 assembly)
35 With bite
37 Took action
38 60's coll. radicals
39 Wisest of the centaurs, in Greek myth
41 Brown shade
42 Not be alert
43 Tale of a tiny bellower?
46 Talk effusively
49 Alpine sight
50 Hot to trot
51 Priest of I Samuel
52 Shoulder piece
54 20's beer barrel busters
55 Like some shopping
59 Homecoming visitors
60 Acted like
62 Apple product
64 Shortly before?
65 Traitorous intruder?
68 What an ass declares in cards?
71 Berlioz's "Les Nuits d'___"
72 Beloved subject of Thomas Campbell
73 Jaywalking, e.g.
74 Home run, slangily
75 Not at all like
78 Newswriter's specialty
80 Exploitative employer
82 Rough stuff
83 Tot toter
84 Stitch souvenir
86 Abbr. starting some corp. names
87 Bedtime reading in the forest?
93 Place for a run
94 Call upon
95 Canine cover
96 Calendar abbr.
99 Roaster, maybe
100 Nonabrasive
101 Cross with a loop
102 They exist from hand to mouth
104 It's often left hanging
105 "Got it"
106 Warrant follower
108 High point
110 Takes off life support?
112 "Time to have a foal"?
115 Gold standard
116 Pal
117 Profusion
118 Prince Albert, e.g.
119 Doesn't fold
120 Like cancan dancers
121 Noise pollution
122 Play opener

DOWN

1 Them
2 Held jointly
3 Troublemakers, never
4 Potted plant place
5 1974 Sutherland/Gould spoof
6 Airborne faultfinder
7 Botheration
8 Separates
9 Prodder
10 Tight
11 "Radio Free Europe" rock band
12 Red-white-and-blue
13 Green gem
14 Comfortably inviting
15 New England state sch.
16 One who accepts charges
17 Use Schedule A
18 Put down
24 Common aspiration
25 Singer Lennon and others
30 Essayist Day
34 Smooth
36 Stick-to-it-iveness?
40 Blood pigment
42 Seat of honor location
43 Handy digit
44 Scratched (out)
45 Big cheer
46 Ready, with "up"
47 Burning the midnight oil, so to speak
48 Makes veal, maybe
53 Shaq's alma mater
54 "That's ___ sure!"
55 Source of 85-Down
56 Germanic tribesman
57 Familiarize
58 Tube-nosed seabird
60 7th-century Arab caliph
61 Brown, in a way
63 Phone button trio
66 Set aside
67 Test for a college sr.
68 Part of an e-mail address
69 So far, on a pay stub: Abbr.
70 Hindu habits
73 Handle
76 Sci-fi writer Frederic
77 It makes one hot
79 Item that's often hidden
80 Athens attraction
81 Voice stretcher
83 Like many a sports report
84 Comparison basis
85 Stopper
87 Center strip cuts?
88 Gorge
89 Trumpet blast
90 Barely enough
91 One step
92 Flubbed
96 Affixed
97 Boot
98 A matter of will?
100 Nubs
103 Author Jong
107 "When I was ___ . . ."
109 Seasoned hands
111 Word from a con
113 Fix
114 A crowd, for Caesar?

by Nancy Salomon

ACROSS

1 Arises
6 Florida fruit
12 Officer of the Ottoman Empire
15 Jerk
19 Private sector?
20 Hit actor of 60's TV
21 The Jets or the Sharks
23 Home of the Black Bears
24 Florida fruit
25 One of the "three faces of Eve"
26 House detective's item
27 They get their kicks
28 Opera featuring the "Prisoners' Chorus"
29 Au courant
31 Eric Dickerson's alma mater, for short
34 Try
35 Crooks' patterns, to cops
38 It may be due
39 First name in erotica
41 Computerniks push it
45 O'Neill masterwork, for short
47 Singer Jackson
48 Scratch
49 Like rich desserts
51 Semiotics study
53 Assassinated Swedish P.M.
54 Like a combination lock
55 Battery type
57 Three-ply snack
58 Kaffiyeh wearers
59 Request from an ed.

60 Directional suffix
61 Tails
64 Lush
65 Allowed
67 Hydrocarbon suffix
68 Spooks
70 Evelyn who played Scarlett's sister
73 Gizmos
75 String of pikake flowers
76 Set foot (on)
80 Forest clearing
82 "The Postman Always Rings Twice" wife
83 Burns's birthplace
84 Painter Veronese
85 First name in TV talk
86 Tipped off
89 Arrive angrily and abruptly
91 ___ de Castro (storied noblewoman)
92 Soccer score, perhaps
93 Party dance of old
94 Mountaineers' wear
97 "The Maids" playwright
98 Excites
100 Draft org.
101 Project
102 Vote in the Senate
103 Dwindles
106 ___ "Le Morte d'Arthur"
110 Iceberg's location
111 Noted heart surgeon
115 Individually
117 Poet Levertov
118 Yves St. Laurent fragrance

119 Thanksgiving aftermath
120 Run on
121 Utah's ___ Mountains
122 Latin trio member
123 Draft org.?
124 Judge
125 Append

DOWN

1 Word with chop or sweat
2 The O'Haras' home
3 Asteroid discovered in 1898
4 Test group?
5 What CBers watch for
6 Some addresses
7 Rodeo item
8 Bridge supports
9 Like some rewards
10 What solar flares are measured in
11 Ship's log entry
12 "So that's it!"
13 Make the rounds?
14 Still serving
15 Vehicle for Blanche DuBois
16 Part of a pump
17 Amahl's visitors
18 Melville novel
22 Added to the database
30 Rajah's spouse
31 Medic
32 Restrained mood
33 In vain
35 They'll knock you out
36 Neighbor of Silver Springs
37 Hingis rival
40 Jean or Jacques
42 Greece, to the Greeks

43 Macho military type
44 Where Hemingway wrote "A Farewell to Arms"
46 German wine valley
47 Dan Beard's org.
50 Variation of the samba
52 Pea-___ (dense fogs)
53 Spread
56 Treasury of sorts
60 Prefix with friendly
61 1990's dance craze
62 In tune
63 George ___
66 Julian calendar date
69 Ringo's original surname
70 Best boy's colleague
71 Turgenev heroine
72 Lyricist Carole Bayer ___
74 Part of E. I. du Pont
77 Easy wins
78 Hodgepodges
79 They'll bray for you
81 Spinners
83 Suffix with 24-Across
84 Lost momentum
87 ___ loop (skater's jump)
88 Contest hopefuls
90 Sound of impact
95 Emanations
96 "A Tidewater Morning" author
98 Purse items
99 Exodus commemorations
104 Gentry

by Nancy Nicholson Joline

ACROSS

1 Calculating machine inventor, 1642
7 Reach
14 Protest
20 Delphi temple god
21 Invented word
22 Fingerprint features
23 Supper
24 Job for a restaurant server?
26 Pesticide
28 Had dinner at home
29 Three-way joint
30 Professional org.
33 Milne marsupial
34 Yugoslav novelist ___ Andric
35 Mildew cause
39 Job for a statistician?
43 Hurting the most
44 Alan and Adam
45 Blintzes, e.g.
49 Dustup
50 Player for coach Marv Levy
51 Embargoes
52 Job for a plastic surgeon?
57 Skid row look
60 Tomato-impact noises
61 ___ man
62 70's All-Star ___ Otis
63 Most like a wallflower
64 Worry
66 Job for a mathematician?
72 Plays the siren
73 Quark/antiquark particles
74 Rudolf's refusal
75 Man-mouse link
76 Food on a tray

77 What squeaky wheels get
82 Job for a relay racer?
85 Like Mongolia
86 Photography woe
87 Scull
88 Summoned
90 Jack
92 Styx ferryman
95 Job for a critic?
97 London institution
99 Rhine feeder
100 Second-century date
101 Thumbs up
102 Airport info: Abbr.
103 1978 disaster film, with "The"
105 Ripoffs
108 Job for a debutante?
113 Panama party
117 Screenfuls
118 Caught by surprise, with "on"
119 Athlete's assignment
120 Lohengrin and others
121 Toast opening
122 Tempt

DOWN

1 Course number
2 Goon
3 Bread, maybe
4 Sound of shutters in the wind
5 Minor-party candidate
6 Avon products
7 Parrot
8 Word ending in "o" in Esperanto
9 Compass pt.
10 Solve
11 Check words
12 Chill

13 Not strong
14 Have a title
15 Scholarly type
16 One to remember, for short
17 Spiels
18 Like the best ruse
19 "Women Who Run With the Wolves" author
25 Collections
27 Landscaper's need
30 Iraqis, e.g.
31 Singing Osmond
32 Shackle site
34 Woes of the world
36 Dew times
37 Push
38 Speaker's name
40 It's west of Dublin
41 Benedictines
42 They're not free of charge
46 Frees
47 Like carpet
48 Outburst
51 Ring holder
53 Synchronized
54 Lone Star State sch.
55 Christmas stocking item
56 Lady of a 1918 hit
58 Big name in morning radio
59 "___ won't be afraid" (1961 pop lyric)
60 Classic Alan Ladd western
63 Dish out messily
64 Ruckus
65 Place for bouquets
66 Delete, with "out"
67 Money in the making

68 Mrs. Katzenjammer, e.g.
69 Wards (off)
70 Manner of speech
71 Stage of a race
76 Bank
77 1982 Disney film
78 Al from New Orleans
79 Cosmetics brand
80 Urbane
81 Marine fliers
83 Chesterfield or ulster
84 Mata ___
85 Way off
89 Violate, with "on"
90 Cold symptom
91 Bibliophile's concern
92 Some trim
93 Screenwriter Mankiewicz
94 Leaves home?
96 Hotshot
97 Kind of approval
98 Buckle opener
99 Passion
104 It's just for openers
105 Unbending
106 Shot shooter
107 Branch
109 Swellhead's excess
110 Anthem preposition
111 Letters before many state names
112 "___ Girls" (Kelly musical)
114 Tackle moguls
115 Shamus
116 "___ we having fun yet?"

by Nancy Salomon

ACROSS

1 1962 Tommy Roe hit
7 "I'd rather not hear about it!"
14 Go with the flow
19 "Casablanca" producer
20 Meteorological effects
21 "Beggars can't be choosers" et al.
22 Start of a verse
25 Ring thing
26 Toothpaste-approving grp.
27 "I Know" singer Farris
28 Christian ___
29 "Olympia" painter
31 Every, in prescriptions
32 Tot's transport
36 They may have soft shells
37 Filippo Lippi's title
38 Finger, so to speak
42 Muezzin's call to prayer
43 Unnerve
44 Plum pudding ingredient
45 From Umbria: Abbr.
46 Verse, part 2
52 Dolly, for one
53 Lust after
54 Sailplanes
55 Stag
56 O.K.
58 Attribute
60 Mug
61 Designer in J.F.K.'s White House
63 Take under one's wing
65 Thin
68 Nice touch

70 "Caught" star Maria Conchita ___
73 ___-garde
74 Netanyahu's predecessor
75 Starbuck's captain
76 Its capital is Altdorf
78 Verse, part 3
83 Galley feature
84 "How now! ___?": Hamlet
85 Caesar's wings
86 Malodorous
87 Christian Science founder
88 RR stop
89 Jelly Roll Morton biographer Alan
91 Locale of Ptolemy's lighthouse
93 Good name for a chef?
94 Hardly a sissy
95 West of Hollywood
96 Patch up
99 Princess Yasmin ___ Khan
100 Obvious clue
105 End of the verse
109 Person in a booth
110 ___ Trail (Everglades highway)
111 Testify under oath
112 Nervous, with "up"
113 Clytemnestra's killer
114 Sprung up

DOWN

1 Draft
2 Harness part
3 K-6: Abbr.
4 St. Pierre and Miquelon
5 Refuse
6 Classify
7 All there

8 Plunk
9 One of Knute's successors
10 Cheese made of 52-Across's milk
11 Cuts into
12 French Revolution leader
13 Toledo-to-Akron dir.
14 Extra
15 Not-so-mild oath
16 Stravinsky ballet
17 A Dumas
18 Lao-___
21 Lively, to Liszt
23 Dona ___ (Las Cruces' county)
24 The Magi, notably
29 Hampton Court feature
30 They're nonreturnable
32 Kind of warden
33 Conductor Seiji
34 Christmas tree hangings
35 Even one
36 Napoleon relative
37 W.W. II tyrant
38 Certain rating
39 Friend of Aramis
40 See 72-Down
41 Bugs bugs him
43 Desktop publisher's supply
44 Social climber's concern
47 Affirm under oath
48 Ragwort variety
49 Strange "gift"
50 They may be modified
51 Richard Leakey's birthplace
57 Set back?
58 Making no progress
59 Sticks in the mud

60 Stalin's persecuted peasant
62 Bygone delivery person
64 Source of the Truckee River
65 It may be toxic
66 Work around
67 Broken
69 Shakespearean verb ending
71 Babydoll
72 With 40-Down, Down East university town
74 Discompose
75 Bon Ami alternative
77 Rubs the wrong way
79 More odious
80 Crimson Tide, for short
81 Panache
82 Blue Eagle inits.
89 Mesquite or mimosa, e.g.
90 Muscateers?
91 Shanxi shrine
92 Marilu of "Taxi"
93 Socked away
94 Helga's husband
95 Thou squared
96 First South Korean president
97 Hard to hold
98 Mayberry's Goober
100 Biol., geol., etc.
101 Name of two ancient Egyptian kings
102 Cries of surprise
103 Kind of wave
104 The Untouchables, e.g.
105 "Naughty!"
106 W.W. II arena
107 Make an antimacassar
108 Cockney residence

by Frances Hansen

ACROSS

1 Heist gain
5 East German secret police
10 "Star Wars" princess
14 Attack moves
20 S
23 Alpo competition
24 P
25 Threatening finale
26 Clinton has two
27 Buys or leases
28 Miller hero
30 Downed
31 Shakespeare, e.g.
32 Here on the authority of
35 Ripken, Jr. and Sr.
36 "And I Love ___"
37 Had the know-how
39 Mo. parts
40 Hot
42 Knots
43 "Cabaret" director
45 Tract
46 1968 track and field gold medalist
48 Former Swedish P.M. Palme
49 J
55 Water around the Ijsselmeer
56 Wrap
58 Medium-range U.S. missiles
59 Some feasts
60 Dolphin leader
62 She's put out to pasture
63 Horror film staple
66 Vocal style
69 Sat at home
70 First "M" of M&M's
73 Heroine of Tennessee Williams's "Summer and Smoke"
74 N
79 Basso Pinza
80 Existentialist concern
81 From Tabriz
82 Wayne genre
83 Whitish
84 Printed
86 Popular museum exhibits
88 Anatomical cavities
91 Irk
92 Big dictionary section
93 Break
96 L
101 Pinball paths
102 Hill and Bryant
103 Horseshoer's need
104 Hostilities
107 Greek architectural feature
108 Circus
110 Wheat part
112 Old-time actresses Markey and Bennett
113 Oscar-winning Gibson
114 Moravian, e.g.
116 Some clouds
118 Bit of fancy footwork
119 Live
120 Correo ___ (airmail)
122 Make eights, maybe
124 Kind of hotel
127 Unlearned
129 M
133 Made out
134 G
135 Positions
136 The best
137 Call it quits
138 Complete

DOWN

1 "Dog Day Afternoon" character
2 Blame
3 Switch settings
4 "The Crucifixion" painter
5 Tariff co-sponsor of 1930
6 Common powder
7 When the sun goes down
8 Near misses, maybe
9 "Wie geht es ___?" (German greeting)
10 Flight
11 Two or more periods
12 "___ be all right"
13 Partner-to-be
14 Toast
15 Alerts
16 "Bravo!"
17 Choctaw for "red people"
18 Attached, in a way
19 Derisive
20 Not just any
21 Remnants
22 Ski run
29 "Buddy"
31 Bit of a drag
33 Thin nails
34 Yesteryear
37 King ___ Trio (popular 40's combo)
38 ___ d'amore
39 Baby
41 Actress Harper
42 Bettors bet on them
43 Dickens alias
44 Traveled horizontally
46 Cold one
47 Heroine of 1847
50 Alley mewers
51 Lover of Pyramus
52 The duck in "Peter and the Wolf"
53 Armor-plated warship
54 Black Sea port, new-style
56 Kind of path or pay
57 ___ about (approximately)
60 Karate school
61 Blows away
63 Run for it
64 First name in bridge
65 Pinup features
66 Over
67 Shah ___ Pahlavi
68 Game-ending pronouncement
70 Have it in mind
71 When shadows almost disappear
72 Grand slam foursome
73 Lawyers: Abbr.
75 Touch, say
76 Largest Greek island, to locals
77 Rawls and Reed
78 1968 Chemistry Nobelist Onsager
84 Santa ___
85 Egyptian menaces
87 Seemingly forever
88 Greek cheese
89 Reaches
90 Online periodical, for short
91 Subject of a 1982 best seller
93 Mapmaker's aid
94 Crackerjacks
95 They follow signatures
96 Underground network
97 Forum locale

by Matt Gaffney

ACROSS

1 River name meaning "where the goods are brought in"
8 "Shane" man
12 He's well-sooted for the job
19 Womb-related
20 Mine, in Amiens
21 Most volatile emotionally
22 "Hey, babe, wanna sit with me on the plane?"
24 Transport to ecstasy
25 Game for two of four
26 "While we're in the air, write an essay on aviation"
28 "Don't waste your breath!"
31 Still
32 Some M.I.T. grads
33 Spree
36 Nods, perhaps
37 "I'm an unattractive woman who'll gab the whole trip"
43 Revolt
45 Burden
48 Deanna of "Star Trek: T.N.G."
49 "Mulholland Falls" actor
50 One of the clan
51 Bad-mouth
53 "___ out!" (ump's cry)
55 Manor near Twelve Oaks
56 "Follow orders in this plane area or else!"
62 Court huddle
64 Twice 79-Down
65 Sen. Cochran

66 Roman called "The Elder"
68 Trackers, e.g.
69 "Prepare to do a spoof on airports"
73 Accused's retort
74 Middling
75 Cross letters
76 Sine ___ non
79 Pilot's wear
82 "Executives, today's lesson is on jet financing"
86 Years of Nero's reign
87 Found groovy
89 Bush, for one
90 Bits
91 Bank deals
93 A Bear
96 Prefix with biology
98 Housekeeping
99 "First I'll read, then watch the movie, then . . ."
101 Fen-___ (diet drug combo)
103 Through working: Abbr.
104 Astonish
105 Spanish article
107 Lions and tigers and bears, e.g.
109 "What's that knitter doing during air turbulence?"
114 Rhyme scheme
118 Conspicuousness
119 "My suitcase is better than yours"
122 Pollen, e.g.
123 Lake near Jacobs Field
124 Put into motion
125 North Pole family
126 Pick-me-up
127 Bums steers?

DOWN

1 Darts' places
2 Siouan speaker
3 Jets, e.g.
4 Gold braid
5 Among, in poetry
6 "Wheel of Fortune" buy
7 Used a thurible
8 Wash against
9 Part of a Latin trio
10 "Indeed!"
11 Examine closely
12 Assemblage
13 Psychoanalyst Karen
14 Joy of wild animals?
15 Split
16 Chow ___
17 Secy.
18 Last in line, usually
21 "Don't blame ___ voted for·. . ."
23 Zeit or polter follower
27 One telephone button
29 They're missing from a roll
30 Contest
33 American finch
34 Beeish
35 Diving bird
38 Lichtenstein, for one
39 ___ condolence
40 Spills the beans
41 Gillette brand
42 Landing ___
44 It's "here" in Le Havre
46 Pitches
47 Greek letters
52 Basic sugar
54 Hardships
57 Discontinued, with "out"
58 "Wild!" to a dude

59 Ice cream brand
60 Teller
61 Airport monitor abbr.
63 Lacking
67 Tom Joad, e.g.
69 Harassing
70 Watch chain
71 1997 Rose Bowl winner: Abbr.
72 50% of Bonn
73 Porch with a view
76 Doha's land
77 Treatment
78 Plus
79 See 64-Across
80 Hydroxyl-carbon compound
81 Small English coins
83 ___ d'Orléans
84 Veto
85 First name in horror
88 Lass
92 Trees, e.g.
94 N.F.L. sacker Bryce ___
95 Poe's "___ Lee"
97 Aria area
98 Mayo, for one
100 Pang
102 Jet's home
106 Computer game pioneer
107 Sire
108 French toast
109 Convention site
110 Stewpot
111 Place
112 Not spec.
113 Pre-weekend cry
115 Canaanite deity
116 Fishing luck
117 Home of the Cyclones
118 Small pouch
120 Old French coin
121 Change for a dol.

by Mark Danna

ACROSS
1 Signals at sea
8 "War and Peace" heroine
15 Indian dwelling
20 Like Miss Congeniality
21 Christie and others
22 Madonna role
23 Tar?
25 Connoisseur
26 Reception site, maybe
27 Catty comments
28 Even
29 Red ___
30 Tolkien creatures
31 Sprint competitor
32 Crazy, in Cannes
33 Distance between pillars
36 Yorkshire river
37 60's org.
38 Heyum?
41 Some are "great"
42 Common setting for a joke
43 Mme., in Madrid
44 Check out
46 Not separately
50 Last choice on some lists
53 Come-___
56 Destined
57 Commitment
59 Encouraging words
61 Sleuth Lupin
62 Kind of mail
63 Minnie?
66 Phone trio
67 A.A.A. recommendations
68 Eliot's Grizabella, e.g.
69 Popular White House souvenir
70 It precedes "com"
71 Part of a comparison
72 "Exodus" role
73 Furner?
76 They move in a charged atmosphere
77 Request of an equestrian
79 Corn ___
80 Multipurpose truck, for short
81 "Home Alone" actor
82 Meg, among the "little women"
83 Stranger
85 Teach, with "up"
87 Strong
90 Prog. Cons. rival, in Canada
92 Med. drama sites
93 Guns
95 Purty?
99 L-1011 alternative
102 Athos, to Porthos
103 Salon offering
104 Cable inits.
105 Less than diddly
106 Bank posting
107 Broadcasting feed
109 "Aladdin" prince and namesakes
111 Whip
112 Two-dimensional extent
113 Mexican waters
114 Hail?
117 Critical
118 Becomes understood
119 "Your Show of Shows" name
120 Person with a net, perhaps
121 Begins to like
122 Waterloos

DOWN
1 Dissipates
2 Threaten
3 Fairy tale characters
4 All's partner
5 16th President, familiarly
6 Inklings
7 ___ Lake, N.Y.
8 Nopes
9 ___-old
10 It's only skin-deep
11 Museum room, maybe
12 "Leaving Las Vegas" actress
13 Participatory
14 "Don't ___!"
15 Hercules
16 Elliptical
17 Dah?
18 Pied-___
19 Port on the Loire
24 Dweebs
32 Kind of house
34 Movie ratings
35 It paves the way
38 Spar
39 Show disapproval
40 Caterer's need
41 "Hamlet" has five
42 Deposits
45 Drogheda's locale
46 Welcoming or parting gesture
47 Like some corners
48 Mayun?
49 Poland Spring competitor
51 Hit a four-bagger
52 Nicholas Gage book
54 Intensify
55 Restrains
58 Available
60 Mubarak's predecessor
64 Turn topsy-turvy
65 Dog treats
68 Procession
71 La Scala features
73 It may be feathered
74 Was bossy?
75 Antique shop item
78 Perfect ones
81 Actor's goal
84 London greeting
86 Occasion calling for grace
88 Easter starter
89 Onetime U.N. effort site
91 Cause for hitting the forehead
93 Sack
94 Baryshnikov, e.g.
96 Actor Alan of "Hope & Gloria"
97 Haunt
98 Like some cousins
99 Allahabad attire
100 Tristram Shandy's creator
101 Rags
103 Toughie
106 Roam
108 Overhang
110 Limp, as hair
111 Pro ___
114 Attention-getter
115 It may be thrown
116 Napoléon, for one

by Nancy Joline and Peg Conner

ACROSS

1 Theater worker
8 Hank Aaron or Jesse Owens, e.g.
16 "Wild Thing" group, with "the"
22 Day in Hollywood
23 Breakdown
24 Capital of Zimbabwe
25 Part 1 of a prophecy by Martin Luther King Jr.
28 Marshal Dillon portrayer
29 Cone-shaped heaters
30 Grocery area
31 More than suggestive
32 Track pick, informally
33 Sharp
34 Jalopy
36 Fr. holy woman
37 Prophecy, part 2
48 Holmes girl
49 Soup holder
50 What Moses did
51 Prophecy, part 3
58 Bob Hope's "___ Russia $1,200"
59 1/6 fl. oz.
60 Extinct New Zealanders
61 Brown of renown
62 Sludge
64 Swindle
67 Seesaw quorum
69 Prepare to surf, perhaps
71 Category
72 Joint protection
73 Unpopular slice
75 Wreck
77 "___ here" (store sign)
78 Time to act
79 Prophecy, part 4
83 Big name in games

85 Mer makeup
87 Riveter of song
89 Some wait for this
90 Cooperative interaction
93 Hundred smackers
95 Halfhearted
98 Charisse of "Silk Stockings"
100 Laszlo player in "Casablanca"
101 Kin's partner
102 Child's play
103 Grape brandy
105 Kind of trip
107 Pretense
108 Prophecy, part 5
114 Salad topper
115 Where suits are pressed
116 Laundry woe
117 Prophecy, part 6
126 Split
127 Memorable 1995 hurricane
128 Buffoon
129 Half and half
130 Famous redhead
132 Make sense
135 Poker challenge
138 Shade
141 End of the prophecy
145 Whip
146 Bête noire
147 Correction, of sorts
148 "Grand" hotels
149 Well-worn
150 Biased

DOWN

1 Yielding
2 Enthusiastic
3 Moon shade
4 Make way?
5 Architect ___ van der Rohe
6 Literary olios

7 "___ Kelly" (Jagger film)
8 Vinegar radical
9 Item of interest
10 Mrs. Alfred Hitchcock
11 Short orders
12 "Wonderful!"
13 Film rating org.
14 Spot of wine?
15 Missouri town near the George Washington Carver National Monument
16 "Lyin' Eyes" singers
17 "Awesome!"
18 Like some votes
19 Most festive
20 Wall Street analysts' concern
21 Letter getter
26 Cameo carvings
27 Red or Card, for short
33 Geared down, perhaps
35 Crusty ones
38 Had a heart but used a club?
39 Some trains
40 Brit. award
41 8½"×11" size: Abbr.
42 It's often served at home
43 Two-toned treat
44 Savage
45 Plaster of paris
46 Fotomat abbr.
47 "Love thy neighbor" is one
51 Speedily
52 Admitted
53 Make up one's mind
54 Detached
55 Hole in the wall?
56 Unrivaled

57 The first Mrs. Copperfield
58 "E-w-w-w!"
63 Code breaker
65 Here and there?
66 11-Down extra
68 Very early
70 Old car with a 389 engine
71 Senator who made the rounds
74 "i" lid
76 "For ___ sow . . ."
79 Model Cheryl
80 Cool, once
81 Violinist Paganini
82 Operative
84 Tennyson's "___ and Enid"
85 Theologian who opposed Martin Luther
86 "Oh, right!"
88 Wishing spot
90 Excluding
91 Tomorrow's woman
92 Giant gains: Abbr.
94 Mary Tyler Moore catchphrase on "The Dick Van Dyke Show"
96 Elaborate Japanese porcelain
97 Lifeboat support
99 Snuggery
102 Clairvoyants
104 Soothsay
106 Unified whole
109 Venus's home
110 Shavetails: Abbr.
111 Berlin-to-Cologne dir.
112 Problem of the middle ages?
113 "___ geht's?"
117 Something to catch or save
118 Unrefined

by Ed Early and Bob Kahn

119 "Peer Gynt" dancer
120 Fake fanfare
121 Dracula's mother-in-law?
122 Mutually fee-free
123 O.B.E., for one
124 Performance extension
125 Thatched
131 Powwow
133 Wrist attachment
134 Swamp thing
135 "___ hollers . . ."
136 Rubber Duck, for one
137 Baïonnette, e.g.
138 Prowling Wolfe
139 River to the Caspian
140 "Now I see!"
142 It goes to extremes
143 Polo Grounds legend
144 "___ Ramsey" (70's western)

SEEING DOUBLE

ACROSS

1 Where the 1986 World Series was won
5 Lot
9 Automotive pioneer
13 Prepare to go home, in a way
19 Onetime America's Cup champ
21 Kind of service
22 List ender
23 Coffee addict's meal?
25 Special correspondent
26 "Soap" spinoff
27 Humpty Dumpty short?
29 Like ghost stories
33 Saying nothing
35 Nets
36 Awakened
37 Computer program input
41 Ticket place: Abbr.
42 Sch. subject
45 Plowing woe
46 Hydrocarbon derived from petroleum
47 1962 NASA success
49 An otherwise well-behaved liar?
53 One-on-one sport
55 Chanel fragrance
56 "___ precaution . . ."
57 "Voices Carry" vocalist Mann
58 Actor Epps
59 Luke's "90210" role
60 Panay seaport with a repetitive name

62 Landscaper's tool
64 Cupronickel, e.g.
65 Method for mixing cards, Illinois-style?
70 Divided into sections
72 Highflier's home?
73 Oceanus and brothers
75 Some construction beams
76 Part of a wagon train
77 Profit
79 Jump causer
81 Old "Tonight Show" theme writer
82 Grade
83 Tot's plaything?
86 Fumes
88 Gathering places
90 Sale item label
91 Wife, with "the"
92 Crew need
93 No-goodnik
95 Nobel or Celsius, e.g.
96 ___ Ababa
98 Had
99 Sells
101 What to serve stew in?
105 Hard
108 Natural gas component
109 Ice cream as still life?
115 Passes
116 Perfectly healthy, to the Army
117 Person who cracks a whip
118 Can't stand
119 Kind of home or room
120 Russian river
121 Tax

DOWN

1 Gal of song
2 1970's Chinese premier
3 Erhard's discipline
4 Part of a toll-free long-distance number
5 Less exposed
6 Identical
7 Haughtiness
8 Woodworking groove
9 Control
10 Blockers, e.g.
11 Vestige
12 Twilled fabric
13 Verbal dueling
14 God, with "the"
15 Cords
16 Purina alternative
17 "Later!"
18 Brickmaker's furnace
20 Jewish teacher
24 Sentence completer
28 Swiveling part
29 Family head
30 Some Bach compositions
31 Ranch infestation?
32 Underway to over there
34 Consumer
38 French clergyman
39 Bassoon, basically
40 Was overrun
42 Yeast, fruit and nuts?
43 Tree with pods
44 "The Gift of the Magi" feature
48 Monster in the Strait of Messina
50 Scottish landowners
51 Thread: Prefix
52 "___ cloud nine!"

54 One of Henry VIII's six
58 Flirt with, maybe
59 Less sane
61 "Wozzeck" and "Jenufa"
62 St. Patrick's home
63 ___ gratia
66 Land on the Rubicon
67 Guys
68 Smallpox symptom
69 Let go
70 Suffix with endo- or proto-
71 Li'l one
74 Gold coins of ancient Rome
76 Central vein of a leaf
77 One of a ballroom couple
78 Sport ___ (trucklike vehicles)
80 O. Henry Award—winning author Tillie ___
82 Whiplash preventer
83 Flawlessly
84 English poet Dowson
85 Cuss (out)
87 Marmots and such
89 Savers by profession
94 Had too much of
95 "What ___ thou?"
96 Swiftly
97 Deep, unnatural sleep
100 Jean Renoir film heroine
101 Basis
102 ___ Reader (eclectic magazine)
103 Great, in slang
104 Dwindle
106 Rossini subject
107 Singer Adams

by Dave Tuller

110 Basketball Hall-of-Famer Holman
111 Down
112 Somewhat exotic meat
113 Abbr. after a general's name, maybe
114 Aim

ACROSS

1 Rum-soaked cake
5 Tall, slender hound
11 Practical joke
15 Bleached
19 12th-century poet
20 Neckwear accessory
21 Uzbek sea
22 Fashion house ___-Picone
23 "At 9 A.M. breakfast will be supplied by ___"
25 Prohibit
27 Mastic, for one
28 "At 11 A.M. ___ will speak"
30 Comics sound
31 Unusually smart
34 First name in TV talk
35 Like R. L. Stine stories
36 "At 1 P.M. ___ will sing . . ."
39 Govt. property org.
40 River near Chantilly
41 O'Donnell and Perez
42 ". . . a tune from one of their ___"
48 Modern office staples
49 Jackson and Leigh
50 Handle a joystick
51 In post-career mode: Abbr.
52 Dance invitation response
53 Axis Powers, once
54 Jamaican sect member
56 "At 3 P.M. President Clinton will ___ . . ."
61 First name among sopranos

62 The less-used end
63 Nonexistent
64 Key of Mendelssohn's Symphony No. 3
66 Kind of alcohol
67 ". . . on the subject of ___"
74 Initiated, legally
76 Europe/Asia dividers
77 Actress Suzanne
78 Ambient music pioneer
79 Mount Vernon, e.g.
81 Wristbone-related
82 Abbr. on a Mayberry envelope
85 "At 5 P.M. the Philatelic Society will discuss some ___"
87 Knot-tying place
88 Actress Ward
89 Hosts
90 "And at 7 P.M. there'll be a showing of the 60's film ___ . . ."
92 Snail trail
95 Slick, so to speak
98 Some pops: Abbr.
99 Wage news
100 ". . . starring ___ . . ."
103 Goes limp
104 Call to action
105 ". . . unless ___"
110 Grouper grabbers
111 Numerous
112 Dario Fo forte
113 Infamous Roman
114 Cobbler's need
115 Places for coats
116 Lively intelligence
117 Jersey Standard's other name

DOWN

1 Conk
2 Without form
3 Without foundation
4 Gallery event
5 British gun
6 It can be fresh or hot
7 Singer Peggy
8 Put ___ fight
9 Brick baker
10 Dr. Scholl products
11 I love: Fr.
12 Ball partner
13 City on the Ganges
14 Basic: Abbr.
15 Human-powered taxi
16 Province of Spain
17 Tongue-lasher?
18 Access
24 Ticket
26 Slangy tag-team member
29 TV dog
30 Boarding place
31 Sorry individual
32 Barcelona buck
33 Colorful spiral seashell
37 Mary of Peter, Paul and Mary
38 My, to Mimi
39 Lead pumper
42 [see other side]
43 Collins juice
44 Quite awhile
45 Bearish
46 Underground systems
47 Fire escape route
49 Jupiter
50 "___, the heavens were opened": Matt. 3:16
52 Glove fabric
53 Film changes
55 Sheriff Lobo portrayer

56 Wound with sound
57 He's a weasel
58 Flatten
59 Talus area
60 Loss-prevention device
65 Blackbird
68 1984 Peace Nobelist
69 "Dies ___"
70 Familiars, often
71 Writer Singer and inventor Singer
72 Apathy
73 Drives forward
75 Prepare to land
80 Subj. of 60's protest
81 He helped topple Batista
82 Slaps a new head on
83 Dentists' kids, probably
84 Have the guts
86 Prodigious
87 Shift
88 Like some triangles
90 Dam agcy.
91 Hockey's Lindros
92 Hollywood dive?
93 Ostracized one
94 Ready to spit
95 Caterpillar hairs
96 Via
97 Case workers: Abbr.
101 Summer getaway, perhaps
102 School orgs.
103 Big letters in public broadcasting
106 Race car sponsor
107 Columbus, for one: Abbr.
108 Christina's dad
109 Prelude to a hickey

by Meri Reagle

ACROSS

1 Some calisthenics
7 Hardly stars
14 Promote
20 Avid
21 Japanese art of flower arranging
22 Take away
23 Gave in church
24 Indexed early man?
26 Ancient porch
27 "___ of troubles": Hamlet
29 Secret devices
30 It may lead to a strike
31 Twisted person
33 Some campers
34 Wall Street worker
36 Reply to "Is it Mr. or Professor Chomsky?"
40 Together
41 Hill climber
42 Like fabric by the yard
43 How some people seem to know
45 Old despot
48 Hugs
50 Staten Island Ferry litter?
55 Enterprise log signature
56 Toast for the holidays
58 Long time
59 Its cap. is Charleston
60 Showed, with "out"
63 Kind of test
64 They battle the Indians
66 Reply to "How many Senators are there, child?"
70 Big name in computers

73 Friction easer
74 Wire
77 One of the Whitneys
78 From ___ Z
79 Oxford university since 1844
82 Part
84 Molly Pitcher, for example?
87 Sang
89 Indochine locale
90 East, in Essen
91 Electronic snoop
94 Words with word or way
95 Low voice
98 What the overheated passengers called the airline?
100 Nightclub charge
103 Line up well
105 Static
106 Brews
107 Site for Seurats
109 Chairs for prayers?
110 Answer, in brief
114 Question about a flashlight that lacks batteries?
117 Precisely
119 Sharp as a tack
120 "I like that!"
121 Family split?
122 Like the other evil
123 Some kids' bedtime reading
124 Nike rival

DOWN

1 NCO club members
2 Vacate
3 "For ___ us a child . . ."
4 Shocked
5 Common article
6 Some recyclables
7 "Great shot!"

8 Tex. neighbor
9 School org.
10 F.B.I. sting of the late 70's
11 Wall builder
12 Author Bagnold and others
13 Sometimes cracked container
14 City whose name is Spanish for "ash tree"
15 Library ref.
16 Least of all
17 TV debut of 1/14/52
18 "Luann" cartoonist Greg ___
19 Held another session
25 Portfolio contents, for short
28 "The ___ the limit!"
32 Goes to bat
33 Some pointers
35 Wave catchers
36 Moolah
37 In the dark
38 "Wheel of Fortune" songstress, 1952
39 Has
40 Abbr. in car ads
43 Sizing up
44 Like some deities
46 ". . . ___ forgive our debtors"
47 Go crazy
49 "Bottoms up!"
51 Walked awkwardly
52 Bloomsbury group member
53 "The Grapes of Wrath" family
54 More, in Monterrey
56 Continued
57 Sum (up)
61 80's TV adventure

62 Full chorus, in music
65 The first one opened in Detroit in 1962
67 Occupies quarters
68 Israeli city on the Gulf of Aqaba
69 Some radios
70 Bunny boss, briefly
71 Director Kazan
72 Pate toppers
75 Was admitted to
76 "Maria ___" (1933 song)
80 1984 skiing gold medalist
81 "If ___ be so bold . . ."
83 Cracker cheese
85 China rose, e.g.
86 Infantile remark
87 Make an impression
88 Dadaist collection
92 Modern mall features
93 Feel in one's bones
96 Fort ___ (where Billy the Kid was gunned down)
97 Dirty stuff
98 Mishandle
99 Bubble
100 Taj ___
101 Admission of defeat
102 Tiny amphibians
103 "___ coffee?"
104 Babe and Baby
108 Like workhorses
109 Jokes (around)
111 Pin, in a way
112 Clinton denial
113 Look-see
115 Got into a jam?
116 Seine contents
118 Full of: Suffix

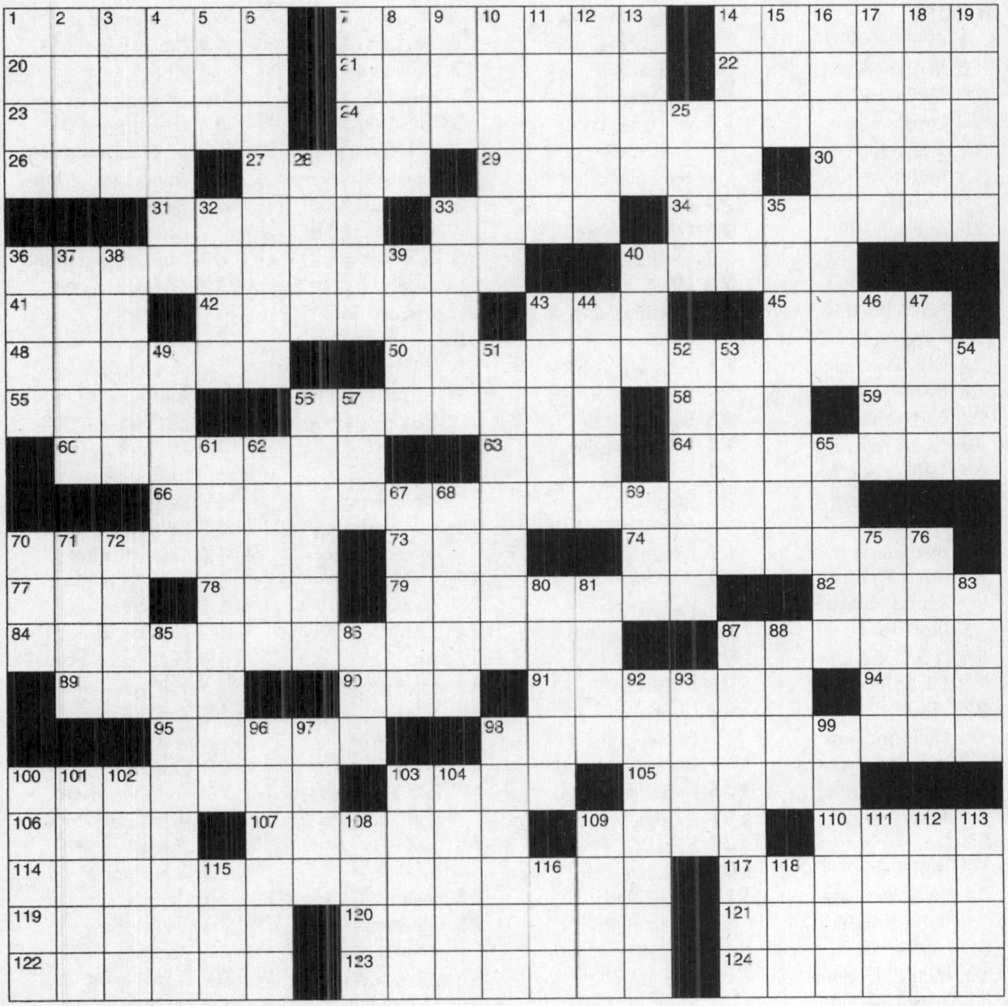

by Manny Nosowsky

ACROSS

1 City district
5 Ricky Martin's "Livin' La ___ Loca"
9 Disqualify
15 End even
19 Lab gel
20 Mil. school
21 Places for matches
22 Foolhardy
23 Great ___
24 Like flies caught by flypaper?
27 Parts cut off
28 Ouzo flavoring
29 1980's pop group ___ Tuesday
30 Aromatic compound
31 Bringing up young nudists?
35 Not live
36 U.S.C. : Pac 10 :: Duke : ___
37 "The Hallucinogenic Toreador" painter
38 City on the Tanaro River
39 Dish served with sauce
45 Inefficient way to harvest sugar?
50 Mother-___
51 Man of Cannes
53 Romance lang.
54 By
55 Wordless response
56 Pearl ___ (aquarium fish)
57 Word with price or brain
59 Forest doings
60 Worthless coupons?
64 "___ noches"
66 Pharmaceutical giant
67 Something that begins foolishly?
68 Part of SST
69 Evening event
71 Cry from a con man spotting an easy mark?
75 Dullard
76 Passes on
78 Loathe
79 Mouth piece
80 Jehoshaphat's father
81 Sign on a grade school door
83 Shine
84 "Must've been something ___"
85 Outback greeting?
89 Elm, e.g.
92 Author Jorge ___ Borges
93 Backpack snack
95 Gray
96 Missing
99 Consider blowing the whistle at work?
106 Pastel shade
107 ___ chi
108 Boost
109 Q ___ queen
110 Bartender's complete guide to spritzers?
114 One up all night at camp?
115 Disillusioned query
116 Mr. of the comics
117 Times of anticipation
118 Art Deco signature
119 Grating sound
120 Small bridge limit, maybe
121 Balance
122 Brand

DOWN

1 Stork or crane
2 Guam's capital, old-style
3 The Amazing ___ (noted magician)
4 Equestrian event
5 Liberty ___ (Lee Marvin role)
6 It's sweet on sweets
7 Lifeboat hoist
8 "___ fit for a king"
9 Hardly the most prestigious paper
10 "___ tu che macchiavi" (Verdi lyric)
11 Suffix with helio- or ethno-
12 Free
13 Comic Mort
14 Lubbock-to-Abilene dir.
15 For emergencies only
16 Devotee of 99-Down
17 Take ___ in the right direction
18 Invitation heading
25 Essential
26 Big name in writing implements
32 "___ dien" (Prince of Wales's motto)
33 Sit in the sun
34 2001 biopic
35 Fed. workplace monitor
38 Bus. envelope notation
39 Places by the tracks: Abbr.
40 "'Tain't nothin'!"
41 Like some muscles
42 Acknowledge
43 Lift, as ice cubes
44 Ape
46 Sephia maker
47 Friendly, as an older relative, say
48 Sister ship of 104-Down
49 Truck stop sign
52 Transforms on screen
56 Blocks in Atlantic City
57 Tailspin
58 ___ Sea, south of the Philippines
59 Receiving party?
61 Benefit
62 Cousin of ante-
63 Burning feeling
64 Noted Los Alamos scientist
65 Rimbaud's "___ saison en enfer"
68 Zoological opening
69 Side dish
70 Yorkshire river
72 Asian autocrat of old
73 Fisherman's wish
74 Olympics sticker
76 Gray removers
77 Doctrine
81 Full of energy
82 Drop
83 "Chicago" co-star, 2002
84 Keeps saying
86 Batting position
87 Next to
88 "Mazel ___!"
90 Most moist
91 One in a dozen
94 ___ Alto
96 Tree with catkins
97 Regional life
98 Blind parts

by Con Pederson

ACROSS

1 Large wardrobe
8 Harder to travel, in a way
13 Household name in Verona
20 Filled online orders, say
21 Barker
22 Unity
23 Party college's nickname?
25 Comeback
26 Idyllic spots
27 Hard wood
28 Musical featuring "It's Today"
29 Tippler
30 Tweed nemesis
31 One side of the Bering Strait
33 "Star Trek" navigator
34 Debarkation points: Abbr.
35 Squeaky wheel, maybe?
40 Mrs. Portnoy, in "Portnoy's Complaint"
42 "__ Dieu!"
45 Ostentatious display
46 Easily-wrinkled fabric
47 Spots
48 Flowerlike polyp
50 Directive to a band
51 Tennis star Jelena __
53 Narrow cleft
54 Talked-about
55 "West Side Story" number
57 Brain passages
58 Radar screen repair?
60 Abbr. on a sale item
62 Parched
63 Come down heavily
64 "The Lake __ of Innisfree"
65 Setter settler
66 Thrash
67 Cook lettuce?
71 Father-and-son actors
72 Cardinal, e.g.
74 Thick
75 Boldness
76 Food item
77 Generous granter
78 Edith who wrote "The Outcasts"
79 Bailey bridge material
81 Certain Indian
82 __-test
83 Napoleonic marshal
84 Slow road crosser
86 Appropriate name for a female fertility clinic?
89 Steakhouse selection
90 In a minute
92 Person of action
93 Author Robert __ Butler
97 N.L. city
98 Coppertone nos.
99 Three-toed animal
102 Harry Potter's potions professor
103 Relentless flood
105 Cause of Leah's many pit stops?
108 "King Lear" daughter
109 Stand out
110 Oblique
111 Run longer than expected
112 Please, in Potsdam
113 She looks to the future

DOWN

1 Wan
2 1970's TV spinoff
3 Palefaces?
4 Willingly taking
5 Wall St. opportunities
6 Make the calls
7 Summer hrs. in D.C.
8 Pain reliever
9 L.B.J. biographer Robert A. __
10 Turkmenistan neighbor
11 It "slayeth the silly one": Job
12 It may be seeded
13 Marine formation
14 Ill will
15 Love-crazy Le Pew
16 Half due
17 Without kids?
18 1991 joiner of the United Nations
19 African pests
24 Big pickle producer
28 Bell insert
31 Dress style
32 Net-surfer's stop
33 Lather
34 Garnish, possibly
36 Does pressing work
37 Hog the mirror
38 "Black Water" novelist
39 Ammonia derivative
41 Jack of "The Great Dictator"
42 Poughkeepsie college
43 Raising hell
44 Like chili peppers?
49 Bog down
50 They're found in the brush
51 Lace mat
52 Previously
54 Unfixed
55 Show case?
56 Molasses
58 Get on
59 Dentist's order
61 How some people get tattoos
63 High sch. disciplinarian
65 Gem devaluer
67 Hoops
68 Fix
69 "I don't __ bit"
70 Hatred
71 Fragrant oil
73 Tries to lose
75 "Norwegian Wood" instrument
77 __ Carlo Menotti
78 Golfer Ballesteros
79 Exotic
80 It's big in the Ivy League
81 Certain co. plans
82 Embarrassing guests
85 Vivacity
87 Like some mushrooms
88 Over there
91 Yard __ (pub order)
94 Borscht server
95 Slender blades
96 Unhip types
98 Song from Dylan's "Desire"
99 Head to the terminal, say
100 It's accessed with a no.
101 Sappho, e.g.
102 Goalie's feat
104 Come together
105 One of the Bushes
106 Not-so-big shot
107 Wrangler competitor

by Alan Arbesfeld

1

```
S O A R S ■ S P A T ■ T R A M ■ L I S A S
A T R I A ■ T O U R ■ H A L E ■ E V E R T
S O A P Y ■ A L D A ■ O R C A ■ M A N I A
H O M E W O R K I S D U E O N M O N D A Y
A L I ■ H O T ■ T H O ■ A S I N ■ I N E
Y E S ■ E Z R A ■ T Y R A ■ I N T O N E D
■ I N E E D A V O L U N T E E R ■
A J A R ■ K I N ■ U S D A ■ A T E S T
C O B A L T ■ E T T U ■ I B M S ■ O A T H
A N Y Q U E S T I O N S ■ S A L E ■ R E E
D E S I R E D ■ C O D A S ■ Y O D E L E R
E S S ■ E M A G ■ N E X T T I M E T Y P E
M E E T ■ S K I P ■ R E A R ■ O N H O L D
E S S E N ■ B E N S ■ R I A ■ O N E S
■ S E E M E A F T E R C L A S S ■
B E A S T L Y ■ S L A B ■ K I T H ■ T O M
A T M ■ C A S K ■ N B C ■ E N O ■ E P A
Y O U D O N T N E E D T O K N O W T H I S
S I L A S ■ E E N Y ■ I D E A ■ B A R A K
A L E R T ■ R E N E ■ D E N T ■ I R A T E
T E T E S ■ Y S E R ■ E R T E ■ Z O N E D
```

2

```
W[HO] S W[HO] ■ G D A N S K ■ ■ T[H]O M M C A N
A R E A S ■ R U B A T O ■ S E A R C H M E
S A I N T N I C[H]O L A S ■ T A R T A R U S
A C N E ■ A S T R A Y ■ T A S S ■ T I L T
T E E S[H]O T ■ ■ S C A L E ■ ■ S E E
■ B O U G H S O F[H]O L L Y ■ E T T A
[H]O O H A S ■ T R U F F L E ■ A D A M S
B R A N ■ H E A R O F ■ M A R I N A
O I L I N E S S ■ E R R I N G ■ S H A
C O L O N Y ■ A P[H]O R I S M S ■ U S E D
A L E N E ■ C[H]O C A[H]O L I C S ■ O N[H]O L D
M E L S ■ [H]O R S E S[H]O E S ■ P U R P L E
P S U ■ A M E N D S ■ T E A R O P E N
■ J A M E S I ■ [H]O R R O R S ■ B E N D
■ S A N T E ■ A T L A R G E ■ P E R E S
[H]O C H I ■ C[H]O O C[H]O O T R A I N S ■
L U C ■ A W I N G ■ A S L O P E
E T[H]O S ■ A G E D ■ R O A S T S ■ E R A S
S T R A P S I N ■ H A P P Y[H]O L I D A Y S
U L U L A T E S ■ A M I E N S ■ [H]O G T I E
P E S E T A S ■ T S E T S E ■ P E E N S
```

3

```
L A P S E S ■ A M B L E D ■ R A M P A G E
I C E A X E ■ S E R I E S ■ I M M O V E D
R E P R O A C H M O T E L ■ P E D X I N G
A S S A D ■ L E O N ■ ■ R O N ■ L I E
■ H U M A N I T A R I A N R E P A I D
E R A ■ S O P ■ R E S O R T ■ A R A ■
R I F F ■ O P S ■ S W E E T ■ I M S E T
G O T T A R E P E A T A N D R U N ■ O N E
S T E M S ■ D U M B ■ N A X O S ■ F U S E
■ R E C T ■ R A I N ■ L E T I N O N
R E P A I F I N G D I R T Y L A U N D R Y
A C A D I A N ■ L O W E ■ S P A S ■
C A R E ■ C A S C A ■ B O R A ■ A L G E R
E S T ■ R E P L A C E T A B L E C L O T H
R H Y M E ■ T I R E D ■ A F T ■ Y O R E
■ B M ■ D E T E S T ■ A U K ■ D E A
R E P L A Y S I T O N T H E L I N E ■
A T E ■ F U N ■ P E L F ■ I V A N I
T H E M O O N ■ R E P E L S A L V A D O R
S A T U P O N ■ B E R T I E ■ S E D A T E
O N E M P T Y ■ S W E E P S ■ U S E R I D
```

4

```
S E C T ■ A D O L P H ■ T I L L ■ C A R B
E L L A ■ S O N O R A ■ I S A Y ■ A L O U
R A I S E T H E P O T ■ E N T R E N O U S
B L O T T O ■ F E E D T H E K I T T Y
■ E R U P T S ■ S R I ■ S E N ■
U S C ■ E N S I L E ■ O N C E ■ D E B T S
N I A ■ D I V A S ■ S W A M I ■ S U E T
M E L D S ■ S O L T I ■ I R O N S ■ C P U
A G L O W ■ O R N A T E ■ S H A K E N
N E T G A I N ■ M A T C H T H E A N T E S
■ H E N N A S ■ G R E ■ S I R R A H ■
B R E A K T H E H O U S E ■ S T O K E U P
R E B R E W ■ R O N D O S ■ N I O B E
I V E ■ R O W E L ■ E V A D E ■ A N D O R
N U T S ■ S A N Y O ■ E L A T E ■ D A M
G E S T E ■ D A T A ■ R E M A I L ■ S T S
■ E D S ■ O H O ■ N E L L I E ■
D R A W T H E F L U S H ■ E N T E R S
M E S A V E R D E ■ C U T T H E C A R D S
V E E F ■ E N I D ■ A M A Z O N ■ I M A N
S L A T ■ P O C O ■ R E B U T S ■ L A S S
```

5

```
A L L A T   H E M I C   D A P P L E
M E A N E R   P A C I N O   P A P E R E R
I N T O N E   I R O N O N   I M P R O V E
D I V I N G B E L L E   T A K E S   S A C
  N I N   I O T A   P O R E   P E N T
F I A T   S W I N E F L U E   S P L A T S
C T N   A T E E   S E A R S   C A E N
C E S A R E   S A T A N   A R C A D E S
    C I R C   B O R N E F R E E   C A T
A P R I L   O A R   E L A T E D   O R R
L A U D   S U M A C   R O S I N   A N T A
P E N   S T R A D A   I T S   F I S H Y
H A N   C A S T E L O T S   T A L L
A N I M A T E   C A R E T   R A S C A L
  N A P E   W R I T E   R A S P   H C L
A N G L E S   E I T H E R O R E   R E E D
S O L E   B P O E   E T O N   A S T
S R A   P R A T T   W E S T W A R D H O E
E M P E R O R   A V I A T E   L I N I N G
T A S T E R S   C A L V E D   S T E R E O
S L E A Z Y   T Y L E R   T R E S S
```

6

```
W A I F   S E T T O   C R A B   L E N T
A L T I   A F O U L   S H U L A   C L A Y
I D E N T I F I E D I T A S A G S H A R P
T O R N A D O   S T R I P E S   L A N C E
    T H R O   O A F   R O I
W R O T E I T D O W N F R O M M E M O R Y
E U R O S   D A N   I N O N   T A O
E S T D   F I S T   S A N E R   S A T Y R
U S E O F T W O H A N D S A N D A N O S E
N E G   I R O N   Y O D E L   E N T
S T A N D O N   L E C I D   H A S I D I M
    A G O   M A S O N   R A R E   O N O
W H I L E P L A Y I N G B I L L I A R D S
H A D A T   A D O R E   A B L Y   R E O S
O I L   U S A F   S L O   S A M O A
A R E Q U I E M F O R H I S P E T B I R D
    U T E   M A I   E L A L
C L E A N   M O A N I N G   A R E A R U G
B Y T H E R O L L I N G O F T W O D I C E
E R O O   E D G E S   L O T T A   Z E S T
R A N G   P E A S   E S S E X   E N D S
```

```
F O N T S █ S U P S █ D R A B █ █ T O S S
I N O I L █ T H A T █ O E N O █ D A R N S
C I N C O █ Y O G A C L A S S █ O X B O W
H O C K T H E H E R A L D A N G E L S █
E N E S C O █ S T R I D E █ U S A █ █
█ █ A L K A █ O A S █ P L O W M E N
█ A F R A I D O F T H E D O C K █ E R O
D C L █ D O F F █ D I S H █ H A N S
A C A █ I N R I █ E R U S H █ A U D I T
L E W I S A N D C L O C K █ E C H O E R
S A N █ V I P █ A E C █ A L E █ W P A
H I T M E N █ M A K E S P O C K S F L Y
O L M O S █ P O L Y F █ R A C E █ D O L
T A O S █ C O M O █ M E S O █ I C E
A M C █ G R E A T W H I T E S H O C K
T A K E A I M █ H E S █ S T E M
█ L U C █ C O A C T S █ W I S E T O
B O C K S U P T H E W R O N G T R E E
G R A P H █ A I R S T R E A M █ O A T E S
P A R E E █ B N A I █ E D Y S █ S T E N T
A W E D █ U G H S █ D E S K █ H E S S E
```

```
O L A F █ Y U P █ B A R O █ S H E █ S R A
M A S E R A T I █ O V E R S E A S █ H E D
N O S Y O R I N Q U I S I T I V E █ A M O
I S T █ D R L A U R A █ G O N E █ S P A R
█ █ C E O █ F I N █ M I D E A S T E R N
W I N D O W C O V E R I N G S █ K O O K S
O D O R S █ H R E █ I S A Y █ I N F █
E S S O █ T I E R █ P O L █ O R D E A L S
█ M S E C █ █ U N E █ A B I E
I S H █ T A K E █ P O S T G A M E
S C O R E P A D █ U N P E E L E D
L A T E W O R D █ P E O N █ L Y S
A L E C █ T E Y █ K N O B █
M E L R O S E █ S W F █ P E N D █ R A G E
█ F U N █ H T M L █ O T E █ G A B L E
S T O I C █ H E A D O F T H E P R I S O N
C A R T E S I A N S █ A P E █ L A D
A N D S █ C A R D █ S T I R S U P █ A T T
R K O █ D O T S I N T H E N I G H T S K Y
E E G █ B L U E N I L E █ E M I S S I O N
D D S █ L D S █ S H O R █ T I N █ E A S E
```

9

Grid 9:

C	A	N	E	■	M	E	N	S	A	■	B	R	A	V	A	■	A	G	A	R
A	R	A	T	■	I	C	A	H	N	■	R	U	P	E	E	■	M	E	R	E
S	I	G	H	■	N	O	P	R	I	O	R	E	S	S	R	E	C	O	R	D
A	S	S	I	S	I	■	U	M	M	■	D	E	T	O	X	■	M	E	D	■
B	E	A	C	H	C	O	M	B	I	N	E	■	■	B	I	T	E	S	■	■
A	N	T	■	E	A	V	E	■	S	I	E	G	■	R	I	S	O	T	T	O
■	■	■	C	A	R	E	S	S	M	A	N	U	F	A	C	T	U	R	E	R
■	S	R	A	■	S	N	O	W	■	Y	E	O	W	■	■	R	Y	E	S	■
P	E	E	P	S	■	■	N	A	T	O	■	S	O	D	A	S	■	■	■	■
R	E	V	O	L	T	S	■	P	I	P	E	T	T	E	S	Q	U	E	A	K
E	Y	E	T	O	O	T	H	■	V	I	D	■	S	A	Y	U	N	C	L	E
P	A	L	E	T	T	E	A	R	O	U	N	D	■	L	E	A	F	L	E	T
■	■	■	H	E	A	V	E	■	M	A	A	M	■	■	T	R	A	C	T	■
E	T	N	A	■	L	E	I	A	■	■	R	O	S	A	■	E	T	S	■	■
G	R	E	G	O	R	I	A	N	C	H	A	N	T	E	U	S	E	■	■	■
G	E	T	E	V	E	N	■	S	T	O	P	■	O	R	T	O	■	W	O	W
■	S	C	R	U	B	■	■	■	S	U	P	E	R	B	O	W	L	I	N	E
A	P	O	■	L	O	A	D	S	■	R	E	V	■	■	B	S	I	D	E	S
M	A	S	S	E	U	S	E	H	Y	S	T	E	R	I	A	■	B	E	T	S
A	S	T	I	■	N	E	M	E	A	■	I	R	I	S	H	■	E	L	E	E
P	S	S	T	■	D	A	I	S	Y	■	T	Y	S	O	N	■	L	Y	N	X

10

Grid 10:

S	A	M	O	S	A	■	S	L	A	P	D	A	S	H	■	A	G	I	T	A
P	E	A	H	E	N	■	N	I	L	E	B	L	U	E	■	T	O	N	E	S
A	N	D	M	A	K	E	I	T	S	N	A	P	P	Y	■	E	N	A	C	T
R	E	A	■	S	L	E	P	T	O	N	■	H	E	S	S	■	E	S	S	O
T	I	M	■	C	E	N	S	E	R	■	T	A	R	■	C	U	S	P	■	■
A	D	E	L	A	■	■	R	A	C	Y	■	■	F	I	N	E	L	Y	■	■
■	■	■	A	P	O	P	■	S	N	A	P	P	E	R	■	O	N	I	O	N
B	I	G	D	E	A	L	■	■	N	E	H	R	U	■	■	I	T	G	O	■
E	V	I	L	■	S	A	V	E	M	E	■	A	N	I	N	■	L	S	A	T
L	O	V	E	S	■	Y	A	X	I	S	■	R	E	T	I	R	E	E	■	■
T	R	E	■	P	A	I	N	T	S	■	H	A	S	S	L	E	■	C	E	L
■	■	I	N	A	S	T	I	R	■	Q	U	O	T	A	■	P	R	O	V	O
A	C	T	I	■	I	S	L	A	■	U	P	H	O	L	D	■	O	N	E	G
N	A	S	L	■	■	A	L	C	E	E	■	■	A	R	I	A	D	N	E	■
A	L	O	E	S	■	F	A	T	L	E	S	S	■	D	E	N	S	■	■	■
■	I	M	S	U	R	E	■	■	A	R	P	A	■	A	T	R	A	S	■	■
■	E	C	R	U	■	S	S	N	■	A	G	O	R	A	S	■	A	V	E	■
A	S	T	R	■	M	I	C	A	■	A	N	I	L	I	N	E	■	D	E	A
I	L	I	A	D	■	D	E	F	I	C	I	T	S	P	E	N	D	I	N	G
L	I	M	N	S	■	O	N	E	T	A	S	T	E	■	A	S	I	A	G	O
S	T	E	E	L	■	L	E	S	S	T	H	A	N	■	R	E	E	L	E	D

11

	C	H	A	R	T	E	R		T	H	A	T		I	N	U	S	E
	T	H	E	N	E	R	V	E		H	O	L	E		N	I	G	E	R
W	R	O	N	G	T	O	E	V	E	R	S	P	L	I	T	T	H	E	M
O	U	R		L	O	I	S		G	O	T	O		T	H	E		P	I	U
K	E	E	P	E	R			B	O	N	E		B	E	E	R	C	A	N	S
		I	S	T	O	B	E	S	E	L	D	O	M	L	Y	U	S	E	D
	A	E	C		J	A	L			R	O	S	E		R	T	S
I	S	M	O	R	E	O	R	L	E	S	S	O	K		A	A	A
G	U	I	N	N	E	S	S		W	H	O	N	E	E	D	S	T	H	E	M
U	N	R	E	A	L		R	E	A	D	E	R	S		L	E	O	V	I
A	D	A		S	O	S	O			O	S	L	O			P	E	S
N	E	T	T	Y		S	P	O	R	T	I	N		G	I	J	A	N	E
A	R	E	I	M	P	O	R	T	A	N	T		C	A	R	R	A	C	E	R
		M	A	R		A	R	E	N	T	N	E	C	E	S	S	A	R	Y
	C	S	I		E	L	I	O		L	O	O		C	B	S
T	O	E	N	D	S	E	N	T	E	N	C	E	S	W	I	T	H
E	L	E	G	I	S	T	S		L	E	A	R		L	O	A	F	E	R
O	L	D		E	K	E		A	T	A	D		I	D	L	E		A	Y	E
	A	L	L	T	I	M	E	W	O	R	S	T	M	I	S	T	A	K	E	S
	R	E	S	E	T		S	O	R	E		A	N	N	E	A	L	E	D
	S	T	U	D	S		P	L	O	D		N	O	T	E	P	A	D

12

E	R	I	T	R	E	A		I	T	S	L	A	T	E		P	A	G	E	S
V	E	T	O	E	R	S		N	A	T	A	S	H	A		A	R	O	M	A
I	N	C	O	M	E	T	A	X	R	A	C	K	E	T		S	I	D	E	D
C	O	H	N			U	N	S	E	R		F	O	S	S	E		L	E	I
T	I	E	S	I	N	T	O			T	A	O			H	O	M	E	R	S
S	R	S		T	H	E	N	O	E	L	P	R	I	Z	E		A	S	S	T
		T	E	L			K	N	E	E		D	O	A	L	L	S
	G	R	I	M		C	H	I	T		S	A	I	N		E	T	A	S
O	R	I	N		C	H	E	E	S	E	U	R	G	E	R	S		M	U	S
M	A	N	H	O	L	E	S			W	I	T		D	I	S	S	E	C	T
A	N	K	A	R	A		S	P	R	I	T	E	S		S	O	U	R	C	E
H	O	O	T	E	R	S		H	U	N		T	E	E	N	S	I	E	R
A	L	F		L	O	O	M	I	N	G	D	A	L	E	S		I	C	E	E
	A	D	E	S		C	E	L	S		I	C	O	N		M	E	A	D
	I	D	E	A	L	S		O	H	O	H		S	E	Q
S	I	S	I		L	E	A	K	F	O	R	E	C	A	S	T		R	D	A
G	O	A	T	E	E		N	F	L		L	O	W	S	P	E	E	D
T	D	S		N	E	A	T	O		L	O	P	E	R		A	C	E	D
M	A	T	T	E		F	A	T	H	E	R	O	F	T	H	E	R	I	D	E
A	T	E	A	M		A	L	T	E	R	E	R		A	M	M	E	T	E	R
J	E	R	R	Y		R	E	S	T	S	O	N		S	O	I	R	E	E	S

13

```
W N B A   G E R E   A C M E   M O M E N T
O E U F   O L I N   S L I P   A M A L I E
W A R R E N F A C T I O N S   R A C I N E
S P R I T E   S R I   P O T   C H O S E N
    C A A N   Y E S   L E S H A N
    B A T T E N P R A C T I C E   W Y E S
I C O N   G I T   L L A N O S   H A R A
M I N S T R E L   A M A   N A B O K O V
A T E   R A V E N M A N I A C   Y O U D O
M Y D E A R   I O N   V U E   A P T E R
    T I E R A C K   C A S S I N I
I T S O N   A G E   F A N   T O E I N G
S H A N E   P A R T O N S H O T S   C O M
L A N D E R S   A L A   A L O E V E R A
A N D I   A T B A T S   A T L   I R A N
M E S S   C A R R I O N C H A R G E S
    O V E R I T   M E T   S O M N
E S C R O W   E C O   H I E   D A N I E L
S T A D I A   F I S S I O N L I C E N S E
S O R E L Y   E N T O   N O O N   S O P S
O P E R A S   R E E D   S S T S   E R N S
```

14

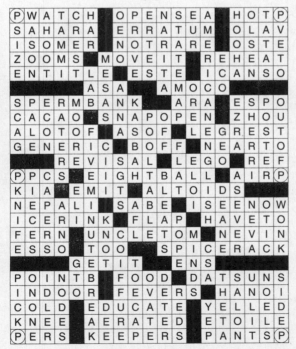

```
(P) W A T C H   O P E N S E A   H O T (P)
S A H A R A   E R R A T U M   O L A V
I S O M E R   N O T R A R E   O S T E
Z O O M S   M O V E I T   R E H E A T
E N T I T L E   E S T E   I C A N S O
    A S A   A M O C O
S P E R M B A N K   A R A   E S P O
C A C A O   S N A P O P E N   Z H O U
A L O T O F   A S O F   L E G R E S T
G E N E R I C   B O F F   N E A R T O
    R E V I S A L   L E G O   R E F
(P) P C S   E I G H T B A L L   A I R (P)
K I A   E M I T   A L T O I D S
N E P A L I   S A B E   I S E E N O W
I C E R I N K   F L A P   H A V E T O
F E R N   U N C L E T O M   N E V I N
E S S O   T O O   S P I C E R A C K
    G E T I T   E N S
P O I N T B   F O O D   D A T S U N S
I N D O O R   F E V E R S   H A N O I
C O L D   E D U C A T E   Y E L L E D
K N E E   A E R A T E D   E T O I L E
(P) E R S   K E E P E R S   P A N T S (P)
```

15

```
P L E B E . C L A N G . F R E T . S A P
D O N A L D . E I G E R . L E T O . P L O
Q U A K I E R S T A T E . O S C U L A T E
B E C K . N O A H S . H O I . C A R A T
A L T E R . D R E S S I E R D R A W E R S
C L E R I C . L I N D Y . E O N . . . .
H A D . C O S B Y . O L D E S T . O R E S
. . F O R T E . S W E A T I E R V E S T
. T O O . D O G M A . R Y A N . C E S T A
T R I G . O L E A R Y . . . P A R T O N
H U L L . B I T T I E R P I L L . B O N D
I M P A L A . N A R N I A . U R I S
S P U M E . P O C K . T O A N Y . Y E A
B U M P I E R C R O P S . W E E K S
E P P S . R E T I R E . K E R R I . F E D
. . S L O . M E N D E . S T E E L Y
C O C K I E R S P A N I E L S . S U D A N
A V A I L . D O S . O N E U P . R O N A
C O S M I C A L . B O X I E R S H O R T S
T I E . C O I F . B R I N K . I M P A R T
I D S . A N N A . S O N G S . M E S A S
```

16

```
A L E W I F E . F L E W I N . M A R L I N
R E N A M E S . I O L A N I . E R O I C A
I A N T H E T E R R I B L E . G A B L E R
O N E T O T E N . N C A A . B A B I Y A R
S E A S . E T D . I S T O O . N O G O
O D D . H O M E O F T H E B R A E . F E W
. . C O O . R O O . I N H E A T .
M A D I S O N . N E P A L . E Y E S H O T
A G R A . L O N E S O M E D O E . T E R I
A R I . F A R O . R O T I . S P R A I N
N E E D Y . A L B A T R O S S . G O L F S
D E R A I L . T O M E . C H A S . L I T
P O E M . O P E N I N G M O E S . D E C A
A N D O R R A . E D D I E . S P R A Y E R
. . U N H A N D . L E S . E O N
S A C . E N D I N G M A C H I N E . W C S
T R A M . A F I R E . E A T . S H I H
O C T O P U S . C O M A . K A S H M I R I
O H I O A N . Y O U O N L Y L I E O N C E
G E O R D I . E L N I N O . I L L T E L L
E R N E S T . H E D R E N . C O D E R E D
```

17

```
H I D E H O ■ L A T E R O N ■ P R E S S U R E
O C E L O T ■ E X O T I C A ■ R O T H I R A S
W E N T S T R A I G H T U P ■ O B E I S A N T
E S T O P ■ A H S ■ ■ L E S S ■ ■ A A N D E
■ ■ N I N N Y ■ S A W A S L I G H T L O S S
S C H ■ T U G ■ A P G A R ■ O T O E S ■ ■
T O O K A B E A T I N G ■ ■ ■ P L U R A L S
A V R I L ■ ■ M O N I E S ■ F O A L ■ E D I T
S E A T ■ A S A N ■ ■ S P R I N T ■ S P O S A
I N C H E D A H E A D ■ F E L L S H A R P L Y
S S E ■ P E L L ■ D O H ■ B E Y ■ E M O T E S
■ ■ M O S T ■ W E R E H O T ■ A L I S ■ ■
O N E A C T ■ C A L ■ P A Z ■ T A P A ■ C R I
L E D T H E R A L L Y ■ G O T H A M M E R E D
O A S T S ■ R A K E I N ■ ■ O I S E ■ S O T O
G L E E ■ B A N S ■ P I L A T E ■ A S C I I
Y E L L S A T ■ ■ ■ G A V E U P G R O U N D
■ ■ ■ C R E T E ■ S E G O S ■ L E M ■ S A O
R E A C H E D A N E W L O W ■ D A N S E ■ ■
A N N U L ■ ■ L O R E ■ ■ I A N ■ D E E R E
S U S P E N S E ■ G A I N E D M O M E N T U M
P R E P P I E S ■ O R V I L L E ■ M A I N S T
S E L A S S I E ■ T S E T S E S ■ C L E A T S
```

18

```
R A I L S A T ■ D R I L L ■ A P O G E E S
A L T O O N A ■ E A S E S ■ C A R O U S E
D I S G U S T O F W I N D ■ C L A I R O L
S A Y I T ■ L I L T ■ R E A C T ■ ■
■ ■ C H A R L E S I N D I S C H A R G E
A H S ■ E S T A S ■ C O P S E ■ L A O S
N O T O N C E ■ Q T I P S ■ ■ N O N U S
G O L F D I S C O U R S E ■ I R O N O R E
S H U T ■ A V I A ■ P R E T E N D S
T A K E ■ S I R E N S ■ A R I A S ■ ■
■ S E R M O N O N T H E D I S M O U N T
■ ■ A N I L S ■ E X U D E S ■ L E A P
A P O S T A T E ■ S A M E ■ ■ N A N A
L I F T E R S ■ T R U M P D I S C A R D S
I N G O D ■ R E A P S ■ S P O R T E D
S N A P ■ F A I R Y ■ O S L I N ■ O M E
T A B L E O F D I S C O N T E N T S ■
■ ■ I N S T S ■ O D E A ■ A C T A S
C I A G A T E ■ B L O O D D I S C O U N T
T I G H T E R ■ B E R R A ■ R O T U N D A
R I O T E R S ■ S A S S Y ■ E C S T A S Y
```

```
L I F T S . A L G A . A G A P E . U S S R
A P R I L . S E E S . R E P O S . S O L O
B O O T E E I N T H E B E A S T . A D O S
. L E A F . S E C . T S O S . A V E
. T H E P R I N T S O N T H E P O P P E R
S E E D Y . C O O . U E Y . P H O N E
A C R . . C A N . M K T S . G S H A P E D
T H E T A U R U S I N T H E H A I R .
. S A B L E . T R O Y . M A D E . P O T
C H A S E D . G R E W . R I L E . G O B I
L I T T L E R E A D W R I T I N G H O O D
O K I E . S O N Y . H U N S . D O O L E Y
P E P . M A Y O . A I T S . M I D S T .
. J A C K A N D T H E B E N S T A L K
I S A I D S O . A W E S . A L G . B A A
M A M B A . D N A . M R T . M O L D Y
T H E E M P E R O R S N U K E L O W E S
H A N . S E X Y . H O E . D I R E .
E R I S . R U M P L E D S T I L T S K I N
R A T E . P L O T S . A L E C . A T O N E
E N Y A . S T P A T . T I N E . L O N G E
```

```
A R I . E L I O . W H A M . S H E D D
S U L A . M I N X . H I L O . S C A R E [ON/OFF]
P I L L S B U R Y B A K E [ON/OFF] P A L A C E
I N T O T O . E M O T E S . D I N E S I N
R E R E A D S . O K A . I N T R U D E
E D Y . P I K E R . D A T I V E . R E S
. W H E E L [ON/OFF] O R T U N E . C [ON/OFF] E R S
A U D I . S E N . S A N T E . B I C
C R E P T . T O B A G O . F E N D E D [ON/OFF]
T A P E R [ON/OFF] R A G . I S A A C . L I E
E N O . U S E T H E [ON/OFF] S W I T C H . U R I
D I S . S P U E S . H A S [ON/OFF] E N D E R
[ON/OFF] C E N T E R . T E A S E T . S E E S [ON/OFF]
. A M C . B E E C H . N I E . I S T S
L A R G E . S A W N [ON/OFF] S H O T G U N
E C O . L A R E D O . O R L O P . S W F
[ON/OFF] C A M P U S . M O M . E M P O W E R
A R R E A R S . B A I L E E . A E R O B E
R U S T L E . D E S S E R T A N D C [ON/OFF] E E
D E A R E R [ON/OFF] S E T . E T U I . H E R S
O S T E R . S T A S . D A D A . D S T
```

21

```
E P O P E E   ▓ N E D ▓   ▓ T E E T H E S
M A R I N E S ▓ I C E S ▓ P O W E R A D E
Q U I C K C E N T U R Y ▓ A G E L I M I T
U L N A E ▓ Q U R A N D U R A N ▓ P R E S
A V G ▓ ▓ A U T O ▓ R E S ▓ P L A ▓
D I S A B L E ▓ S C A N ▓ N E E D L E
▓ Q U I L T B Y A S S O C I A T I O N
O C C U R S ▓ R E S T S ▓ D O N ▓ S O T S
P A R A ▓ T O A T ▓ H O T E L
Q B E R T A N D R O E P E R ▓ V I A B L Y
R O P I E S T ▓ O L D E R ▓ S E A B L U E
S T E A M S ▓ Q U E S T B A T H R O O M S
▓ P I V O T ▓ N A P E ▓ L I E N
I N I T ▓ S I P ▓ I M A G O ▓ C R I S T O
Q E D H O T C H I L I P E P P E R S ▓
S A L E M S ▓ P O T S ▓ R E S H O O T
▓ O S S ▓ M O O ▓ L E I S ▓ U R U
R A V I ▓ Q A N D A B E A R S ▓ O A T E R
A P E R T U R E ▓ Q U I T Y O U R S E L F
M I T E R I N G ▓ I N R E ▓ N A S T A S E
A G O N I Z E ▓ T E X ▓ R O O T E D
```

22

```
P R I E S T ▓ B O S S ▓ E V E R ▓ W O K
R O N D O S ▓ C R A T E ▓ D E L A W(A)R E
U N C E L E B R A T E D ▓ I R I S H S E A
D I O R ▓ T A O ▓ R A M B O ▓ H I H A T
E N G(L)I S H C H A N N E L ▓ S O L I D S
▓ E R E ▓ K E N ▓ S T E E L M E N ▓
B R R ▓ A S S E R T ▓ N O O D G E S
A H E M ▓ O R B I T S ▓ S C A N ▓ T A U
C E L I B A C Y ▓ C(H)I C K E N ▓ R O S E
H A Y F O R K ▓ E L O I ▓ A U N T S
▓ F A M O U S C R O S S I N G S ▓
M O S E S ▓ S O H O ▓ N A U T I C A
A P E D ▓ T A G T E A M ▓ H A N N I B A(L)
G E L ▓ A I D A ▓ E D I S O N ▓ C A R P
I C E D T E A ▓ S H O E R S ▓ R D S
▓ C O(L)U M B U S ▓ E E K ▓ U P I
C A T N A P ▓ O N E A R M E D B A N D I T
O R I O N ▓ O R A L B ▓ D O I ▓ S O M E
A B O R T I V E ▓ J U L I U S(C)A E S A R
C O N S I D E R ▓ U S U R P ▓ O T T E R S
H R S ▓ C A N S ▓ K E G S ▓ N E S S I E
```

23

```
CUSS  LOKI   ABOMB  KAFKA
OSHA  IWIN   RANEE  ILIAD
DEARSANTA    THEANSWERIS
 BRITISHWAITINGLINE
 YESES   EFS    AYS  WAH
 NOES   ATRIAL    PALE
 SECONDPERSONSINGULAR
EEEE  STAY   ISH  EUCLID
ARYL   VNECK   PROWSE
TAOIST  OOLA  AMAT  WES
OPRAHWINFREYSMAGAZINE
NEE  TOTE  KILO   EVONNE
 MIRAGE  NANCY   WOES
CALICO  ATA   ITOO  INAT
DRINKWITHJAMANDBREAD
LOVE  MENACE  SASE
IDE  BRA   COM   ENATE
 WORLDWIDEWEBPREFIX
RAINYSEASON  NONVERBAL
BORIC  INLET  SHOE  OILY
ILENE  TEARS  ARMS  SATE
```

24

```
ASEA  RIDER   SHARE  ABIT
SENDSANOTE   HONOR   CONE
PROJECTMANHATTAN   CRUX
CUR  NIH  STARTER  DEIST
AMMO  EEL   SPIN  MOSSES
 DISCOUNTSENIORS
LAMENTABLE   ANTI   PAO
AMISS  NEEDLES   TETHERS
PARSEC  DESERTCOLORADO
 AAH   ALERT   ECOL
ESL  MINUTENEWYORK  ERE
ATTN  ILOSE    DEP
RECORDBADTRACK  STUPOR
PROVERB  DESPOND  TRADE
SNL  CALX   PLURALIZED
 SAKEFOROLDTIMES
DAPPLE  APOP   EPH  TEAR
RURAL  ICETEAS  FEM  DIO
ARID  ENTRANCESERVANTS
MAZE  CROAT  TAKESPLACE
ALES  TERSE  STADT  ASHY
```

25

```
I N A W E   S O S   A L E S   T O P P S
N A S A L   I R A   L U C Y   F A C E I T
S I T T I N G B U L L I O N   S K E W E R
T R I E D O N   D E I G N   T H E A T R E
      R E T   M I S S I O N M A N N E R S
S E A L   A F U S S   A C R O   R E S
C A B O O S E S   A U N T   P P P
R U N O F T H E M I L L I O N   R A N A T
A D E   F E R   A I M A T   C H I C A G O
M E R I T   O L I O   G O S S I P E D
      M O U N T A I N P A S S I O N
M R P E A N U T   D E L A   N O I S Y
P A R A G O N   G I J O E   T U E   N H A
S T E N O   N O T I O N F O R P R O F I T
      T O G   N O S Y   S E T S F R E E
A D O   D A L E   A M I S H   F A D S
D E P O S I T I O N S L I P   E W E
O M I T T E D   R I P E N   G R A N D M A
B E A T A T   P O N Y E X P R E S S I O N
E A T E R Y   I N T O   E G O   T E M P T
S N E R T   C O H N   S A W   E S S E S
```

26

```
A F R O   M R M O M   I C A N   O J O S
S E A R S   O U T I E   N A M E   V I N O
K R Y S T A L B A L L   S T A B L E M E N
T A E   O R D E R   M I E N   A R S O N
O L D F O G Y   A N N A G R A M M   H U E
      A G O   B R I O C H E   L A M O N T
W A R R E N P E A C E   T R E X   O R C S
E L I   R E T E L L   S V E L T E
B I G G R E E N   O S S A   N E Z
E V E R E T T   J E R R Y R I G G S
R E L I C T   P A L E R M O   R A K I S H
      D O U G G R A V E S   D I G I N T O
      R I D   L A S T   B A S E N J I S
      D O R E M I   E S P R I T   U N E
P E S O   A M O R   P A I G E T U R N E R
E V E N T S   R E C E I V E   A P E
T A B   S K I P T O W N E   A P R I C O T
S L U N G   S H I N   R A D I O   A B A
H E S I T A T E R   A P R I L R A I N E S
O R C A   R O U E   T R A D E   R O A S T
P A H S   P O S E   M E T E R   U L E E
```

27

```
B E S T S   J A M B   S E N D   T O I L S
A S C O T   A P E R   H U E S   U P L I T
S T A N D U P S T R A I G H T   R H O N E
E E L   N A E S   D R E I   S N I V E L
R E P O M A N   E D E N   G E T R E A L
      M I R   A N D S   E P O C H   I G A
C L E A N M Y P L A T E   A N T E A T E R
E L A N D   A N E M O N E S   O O F
N A S   M I N E R S   D E S E R T R O S E
T N T   Y O G A S   Y O K E L   H I N N Y
R E E L O U T   S E W   E L E C T E E
A R R O W   Z E R O S   R A C E R   H E B
L O S A N G E L E S   C U L T I C   E R A
      N B A   E V A G A B O R   H A G E N
R E A D U P O N   D O M Y H O M E W O R K
E L S   S E D A N   N A S A   E E O
S E A F I F E   O B E Y   B A K L A V A
P A R E N S   G R U B   M O E N   L E W
E N U R E   S E T M Y S I G H T S H I G H
C O L D S   P R O P   U C L A   D U B A I
T R E E S   Y E N S   V E E R   S T I N T
```

28

```
G L O   G O A L S   S T E A M   D I N
R E V   A L L I E   S T R A T I   A R N O
A S E   L I L A C   T I A R A S   M I T T
M A R I A V O N T R A P P   P R E V U E
M B A S   E W E   A L E S   P R I C E R S
A R R A S   V I A L   W E I G H I N
R E M O D E L L I N G   H A N S E N
      I M E A S Y   S P O R T   T U B
B A C K   M A N E   S E E M   E O C E N E
A D A R   A D A   A C E S   D A H L I A
D O R A L   S I N G A P O R E   S A L T S
E N D U E D   O I L Y   E L S   F E E T
M A I T A I   P O L E   A S I T   E R R S
S I N   C H O K E   A L O H A S
      A W A K E N   O F F D U T Y C O P S
      C L A M M E D   E P O S   M A N I C
D E C R I A L   O V E R   S A C   S E E R
I S O M E R   H E R E F O R D S H I R E
P S A T   T I R A N A   A L E R T   O C A
I N C H   I N U R E S   C A N O E   T E M
N A H   N A M E D   T R A M P   A D S
```

```
A P B S · S T A M P · B A N C O · W I S P
S H E P · L I B E R T Y B E L L · E N T R
P O N E · A M E L I O R A T E D · I D E E
I N J E C T E D · C E N · S A M I S E N S
R E A D I E R · S Y🔔E S · T E N S P O T
A T M · A S S A I · · A S S N S · E P I
T R I · · U N P L U G S · · N A G
E E N · P A🔔S · R E N · W🔔E R · D D E
D E F L A T E · N O T S O · I C E L E S S
· R I S E R · S O F T Y · N O T I N ·
T O A D S · · A F R O S · · E P C O T
A N N · B🔔U P · S E P · A I🔔S · E M U
R F K · Y O D A · P E P · S M U T · H E B
M I L · S O G · I D A · S A P · A L E
A L I S T · N O P R O B L E M · A B L E R
C E N T E🔔 · D A I M L E R · 🔔B O L T S
· 🔔E D · A S T🔔E N T · D U🔔 ·
D A T · T O P · · B I T · E S S
A C H I E V A B L E · O N I O N T A R T S
I C A N R E L A T E · R O S E G A R D E N
S T R E S S M A R K · O V E R S L E E P S
```

```
B E G U M S · E S C U D O S · S A P P H O
A R A R A T · P A I S A N O · P O U R E D
C O L A D A · E D G A R A L L A N P O N Y
K I L L E R B E A N I E · I R E · T B S
E C O · A M A · T A R · T R E K · B E A S
R A P · N A I L · · M E A T · D E A N E
· · C O N T E M P T O F C O U R T N E Y
R O B O T · · I D E A L L Y · R A H ·
E R A S E R S · X A C T O · D I C E S U P
W I T H O U T A C L O O N E Y · L E N A
R O T · F E E S · · A N E W · A S P
A L E S · T H E K A R A T E K I D N E Y
P E N P A L S · X A N A X · S E D U C E R
· E R A · P I T C R E W · E L E N I
R E M E M B E R T H E A L I M O N Y ·
I P O D S · J O E Y · T A R T · B U S
T I V O · L E W D · P R O · I C H · E N T
A G E · R O C · F R O M O N H E I N I E
L O O K O U T B O L O G N A · I G N I T E
I N U I T S · I H A V E I T · D A G G E R
N E T P A Y · T O Y O T A S · S P E N D S
```

31

```
I L I A C . A F T S . P U M A . I M A C S
W A N N A . G A Z E . O R E L . T A R R Y
I V A N T H E T E R R I B L E . S R T A S
N A N A N A N A . . A R A B . I N T E N T
. . . . A R T H U R C O N A N D O Y L E
V S H A P E S . T O O T . L O U R .
E T O N . . A U T O . O M E N S . Q B S
N A P O L E O N B O N A P A R T E . U L E
N Y E . A C U T E R . L T R S . S A I N
. . G T O S . . H A I G . A T K I N S
S A M U E L T A Y L O R C O L E R I D G E
P I U S X I . L E A P . O S I S .
A R C H . E L A M . A D J O I N . A D D
T E K . E L V I S A A R O N P R E S L E Y
E D S . T A I N T . C B E R . A P S E
. . M A S C . T H O R . T O P T H I S
. C H R I S T O P H E R R E E V E .
P U E B L O . R A I N . N E A T I D E A
R O L L E . L A U R E N C E O L I V I E R
A M O U R . E L L S . P E R F . T E N E T
T O T E S . O B I T . R O O F . E S T E S
```

32

```
P R E S . M O R O S . G U N . M O R K
A E S O P . S A I N T . O N E S E A S O N
R A M B L I N R O S E . P A S T E L H U E
A M E B A S . S T P A U L . T O O L A T E
. . E Y R E . E D N A . O N C E .
S N E R D . C A N C E R C U R E . A G E R
L A X . A C U T E . D I E S . D E B O N E
O P I A T E . W A C . P S I S . B L O T S
T A T L E R . I R A T E . A C C R E D I T
. E A S E . L E N O . O R O . O R E
O W N S . B A L D I N G P A T E . B L E D
N I M . S R S . G I R L . S W E E .
T E A M M A T E . C A V E D . T I E B A R
I S S U E . O L E O . E S E . E N R O B E
M E S S E D . S A M E . T R A D E . Y E N
E L E C . O V E R E X P O S E . G E S T E
. A L T I . C O P A . S A L E .
S T A T U E S . A N I M A L . S A L A M I
L A M E B R A I N . R E S U M E S P E E D
A P P L E S E E D . E L I T E . S O R R Y
B E S S . D R Y . D A N Z A . T O L L
```

33

```
B A G S   P R I S O N   S L O B S   R H E A S
O R E O   C O N T R A   E A R L E   H E L L O
M Y O U T P U T I S D O W N B U T   E A S E L
B A R R I S T E R   A R A C E   S T O R A G E
A N G E L     R I O   A G E   B U R S T
Y S E R   M Y I N C O M E I S U P I T A K E A
      T E E M   T R A   T O T   P A C E R S
P O M P O U S   F E B   A O R T A   T H A N T
S H O R T P O S I T I O N   T I M E   E N E R
A S N O T   R E S   T A T E   N A N U   E S O
L A T T E     A C E   F I L L   I O N A
M Y E A R   C L A S S   C L O W N   T R I S H
      X E N A   L S T S   A A A   A R N I E
S A W   D U M A   O J O S   V I C   N I G E R
A V O W   T E R M   O N T H E L O N G B O N D
M I R E S   O R A L E   I O S   C O L A D A S
B A L B O A   I D A   L E O   S O R E
A N D M Y R E V E N U E S T R E A M   D C I I
      A B B I E   D N A   S U D   M E A N T
C L O S E S T   O L I N S   A U T O P A R T S
O U T T A   H A S I T S O W N C A S H F L O W
S I R E N   E Z I N E   A I D E R S   T I N A
T S A R S   R O S E S   R E A D T O   O N E R
```

34

```
M A N   S C A L P S   A C T I I I   C O G
E L I   A L L S E T   F L A C O N   A R R
N U T   B E A U T Y P R O T E S T   R E E
U M P I R E   I L L   M A P   R I D G E
    I N A S T A T E O F P R O F U S I O N
R O C S   E E L   D W I   P A D R O N E
O A K U M   A D O   E E E   N E A
T H E L I B R A R Y O F P R O G R E S S
H U R T L E   G A P   I A N S   L O A F
    A N A   A R T   S T E   R I N G O
A B S E N T M I N D E D C O N F E S S O R
F A C T O   A S I   D E O   D A S
B N A I   A I L S   T A P   S E A M U S
  G R O S S N A T I O N A L C O N D U C T
    L O S   M S S   L E A   T E S L A
S K I A R E A   N I N   E S S   L I A R
C O N T E S T A N T W O R K E T H I C
O A S E S   H U E   A S H   R E E C H O
F L U   P R O F E S S I O N B O X   I O N
F A R   O N M E D S   E N R O B E   T S E
S S E   T H E U S A   R E A P E D   Y E S
```

35

```
 ASSIST SLED  SPITON 
QUELQUECHOSE HOOKNOSE
TDWATERHOUSE OKCORRAL
SINGE SIR EMCEE  ISTO
    SLEETY HLMENCKEN
 ABATE FIE AREOLAE  
AMFM CSLEWIS SNOG PTA
REGISTRY NEDS  SUGAR
PROTEUS LANCE INAPTLY
 OYER PERK NINOTCHKA
MCD  EZBAKEOVENS  IAN
CORNBREAD EWER TBAR
CHINESE TAPER FAUSTUS
ONCEA CODE BULLPENS
OSH URDU JREWING CELT
  STBARTS GAG IVANV
MXMISSILE OLDSAW
ARUN MINSK TOO BUGLE
YATITTLE UNRESOLUTION
EYESORES SECRETAGENTS
 DEPART SEAS HISSAT
```

36

```
ABBA OPERA SNEAD BUSS
FLAN DUPED TITLE APET
CUDDLEFISH ANTIMADDER
 REROOFS ESTEE ARMADA
  ORNE ESTER CREATED
PALIN DAVIES CLEANER
SPADES NAVE PLUS
AICS PODDEDPLANTS KAI
TAC OBOE HUSK ATILT
 EASIER ATOMS STUDIO
TAFDILY PLANE STANDIN
HODADS RAINY GURNEY
ANAME AARE TREE HAT
TEY BUDDINGHEADS MAXI
 NIAS RUMP SPEWED
MALODOR HAMPER ANKLE
SERAPES RATIO ASCH
ATONER TONED APPEASE
SHUDDERBUG OFFPUDDING
HONI ABASE RARER EROO
ADDS TIRED SNORT NEST
```

37

```
L A B E L   H A S T E   B E E F S     M R E
E N U R E   U S U R P   U N C U T     O E R
I D O N T L I K E Y O U R T O N E     L P S
S A Y S H I T O     N E T S   N E S T E A
      T A P   V I N Y L     A I L M E N T
A L F   L O N E S O M E D O V E   A N T Z
L E A F   E R A T   O N A R O L L
A T L A N T A   A D D I C T S   S L A K E
M O S Q U I T O C O A S T   T E L A V I V
O N E S I D E D     B L O C   T O D A T E
      I R E S T   A R O A R
C O O K I E   S C O T     S N A K E P I T
C A R E E R S   E B O N Y A N D I V O R Y
S T A N S   T I N Y T I M   L E X I C O N
    N O T A O N E   E C C E     L U N A
E G G S   L O V I N G C A R E S S   S S N
T O E H O L D     A R E S O   E O S
H A Z A R D   A S T O     U P G R A D E S
I L E   D O N T T O U C H T H A T D I A L
C I S   E N E M Y   N I M O Y   O T E R O
S E T   R E E S E   D A M N S   F O U N T
```

38

```
P A S T E D   A W A K E N   A T T A C H E
I N C O D E   C A L I C O   B R O N Z E D
K N O W S F O U R G N U S   M A S T E R Y
E A R N   T W A S   S E M   D E I C E S
    E S O   E T H O S   R E T E A C H
A B C   B A R E I N N M I N E D     B R O
B R A C E R   P O L E N T A   A S I A N
E A R L Y I S H   N G O   G R A M P S
D U D E   M I S T R E S S   O R N A T E
    F E D E R I C O   A T E A L O T
A M Y   M E A T B U Y C H A N T S   E R S
P O U T I E R   A P O S T A T E
P O L A N D   G O P L A C E S   A W A Y
A L E R O S   E N O   C Y N I C I S M
L A B O R   B O O N I E S   E T H N I C
S H E   B O R N E T W O L O O S   D N A
    E N L A R G E   E E L E D   Y A P
M E M O I R   E S A   A V E S   R O P E
A B I L E N E   W R Y B R E D F L O W E R
H A S T I E R   A M E L I E   P A M E L A
I N T E N S E   Y E N T A S   D W A R F S
```

39

```
  METS  STAFFS  PAD   HIM
HANOI  INDIAN  OLDJEANS
ANION  SUITCOMPLAINING
LUSTALITTLEBIT  YGOR 
SALVIA  SYD  LAM  STYLI
 LEE  SPA   INBED  EGAD
  GATINSTYLE  SAG  OLE
 DEEM  NACHOS  ASWANDAM
SEATAT  SHERA  RANSOM 
ITSAJOB  IRK  FIG  XSOUT
ARIB  PURSESAIDES  ETNA
MENLO  LEM  TAC  SIOBHAN
 GENTLE  FUNKY  PRYERS
HOTSTUFF  ODDLOT  WARM
UNH  ORR  RAYPERVIEW 
TIED  FOCAL   EAN  HAP
STJOE  GAD  ISO  DRIVEN
 ONLY  MISSINGCOUSINS
DRINKOFDISASTER  SKATE
JANEEYRE  NATANT  SERAC
SET  CON  SCAPES  ORYX
```

40

```
ALLPRO  RESAVE  TRIBAL
LTILES  MINIVAC  HORACE
MYFAVORITEMART  EDITED
ARTIE  ATARIS  OPS  STLO
  NARZ  GATO  JEN  IAN
BATTLEOFBIN  RESTAIN 
ALAS  MRLEE  MIX  LINGER
TOM  TYSONS  AEC  ESTATE
HOPIN  HET  ANNE  THEGAP
SPATULA  SEDATEST  LESS
  STIRS  NOG  DIETS 
ARCA  SPENGLER  DREAMUP
NODSAT  CARL  EVE  STASI
KALINE  AVA  ARETES  VIC
ARAGON  DEM  TIROS  PENA
 UNUSUAL  TOGASPRINGS
MAG  KTS  SOHN   INEZ 
OCHS  OHO  TEEMED  CAIRO
OTTAWA  BOTOFTHEBARREL
LEERED  IRONONS  SPRANG
ADRATE  TASERS   ASONIA
```

41

```
O S C A R _ _ A R M S _ I N G E _ P E R U
H O O V E R _ T O I T _ N E O P H Y T E S
M Y L I F E _ O G R E _ C A T H A R T I C
S A D _ I N A M E R I C A T H E Y O U N G
_ _ C E L E B _ T O N I _ L S D _ _ _ _ _
A R E A L W A Y S R E A D Y _ R E D A C T
K E R R _ E T E _ _ M R X _ L A M I N A R
I L E _ C R E T A N _ D I M E _ I S S U E
T I A R A _ _ T O G I V E T O T H O S E
A T L A S T _ P E L F _ A A A _ O N E S
_ _ _ W H O A R E O L D E R T H A N _ _ _
S A B U _ P L O _ _ A U R A _ U B O A T S
T H E M S E L V E S T H E _ _ E R N I E
A S A B C _ B O S C _ S I G U R D _ N E A
L I N E A G E _ A H A _ U T E _ N A T O
E N O R M E _ F U L L B E N E F I T S O F
_ _ _ T S E _ E D A M _ N O C H E _ _
T H E I R I N E X P E R I E N C E _ W O O
V E R S A T I L E _ N I N A _ U S N E W S
P R I E D O P E N _ T U E S _ S A M L E T
G O N E _ N E R O _ E M M Y _ W I L D E
```

42

```
M O N T E R O _ W O W E D E M _ T E R R A
A R O U S E R _ O O H L A L A _ A L O E S
D E B T O F A S A L E S M A N _ H O O P S
A G U T _ _ C E D A R _ A L A M O _ T E E
M O T O R O L A _ E X S _ Y E L L A T
E N S _ T H E R A T O F K H A N _ E E L S
_ _ S E M _ R O N A _ E N A C T S _
S S G T S _ T B A R _ C A R E _ A T S E A
A P I P _ U S E B O A T H A N D S _ P A S
F I V E O N E S _ C O M _ D U S T E R S
A C E T I C _ S E C U R E D _ R I V O L I
R U B E L L A _ N U T _ R O A S T P I G
I L E _ W E L T C R E A T I O N _ A L E N
S E R T A _ I B L E _ C A P P _ A P E R S
_ _ T R Y S T S _ A D E S _ H U E _ _
E S T A _ P O P U L A R M I T T S _ D R Y
U T O P I A _ E L M _ C O S T F R E E
R E A _ F R A N C _ P L I E R _ L A D S
A L B E E _ T A K E M Y B R E T T A W A Y
I L O N A _ O N E V O T E _ A V A R I C E
L A Y E R _ P A R A P E T _ T A L E N T S
```

43

```
M E S S I N G   U N C A P     P Q R S   E L S E
A T T A B O Y   N I O B E     A T E E   N E E D
C H R I S T M A S T R E E     W I G W A G G E D
R A I S E S   P E R     T R A P P     S A L U K I
A N D O N   S P R I G   E R A T O     A I M E E
M O E N   A T L   C R O S S W O R D     S E R S
E L S   S L E E K   O D S     S P E E C H
      R T E   J I N G O       B A M A   M A S
J U L I U S C A E S A R S A L A D     S M A C K
O R I O N   U C L A N     A S O N   C H E R R Y
E G G     J F K     A S T R A     L E N S
S E A L S O F F K E Y C H A I N S A W D U S T
    M E A L   R E M E T       A R M     P Y E
D O E S N T   O N I T   A U S S I     I R I N A
O W N E D   G S T R I N G S U P S E T B A C K
G E T   A J E T       E A S E L     C C I
      P L A N B S   C A M   Z I L C H   L A B
A G A R   G U I N E A P I G     T O E   S E U L
R A B I D   S T A R R   C H O P S   M E T R O
G U A V A S   P R C A M   E X E   F U R M A N
O C T A G O N A L   F O O T B A L L F I E L D
S H O T   M O R E   E N D T O   E A T A B L E
Y O R E   E S T D   S Y D O W   S M I L E Y S
```

44

```
I T A L I C   S I M P E R   I O N E S C O
N O V E N A   A Z A L E A   T E E S H O T
L E A D I N G L A D I E S   C O M P O S T
E S T   T A O   A R A   P A H   E N O T E
A H A S   P A C K I N G S L I P S   T A R
F O R E T E L L   D T S   L E O I   I S S
    E S T O   S A C   T R U S T S I N
      U D O   N A R C   O P T S   M G M T
D U M P I N G G R O U N D S   Y E S S I R
A P A   E M O   O P P O S E S   L O T S A
E D T   F E U D   I C E   T Y R E   A C C
M A C R O   P O L E A X E   N O V   R U T
O T H E R S   W O R K I N G C L A S S E S
N E I L   T A N G   E T T E   E T A
    N O M A T T E R     S I N   O W A R
R I G   O R T O   M A B   C O U R T I E R
R A P   D R A W I N G R O O M S   O R S O
A G A P E   I N N   E E R   S A T   D I O
T R I L L I N   R U N N I N G B O A R D S
E E F I E S T   E V A D E S   L I P O U T
D E S E R T S   M A S A L A   E L O P E S
```

45

A	T	A	L	O	S	S		C	R	O	C	I		O	C	A	N	A	D	A
S	H	R	I	V	E	L		A	L	T	H	O		L	O	W	E	R	E	D
P	E	N	N	A	M	E		R	E	S	A	W		D	A	L	L	I	E	D
S	O	O	T		I	D	O	L	S		R	E	L	A	X		L	A	P	S
				G	U	Y	S			D	Y	E	S							
M	A	R	G		B	E	S	S				O	A	T	S		S	L	U	E
G	L	O	R	I	A		T	I	S		E	U	P		E	M	I	S	M	S
M	A	K	E	S	T		E	M	O	S	T	O	F		N	A	S	D	A	Q
		A	R	T		R	O	S	S	A	N	O		A	N	T				
G	R	A	T	A	E		S	N	A	R	L	E	R		T	O	E	I	N	G
T	E	N	D	E	R									E	A	R	T	E	D	
E	A	S	I	L	Y		V	A	N	E	S	S	A		S	M	I	T	E	S
		V	I	P		A	P	O	G	E	E	S		E	A	N				
R	O	S	I	T	A		L	A	R	G	E	R	T		A	N	L	I	F	E
P	O	W	D	E	R		O	R	N		A	V	A		T	O	A	T	E	E
T	H	E	E		K	A	R	T			I	R	E	S		W	O	N	G	
				M	E	M	O		B	E	T	H								
T	O	A	D		E	M	M	E	T		A	T	E	I	N		F	O	P	S
I	N	R	A	N	G	E		N	E	T	W	T		L	O	L	I	T	A	S
N	U	C	L	E	A	R		T	R	A	D	E		L	A	Y	S	O	U	T
A	S	S	I	G	N	S		S	O	N	Y	S		S	H	E	K	E	L	S

46

H	D	T	V		U	S	A	F		O	B	J		R	O	S	E	H	I	P
A	R	E	A		P	A	I	L		N	A	E		A	C	E	T	O	N	E
J	O	L	L	Y	M	R	R	O	G	E	R	S		S	T	A	T	U	T	E
I	L	L	S	A	Y		C	R	E	P	T	U	P		A	M	U	S	E	R
S	L	Y	E	R		M	O	I	R	A		R	I	D	S		I	R	A	
				G	O	O	D	M	R	D	E	E	D	S		S	N	A	G	
C	E	R	E	B	R	A	L		S	T	I	N	T	S		I	N	G	L	E
A	N	O	M	I	E				A	G	A		S	W	A	M	I	S		
I	S	A	I	D		B	R	A	N	D	M	R	X		C	O	P	R	A	
R	U	S	S	E		Y	O	W	E	E				B	A	N	D	B		
N	E	T	S		M	R	I	N	B	E	T	W	E	E	N		R	U	S	T
		E	A	S	E	D			R	I	P	E	N		T	A	B	O	O	
	C	D	R	O	M		M	O	D	E	L	M	R	T		E	G	B	D	F
S	I	M	I	L	E		A	M	O					S	T	O	L	A	F	
A	G	R	E	E		D	R	O	P	I	T		F	I	N	E	N	E	S	S
L	A	P	S		M	Y	B	O	Y	M	R	B	I	L	L					
E	R	E		R	E	E	L			M	I	L	N	E		A	D	A	Y	S
S	C	A	L	E	R		E	U	G	E	N	I	A		I	M	F	R	E	E
M	A	N	I	A	C	S		S	P	R	I	N	G	M	R	C	L	E	A	N
A	S	U	N	D	E	R		P	A	S		K	L	U	M		A	T	R	A
N	E	T	Z	E	R	O		S	S	E		S	E	G	A		T	E	N	T

47

```
PROS  NICE  COMPASS  MGS
OUCH  AREA  ABILITY  ERN
SPEARMINT  VITAMIN  REO
TEARIEST  PETES  RAILER
SENDON  AILS  MISPRINT
     TABULA  MBAS  SONES
MAP  MERINGUE  ADEN
SNACKED  ETIOLATE  ISIS
STRAUSS  ANNUL  ACCENT
  ANN  IONIA  GIRTH  NRA
ARMAGEDDON  RACEHORSES
COO  FLEES  BESET  LEU
MUUMUJ  TWEED  ADENOID
ETRE  DESERTED  KEROUAC
  DEER  ANHEUSER  SNL
RABIN  GATO  MATRON
ELECTION  PELE  GOSOFT
BICORN  IHEAR  WHATEVER
ICK  ANOMALY  CAUTERIZE
DIC  NEBULAE  URGE  INES
SAN  TRESTLE  RTES  FESS
```

48

```
HADJIS  CRUSADE  BATHED
AMOEBA  BANANAS  UNRULY
WITHINGENUITYANDGUILE
  SHUDDER  LOA  OGRESS
    EYE  GLENN  TEY
SPERM  MOODY  GIT  BACH
MINT  FARO  DOE  EBRO
INVENTIVENESSANDFLAIR
TOD  CHOS  GOWNS  OLSEN
STIMSON  ADONIS  BRIERY
  ATLARGE  INKHORN
ABLAZE  EOCENE  ONEIDAS
KEANU  CHRON  ETNA  RIA
IHIDMYHOARDSOSLYLYILL
TARP  IAN  POSY  ELEM
ANDA  ERE  MAIZE  NALDI
  ALL  CARNE  ANI
  GRANDE  ORT  ABETTED
BEBLESSEDIFIKNOWWHERE
ORIENT  DENUDES  TIARAS
WISETO  ADELINE  STROBE
```

49

```
B S A   C H A S   S M A R T   G R U F F
R A G   H A S H   E A D I E   R E P L A N
A P I S A T H E A C T I O N   I N T O T O
S I T A R S   B L U T O     R E T O R T S
S E A T O   N A P L E S U L T R A   E E E
I N T E N S E   H A L   N A E   L E N N Y
E T E   T A T A R   M U Y   S A C
  C L A R A S   S A M O S A   R E A M
A C C O U T E R   T U X   P O S   L I S A
G A R A G E D   P E N I T E N T   L S U
G R A T E R   S T A R M A N   I O N I A N
I O N   O N T A R I A N   H O M I N I D
E L B A   M A R   I S L   G A P I N G L Y
S E A T   E T E R N E   B E R A T E
  R O D   T O G   G R E A T   C U M
B A I Z E   I T S   P O O   S H A N A N A
O T S   G E N O A M O T O R S   T E N O N
C H A I R E D   A P A C E   B E A T I T
C A U D A L   E N N A W H E R E A T A L L
E N C O D E   M O I R A   D E E S   T E E
  D E L E D   S L A T Y   Y O R E   A D S
```

50

```
L A B R A T   A N N E A L   F R I S K E D
A N Y O N E   L O A T H E   L I N E A G E
C I T I E S   A R C H E D   O C T A V A L
E T E   W H E N T H E M A N W H O M A D E
S A S S   A B H O R   O I L
  O H A R A   E B O N Y   D I A L
T H E F I R S T D R A W I N G   M E C C A
S E P T E T   E R O D E D   E M E R Y
A R O O   I N S O L E   E T A   L O D E S
R E D N O S E   N A S A   A N T O N
S S E   S T E V E N   W R I G H T   B R A
  M I S D O   D A N A   L I T H I U M
M E L E E   S A T   B I D D E R   A N N O
B L E A R   B E A N I E   S A I G O N
A B E T S   B O A R D G O T I T W R O N G
S A K S   H O U R S   R A Y E D
  A R C   T A T A S   O I N K
W H A T D I D H E G O B A C K T O   M O M
A U R E O L E   R A R E S T   A R M A D A
S L E N D E R   A V I A T E   M E A G E R
P A S T O R S   T E S T E D   S L Y E S T
```

51

```
A B A T E S . . . C L A R E T . S C A M P
S E V I L L A . T R I R E M E . P A N E L
T H E M O U S E H A S M I C E . A R E N A
O E R . N E S T E D . . M E T S . O M A N
R A S P . . T H E L O U S E H A S L I C E
. D E A L S . . E M P . . E N T I C E D
. . S U R E S T . A D D A . D E N . .
. W H Y C A N T A G R O U S E . M A R L .
M A Y S . . S A U R . M I L . . A U G .
C H U T E D . B R E E D B A B Y G R I C E
K I N E T I C . G L O . A R O U S E S
A N D M O T H E R G O O S E . S O B E R S
Y E A . . U V A . M A L E . . B R N O
. S I A M . B E G E T S H E R G E E S E
. N A T . N U D E . L E G E N D .
S T E E L I E . G A R . . M O I R A
W H Y C A N T T H E M O O S E . N A B S
I R E D . A C R O . B R I E F S . C U E
P I L O T . H A V E L I T T L E M E E S E
E V I T A . E L E V E N S . S T O R M E D
S E D E R . S A L A D S . . E G R E S S
```

52

```
D I A L E R . S A T . A L L . M O P U P
A S L O P E . H O R A T I O . S A L I N A
M A D C A P . A N I M A T E . A L I E N S
. D O H . . C H E X A N D B A L A N C E S
B O R A . S A D . I N A . T O Y . E R A
I R A N . F R O S E A N D C O N S . A V G
D A Y D R E A M T . G O O P . . K N E E
. . K E N T . E M B L E M . A M I D .
L A T E N T . P R O L E . P A L E N Q U E
A S H Y . G E N O A . S O N A R . U M A
I C Y . F A R E A N D S Q U A R E . I B M
R A M . A G I R L . D A U N T . H E R O
S P E C T A T E . R E D I D . B H U T A N
. A P E R . D O U R E R . H A I G .
Z E N O . F I R N . E L I A S H O W E
I N D . W H I N E A N D D I N E . A V O N
P C S . H E N . R O E . P E D . N E R D
C O P S E A N D R O B B E R S . D R S
O R A T E D . R O U L A D E . U N C L E S
D E C A L S . A M N E S I A . S H R I N E
E D E N S . W E D . E T D . S L Y E S T
```

53

A	C	R	O	S	S		C	H	A	F	F			D	I	P	P	I	E	R
C	L	A	R	K	E		R	E	S	U	L	T		U	T	R	I	L	L	O
H	E	N	R	Y	W	R	I	N	K	L	E	R		D	O	O	N	E	I	N
T	W	I		B	E	A	M			N	O	S	E	O	U	T				
		J	O	D	I	E	F	R	O	S	T	E	R		D	O	J	O	S	
C	O	D	E	X		A	I	R	E		N	A	M	E	S	A	K	E	
O	R	E	S		S	H	A	R	O	N	S	T	O	N	E	R		C	A	N
N	I	B	S		W	A	R	M	T	O		O	R	C	S		S	K	Y	S
M	O	R	E		E	I	N			R	A	H		L	A	P	S	E	
A	L	A	S		D	R	E	S	S	L	E	R		C	O	P	A		
N	E	W		W	E	S	L	E	Y	S	N	I	P	E	R	S		R	A	M
		R	A	I	N		A	N	T	E	D	A	T	E		A	L	L	A	
S	K	I	R	T		M	O	L			G	U	M		M	A	Y	S	
E	E	N	Y		C	O	R	A		S	E	C	E	D	E		U	N	D	O
T	A	G		P	H	O	E	B	E	C	R	A	T	E	S		S	C	A	N
U	N	E	R	R	I	N	G		L	A	I	R			P	E	E	R	S	
P	U	R	E	E		S	O	N	D	R	A	L	O	C	K	E	R		
			P	A	R	T	N	E	R			W	R	E	N		P	G	A	
C	O	L	O	M	B	O		V	I	R	G	I	N	I	A	M	A	Y	O	R
C	R	I	S	P	I	N		A	C	C	U	S	E		T	A	B	L	E	T
I	D	L	E	S	S	E		H	A	V	E	R		S	N	E	E	R	S	

54

W	E	S	T		I	C	I		H	A	R	A	R	E		T	E	A	M
O	N	E	R		N	O	S	E		I	R	A	N	I	S		R	A	J	A
R	O	T	E		S	Q	U	E	A	L	O	F	A	P	P	R	O	V	A	L
S	C	A	M	P	I		Z	E	L	D	A				E	V	E	R	T	
T	H	E	B	A	S	Q	U	E	S	A	R	E	L	O	A	D	E	D	
		L	U	T	E					L	A	M	P	S			
A	N	G	E	L		D	U	H	S		A	I	M	A	T		Z	E	B	U
S	C	A	R	A	B		M	A	O		N	O	A	H	S	Q	U	A	R	K
H	A	W	S		A	L	E	V	E		I	T	S	A		U	N	T	I	E
Y	A	K		B	R	O	K	E	U	P				D	E	I	S	T	S
		P	A	Q	U	I	N	R	E	L	I	E	V	E	R	S	
R	A	Z	O	R	S			Z	O	M	B	I	F	Y		T	A	N
A	B	O	M	B		P	T	A	S		C	A	S	I	O		H	O	P	I
F	I	N	E	Q	U	A	R	T	S		A	G	E		G	A	E	L	I	C
T	E	E	S		C	R	A	S	S		L	E	N	T		B	A	D	G	E
		S	L	I	C	E						A	B	E	D	
	Q	U	E	A	S	Y	A	S	O	N	E	T	W	O	T	H	R	E	E
A	M	U	S	E			A	P	I	S	H		U	S	U	A	L	S	
Q	U	A	L	M	S	F	O	R	T	H	E	P	O	O	R		N	O	E	S
U	N	I	T		H	A	W	A	I	I		N	U	N	N		T	U	N	A
A	I	D	A		E	A	S	T	E	R			S	T	E		S	L	A	Y

55

```
P R A W N S  C A G E D  A S T A  T H A W
A B L O O M  O R O N O  W W I I  E R A S E
L I F E T I(ME)M B E R S H I P S  N O W I N
      I L L S A Y  C O M I N G(GA)A I N S T
R E F T  E B O N  T A O  E R G
E L I(LI)L L Y A N D C O M P A N Y  N I P P O N
S P E E D S  A N A E M I A  I N A R U T
C R A S S  P A R T I I  A N N E  G N O T E
U A W  A D E  C N N H E A D L I(NE)N E W S
E D A M S  N O N O  O L A  S O N  T I T
R O Y A(AL)L B E R T H A L L  M M E S  R O T S
    P E E L E  S T A I N  I L E N E
R O T H  R I D S  S C E N E S F R O(MA)M A L L
I T O  R L S  T A E  W A C O  E N D U E
S I N G I(IN)N T H E R A I N  R U R  D N A
K O I N G  S E E R  C Y C L E D  B L E E P
I S E L L T  B L E M I S H  S A I N T S
T E R S E R  B E(AR)A R E S E M B L A N C E T O
    A A A  T R A  A E O N  E D E N
C L A U(DE)D E B U S S Y  O S C A R S
H A Z E R  A(MI)M I S S I N G S O M E T H I N G
E V I L S  C A T T  S A L E M  M U U M U U
F A Z E  I K E S  O B E S E  O B T A I N
```

56

```
C H A S E  F C C  U S E D  S C R E W
H A S T A  G U A R A N T E E  H O O C H
I N P U T  A L M A N D I N E  A M P L E
C O I N C O L L E C T O R  R E D M E A T
K I N  R U E  K E N  J O U S T S
    C O T  L A P S E S  S E W N
E L B O W  B O N O  C H I C  I S T
P E A L  C O U N T Y C O U R T  T O M E
I N D O L E N T  E A R N S  T Y L E R
C O M R A D E  B A S I N S  F A C I N G
  I C I E R  O Z O N E  A L L O T
M A N O R S  H A T R E D  V I L L A I N
A L T O S  S I R E N  B E R Y L I N E
O D O R  C O L D C O M F O R T  E R O S
  A N D  A B L E  O U S T  A G E N T
    I M P S  D E M U R S  A P E
B E A N I E  V A R  H E R  A B E
A T L A N T A  C O U N T R Y C O U S I N
S U I T E  S M O L D E R E D  P R I N T
E D G E R  W O L V E R I N E  O S A G E
S E N D S  E T T E  S G T  S A N E R
```

57

```
A F L   G A T O R   A D E E     O K R A
T R Y   R O M E R O   C O M F Y   R O A R
H O C K E Y P L A Y E R ' S F A C E O F F
O N E I D A S   T A X E S   U N B O L T S
S T E A L     W E L T     A S K S
    E T T E   R O O M I E   O R D O
  S I N G E R ' S B O W L O V E R T E E N
S O M E   M A R I A   E I R E   E R A S E
C R E A M   N E L L   R O I   I T A L I A
A T A L O S S   O E D   T E T E
M A N S H O O T S R I O T E R ' S D O W N
    A L M A   S K Y   A S T O R I A
M A S H I E   C C C   A S P S   S U D S Y
O S I E R   S T A R   P O E M S   S E P S
D O C ' S S L I P U P I N S U R G E R Y
I N K S   H A L T E R   T S A R
    N A V E   E S A S   A L I S T
A S T A I R E   E A G E R   D I S O B E Y
F I R M H I R E S W O R K E R ' S B A C K
A D A M   F E T A L   F I N E L Y   R T E
R E P O   D A I S   S N A I L   S S S
```

58

```
T A P E R S O F F   H A S   S A F E   T R E P I D
A L L B E T T E R   A G L I T T E R   H U M A N E
S E A B R E E Z E   R E U S A B L E   E M E R G E
T R Y   E E L E D   D I G I T A L C O M P U T E R
E T E   A L L S O U L S   T I T H A L
  R A D I O   T I T L E   N O N L E V E L
D E P O S E   T E N S E U P   G R O T   E M I T
E M I R   S P A R S E   O R A L   E S T A T E
A M A T I   I D A   S A N E L Y   R O S Y   C T A
L E N I N S T O M B   T A K E S L I B E R T I E S
S T O C K T I P   A S T R A   A S I F   H A R E
  P I E T   S A I D   T A L K   A G A T E S
  B E H O L D   M A R C O P O L O   A L L I E D
P E Y O T L   S A L K   D O T O   A R C O
L E E K   L X I I   M A S O N   C R O S S B O W
U L T E R I O R M O T I V E   G E T I N S H A P E
T I E   U F O S   R E T I R E   R I B   Y E N T A
O N E O N E   B A R N   M A N I A C   A G I N
N E T S   P A S S   R E C I P E S   H A V O C S
  S H U T A W A Y   D I T T O   F I N E R
  S I E N N A   S I N G S O N G   M E R
L I S T E N S T O R E A S O N   A T W A R   A X E
A L C O T T   I D E A T I V E   F A L S I F I E S
B L O U S E   N I T R A T E S   F R E E L A N C E
S E T T E R   I C E S   E R S   E S S A Y T E S T
```

59

```
ASMARA   SYSTOLE  CARA
WHALES   RETIREE  DUDED
KODIAKS  SLOEGINFIZZLE
WOE  LEAS  PODIA  EMCEES
ATAD  RUPP  LYE  UTMOST
REFER  DEITIES  POE
DRAFTPICKLE  CORDOBA
 SASH  TEC  CAN  SILK
 STU  DER  AMAS  STOGIE
SABLE  CASTLEPARTY  BEA
CLUTTER  OUTRE  OPERANT
RIC  THUMBTACKLE  SONES
ANKLES  NEUR  ASS  LGE
PALE  DOR  PMS  HALL
 SENDSUP  BEATLEPOETS
 IAN  STERNLY  ENTRE
 SEDATE  CRT  NERF  SHUE
ACTONE  TROCP  GILA  ESK
GROUNDCHUCKLE  CONNOTE
RINSE  SUBHEAD  STARER
APSE  ASSENTS  SAYYES
```

60

```
FRANCIS  ISLIP  WIDENED
LUCERNE  TIARA  AGESAGO
ASUSUAL  ARRAU  SOFARAS
TE[TEA]TETE  DEFINI[TEA]RTICLE
 CEL  CADS  SCOWS
ABCD  ATMS  MEHTA  SELAH
ZOE  EXECUTE  YAY  ISITI
UNNOTED  PUCE  OXCART
LETON  SCRAPEUP  BAM
 MAYA  CHARLOT[TEA]MALIE
GASP  OLGA  IMAT  TENN
ASWHI[TEA]SASHEET  TSAR
SSE  SMOTHERS  LAPSE
PUEBLO  ERAS  RIPPLED
AMPLE  MOP  OUTLETS  AND
RESTS  ENROL  HYPO  INDY
 FAKER  FEEL  ONE
INTIMA[TEA]PPAREL  ILLA[TEA]SE
SEASALT  ATIDE  CULPRIT
IMPULSE  RECON  ARIETTA
SOAPIER  EDENS  SEETHES
```

61

```
S A V A G E ■ A N T H E M ■ L E G P U L L
A V A T A R ■ C O R O N A ■ A L I E N E E
G O T T H E S U N I N T H E M O R N I N G
A W S ■ A M A T O L ■ ■ D R O I D ■ T I O
■ ■ S N I P E ■ L A R I A T ■ E D E N S
O H O H ■ T O L ■ I R E ■ S T A R R ■
W A S A V E R Y G O O D Y E A R ■ I L L S
L I L L E ■ ■ A N O D E ■ C A V E I N
■ R O L E P L A Y ■ ■ N S F ■ H E N N A
■ O R E O S ■ A O R T A L ■ A S T E R
S L A V ■ D O N T L O V E Y O U ■ M O N K
P A L E S ■ S E R I F S ■ S A N D E ■
A M O R E ■ E R A ■ M O T O R C A R
C A N C A N ■ W A S T E ■ U R B A N
E R G O ■ C A L L T H E W I N D M A R I A
■ M O O L A ■ Y U L ■ C O E ■ Z A N Y
T O W E L ■ O P I A T E ■ E M P T Y ■
E T A ■ D R O S S ■ V O L A R E ■ V I A
M A K E M E F E E L L I K E D A N C I N G
P R E V A I L ■ R A I S E S ■ V O O D O O
T Y R A N N Y ■ E M B E D S ■ E N D I N G
```

62

```
D A L I ■ A N G E L ■ H I R E D ■ S H E A
E T O N ■ W O R R Y ■ I N U R E ■ T E N S
M O N S T E R E O S ■ T O B A C C O R D S
S M I T H ■ M E D I C I N E S ■ I M B U E
■ A E R ■ D E N O T E S ■ C L A S P S
S C E N T E D ■ D E N ■ L A I C ■
C A N T A T A S ■ T E A ■ I D A H O A N
O M A R ■ T O P L E S S O N S ■ I D L E
P E T U L A ■ B R U N E T T E ■ S N O B S
E L E M E N T ■ A G T ■ E T C E T E R A S
■ T O R I C ■ R O U T E ■
P R O M I N E N T ■ S R I ■ T U N E S U P
L E M O N ■ S K I R M I S H ■ I O D I N E
O D I N ■ P S Y C H I C K E N ■ I N C A
P O T A B L E ■ E E L ■ N E R F B A L L
■ R O O S ■ E G O ■ G O A L I E S
H E P C A T ■ C A R R A R A ■ E K E ■
A M A H S ■ S A V E S T I M E ■ I S L A M
D I G I T A L I A N ■ H O O V E R S I O N
S L A V ■ C U R I A ■ E L V I S ■ E R N O
T Y N E ■ T R O L L ■ R E E L S ■ D E E P
```

63

```
O P A L   S T A S   S C R A P   H U M I D
T O N E   P E D I   P O E M E   O R A T E
H O G D A Y S O F S U M M E R   M I T E R
E L E G I S T   T E R P   R I C E   A M I
R E L E T   P I S A   A C I D L Y   D I D
S D S   C H I R O N   C O C O A   D O Z E
      T H E L O U S E T H A T R O A R E D
G U S H   M O N T   K E E N   E L I
E P A U L E T   F E D S   O N E S T O P
A L U M S   A P E D   I M A C   E R E
R A T B U R G L A R   D O N K E Y S U I T
E T E   E R I N   N O N O   T A T E R
D E S P I S E   B E A T   P A D R O N E
    O R E   P R A M   S C A R   I N T L
M O T H E R M O O S E S T O R I E S
O V A L   V I S I T   T A R T A R   T U E
H E N   G E N T L E   A N K H   R E I N S
A R T   I D I G   R A I D   E V E R E S T
W E A N S   M A R E B R A I N E D I D E A
K A R A T   A M I G O   R I O T   C O A T
S T A Y S   L E G G Y   D I N S   A N T E
```

64

```
S T E M S  [KEY] L I M E S   A G A   S H M O
H A R E M   N A B O R S   H O C [KEY] T E A M
O R O N O   O R A N G E   A L T E R E G O
P A S S [KEY]  T I R E S   F I D E L I O
      A B R E A S T   S M U   V I E
M O S   E A S T   A N A I S   E N T E R [KEY]
I C E M A N   B R O W N E   C L A W
C A L O R I C   S Y M B O L S   P A L M E
[KEY] L E S S   A A A   O R E O   A R A B S
S A S E   E R N   M C N [KEY] S U I T   S O T
    L I C I T   A N E   S P I E S
[KEY] E S   D O O H I C [KEY] S   L E I   T R O D
G L A D E   C O R A   A Y R   P A O L O
R E G I S   A L E R T E D   S T O R M I N
I N E S   O N E O N E   H O [KEY] P O [KEY]
P A R K A S   G E N E T [KEY] S U P   S S S
    J U T   Y E A   R E C E D E S
M A L O R Y S   S A L A D   D E B A [KEY]
A L A C A R T E   D E N I S E   O P I U M
T U R [KEY] S O U P   N A T T E R   U I N T A
A M A S   N B A   A S S E S S   T A G O N
```

65

```
P A S C A L   E N D U P A T   O P P O S E
A P O L L O   C O I N A G E   W H O R L S
R E P A S T   H U R R Y U P A N D W A I T
    P O I S O N   A T E I N       T E E
A M A   R O O   I V O   D A M P N E S S
R A N K A N D F I L E     S O R E S T
A R K I N S   R O L L U P S   R O W
B I L L   B A N S   N I P A N D T U C K
S E E D I N E S S   S P L A T S   T O A
    A M O S   S H I E S T   S W E A T
B E F R U I T F U L A N D M U L T I P L Y
L U R E S   M E S O N S   N E I N
O R A   C A N A P E   T H E G R E A S E
T O U C H A N D G O   A R I D   B L U R
    O A R   S E N T F O R   S E A M A N
  C H A R O N   R A N T A N D R A V E
T H E T I M E S   A A R   C I I   Y E S
A R R   S W A R M   T H E F T S
C O M E O U T A N D P L A Y   F I E S T A
I M A G E S   S T O L E U P   L O C K E R
T E N O R S   H E R E S T O   E N T I C E
```

66

```
S H E I L A   S P A R E M E   A D A P T
W A L L I S   A U R O R A S   A D A G E S
I M E E T S A N T A M O R E A N D M O R E
G E M S T O N E   A D A   D I O N N E
    E R A   M A N E T   O M N
G O C A R T   T A C O S   F R A   N A M E
A Z A N   F A Z E   S U E T   I T A L
M A N Y S T O R E S E N T H R O N E H I M
E W E   W A N T   S O A R S   A L O N E
  A S S E N T   I M P U T E   K I S S E R
    C A S S I N I   N U R T U R E
W A T E R Y   C A R E S S   A L O N S O
A V A N T   P E R E S   A H A B   U R I
S O M E O N E M U S T B E J O K I N G O R
T I E R   A R A T   A L A E   R A N K
E D D Y   S T N   L O M A X   P H A R O S
    S T U   H E M A N   M A E
  R E P A I R   A G A   S I G N P O S T
T H E Y V E B E G U N T O C L O N E H I M
S E L L E R   T A M I A M I   D E P O N E
K E Y E D   O R E S T E S   A R I S E N
```

67

```
L O C T   S T A S I   L E I A     S W O O P S
T E N N I S M A T C H P A R T S   K A L K A N
H O U S E H O L D A N I M A L S   O R E L S E
E N S   P R O C U R E S     L O M A N   A T E
    P O E T   S E N T B Y   C A L S   H E R
  C O U L D   W K S   E R O T I C     N O D I
B O B F O S S E       A R E A   B E A M O N
O L O F     W E S T S I D E S T O R Y G A N G
Z E E   B O A   T H O R S   S E D E R S
      D A N M A R I N O       E W E   F O G
A R I O S O   W A S I N   M A R S   A L M A
N E W J E R S E Y B A S K E T B A L L T E A M
E Z I O     E S S E   I R A N I   O A T E R S
W A N   R A N       D I N O S A U R S
    F O S S A E   G E T T O   E S S   G A P
G I V E S P E R M I S S I O N T O   A R C S
A N I T A S   R A S P     E N M I T I E S
S T O A   B I G T O P   A W N   E N I D S
M E L   S L A V   S T R A T I   J E T E
A R E   A E R E O   I C E S K A T E   S R O
I N N A T E   S H E A S T A D I U M G R O U P
N E C K E D   A S S U M E S O W N E R S H I P
S T E A D S   T O P S   D E M I T   A T O Z
```

68

```
P O T O M A C   L A D D     C H A R M A N
U T E R I N E   A M C I   M O O D I E S T
B O A R D I N G P A S S   E N R A V I S H
S E M I   S E A T A S S I G N M E N T
    S A V E I T   Y E T   E E S
J A G   B I D S   C A R R Y O N B A G
U P R I S E   T A X   T R O I   N O L T E
N I E C E     D I S   Y E R   T A R A
C A B I N P R E S S U R E   S I D E B A R
O N E   T H A D   C A T O   G E O S
    R E A D Y F O R T A K E O F F
  L I E S   S O S O   I N R I   Q U A
H E A D S E T   B U S I N E S S C L A S S
A N N I   D U G   E L I     I O T A S
L O A N S   P A P A   E X O   M E N A G E
F L I G H T P L A N   P H E N   R E T
    A W E   U N A   B E A S T S
  H O L D I N G P A T T E R N   A B B A
S A L I E N C E   B A G G A G E C L A I M
A L L E R G E N   E R I E   A C T U A T E
C L A U S E S   L I F T   R U S T L E S
```

```
W I G W A G S █ N A T A S H A █ H O G A N
A M I A B L E █ A G A T H A S █ E V I T A
S P A R E I N T H E T R U N K █ M A V E N
T E N T █ M E W S █ T I E D █ A L E R T
E N T S █ M C I █ F O U █ S P A N █ U R E
S D S █ M E A T F R O M H O G S █ A P E S
█ █ B A R █ S R A █ I N S P E C T █ █
E N M A S S E █ O T H E R █ H I T H E R
M E A N T █ V O W █ O L E S █ A R S E N E
B U L K █ I N N U M E R A B L E █ G H I
R T E S █ C A T █ P E N █ D O T █ T H A N
A R I █ N O N A M E R I C A N █ I O N S
C A N T E R █ P O N E █ U T E █ P E S C I
E L D E S T █ O D D E R █ S M A R T E N
█ I N T E N S E █ L I B █ E R S █ █
R E V S █ G O O D T O L O O K A T █ S S T
A M I █ P E R M █ H B O █ N I L █ R A T E
V I D E O █ A L I S █ B E S T █ A R E A
A G U A S █ P L A C E F O R S I N N E R S
G R A V E █ S I N K S I N █ I M O G E N E
E E L E R █ T A K E S T O █ N E M E S E S
```

```
P R O P M A N █ A L A B A M A N █ T R O G G S
L A R A I N E █ C O L L A P S E █ H A R A R E
I H A V E A D R E A M T H A T O N E D A Y O N
A R N E S S █ E T N A S █ A I S L E █ L E W D
N A G █ █ S L Y █ █ H E A P █ S T E
T H E R E D H I L L S O F G E O R G I A T H E
█ E L S I E █ T U R E E N █ L E D █ █
█ S O N S O F F O R M E R S L A V E S A N D
I O W E █ T S P █ M O A S █ L E S █ G O O K
C O N G A M E █ T W O █ L O G O N █ G E N R E
K N E E P A D █ E N D █ T O T A L █ P A Y
█ D D A Y █ T H E S O N S O F █ S E G A
E A U █ R O S I E █ T I P █ S Y N E R G Y
C S P O T █ T E P I D █ C Y D █ H E N R E I D
K I T H █ T A G █ M A R C █ E G O █ A I R S
█ F O R M E R S L A V E O W N E R S W I L L █
█ O I L █ T R I A L S █ S T A I N █
B E A B L E T O S I T D O W N T O G E T H E R
R A N █ O P A L █ █ O A F █ █ O N E
E R I C █ A D D U P █ I C A L L █ N U A N C E
A T T H E T A B L E O F B R O T H E R H O O D
T H R A S H █ A N A T H E M A █ E R A S U R E
H Y A T T S █ T A T T E R E D █ C O L O R E D
```

71

```
S H E A . S C A D . O L D S . R E P A C K
A U S T R A L I A . W I R E . E T A L I I
L A T T E F O R D I N N E R . P E N P A L
. . . B E N S O N . E G G C A R T O O N
M A C A B R E . M U M . E A R N S . . .
A R O S E . D A T A S E T . S T A . S C I
M I R E . B U T E N E . T E L S T A R
M O R A L F I B B E R . E P E E . C O C O
A S A . A I M E E . O M A R . D Y L A N
. I L O I L O . E D G E R . A L L O Y
. S P R I N G F I E L D R I F F L E .
P A N E D . A E R I E . T I T A N S
L B A R S . M U L E . L U C R E . B O O
A N K A . H I L L . T E E T H E R B A L L
S E E S R E D . A G O R A E . . A S I S
M R S . O A R . S O A N D S O . S W E D E
. . A D D I S . A T E . D E A L S I N
S U P P E R B O W L . S T E E L Y . .
E T H A N E . P A I N T E D D E S S E R T
E N A C T S . O N E A . L I O N T A M E R
D E T E S T . R E S T . L E N A . D U T Y
```

72

```
B A B A . S A L U K I . J A P E . P A L E
O M A R . T I E P I N . A R A L . E V A N
P O S T C E R E A L S . I N T E R D I C T
. R E S I N . . N O R M A N M A I L E R
S P L A T . A P T . L E E Z A . S C A R Y
T H E L E T T E R M E N . . G S A . .
O I S E . R O S I E S . O L D A L B U M S
P C S . J A N E T S . A V I A T E . R E T
. L O V E T O . E N E M Y . R A S T A
D E L I V E R A N A D D R E S S . K I R I
E R A S E R . N I L . A M I N O R
A M Y L . S T I C K T O I T I V E N E S S
F I L E D . U R A L S . S O M E R S . .
E N O . E S T A T E . C A R P A L . R F D
N E W I S S U E S . C H A P E L . S E L A
. M C S . T H E C O L L E C T O R
S L I M E . S U A V E . S R S . R A I S E
T E R E N C E S T A M P . W I L T S .
U P A N D A T I T . I T S C A N C E L E D
N E T S . M A N Y . S A T I R E . N E R O
T R E E . P E G S . E S P R I T . E S S O
```

S	Q	U	A	T	S		N	O	N	A	M	E	S		F	O	S	T	E	R
G	U	N	G	H	O		I	K	E	B	A	N	A		R	E	M	O	V	E
T	I	T	H	E	D		C	L	A	S	S	I	F	I	E	D	A	D	A	M
S	T	O	A			A	S	E	A		C	O	D	E	R	S		L	A	N	E
			S	I	C	K	O		V	A	N	S		A	N	A	L	Y	S	T
J	U	S	T	S	A	Y	N	O	A	M		A	S	O	N	E				
A	N	T		U	N	S	E	W	N		E	S	P		T	S	A	R	
C	L	A	S	P	S		N	E	W	Y	O	R	K	J	E	T	S	A	M
K	I	R	K		W	A	S	S	A	I	L		E	O	N		W	V	A
	T	R	O	T	T	E	D		D	N	A		Y	A	N	K	E	E	S
	A	H	U	N	D	R	E	D	G	R	A	N	D	A	M				
H	E	W	L	E	T	T		O	I	L		M	E	S	S	A	G	E	
E	L	I		A	T	O		O	L	E	M	I	S	S		R	O	L	E
F	I	G	H	T	I	N	G	M	A	D	A	M		R	A	T	T	E	D
	A	S	I	E		O	S	T		H	A	C	K	E	R		I	N	A
	B	A	S	S	O		F	R	Y	I	N	G	P	A	N	A	M	
M	I	N	I	M	U	M		T	R	U	E		N	O	I	S	E	
A	L	E	S		M	U	S	E	U	M		P	E	W	S		R	S	V	P
H	O	W	C	A	N	T	H	A	T	B	E	A	M		T	O	A	T	E	E
A	S	T	U	T	E		O	O	H	L	A	L	A		E	S	T	A	T	E
L	E	S	S	E	R		D	R	S	E	U	S	S		R	E	E	B	O	K

W	A	R	D		V	I	D	A		R	E	C	U	S	E		D	R	A	W
A	G	A	R		A	C	A	D		A	R	E	N	A	S		R	A	S	H
D	A	N	E		L	I	V	I	N	G	I	N	T	H	E	P	A	S	T	E
E	N	D	S		A	N	I	S	E			T	I	L		E	S	T	E	R
R	A	I	S	I	N	G	T	H	E	B	A	R	E		O	N	T	A	P	E
			A	C	C			D	A	L	I		A	S	T	I				
S	P	A	G	H	E	T	T	I		K	I	C	K	T	H	E	C	A	N	E
T	O	B	E		H	O	M	M	E		I	T	A	L		V	I	A	
N	O	D		D	A	N	I	O		S	C	A	N		H	U	N	T	
S	H	O	P	P	I	N	G	T	R	I	P	E		B	U	E	N	A	S
	M	E	R	C	K		A	P	R	I	L		S	O	N	I	C	
S	O	I	R	E	E		T	H	E	R	E	S	T	H	E	R	U	B	E
L	U	N	K		D	I	E	S		A	B	H	O	R		L	I	P	
A	S	A		B	O	Y	S		G	L	E	A	M		I	A	T	E	
W	E	L	C	O	M	E	M	A	T	E		S	H	A	D	E	T	R	E	E
			L	U	I	S		G	O	R	P			A	G	E				
A	B	S	E	N	T		H	A	V	E	A	F	I	R	M	G	R	I	P	E
L	I	L	A	C		T	A	I		L	E	G	U	P		A	S	I	N	
D	O	A	N	Y	T	H	I	N	G	T	O	W	I	N	E		T	E	N	T
E	T	T	U		W	I	L	S	O	N		E	V	E	S		E	R	T	E
R	A	S	P		O	N	E	T	O	N		R	E	S	T		S	E	A	R

75

```
A R M O I R E ■ I C I E R ■ C A P U L E T
S H I P P E D ■ C A R N Y ■ O N E N E S S
H O M E O F T H E R A V E ■ R I P O S T E
E D E N S ■ ■ E B O N Y ■ M A M E ■ S O T
N A S T ■ A S I A ■ ■ S U L U ■ S T N S
■ O I L I N G P O I N T ■ S O P H I E
M O N ■ R I T Z ■ R A M I E ■ A R E A S
A N E M O N E ■ H I T I T ■ D O K I C ■
R A V I N E ■ F A M E D ■ T O N I G H T
I T E R S ■ B L I P S E R V I C E ■ I R R
S E R E ■ P O U R ■ ■ I S L E ■ F L E A
T A N ■ B R A I S E M O N E Y ■ A L D A S
■ R E D B I R D ■ M I D S T ■ S T A R C H
■ V I A N D ■ G E N I E ■ S I T W E L L
S T E E L ■ H I N D U ■ B E T A ■ N E Y
T U R T L E ■ M A D A M E O V A R Y ■
R I B S ■ S O O N ■ D O E R ■ O L E N
A T L ■ S P F S ■ T A P I R ■ S N A P E
N I A G A R A ■ J A C O B S B L A D D E R
G O N E R I L ■ E X C E L ■ B E V E L E D
E N D L A T E ■ B I T T E ■ S E E R E S S
```

The New York Times

Crossword Puzzles

The #1 name in crosswords

Available at your local bookstore or online at nytimes.com/nytstore

Coming Soon!

Will Shortz Presents Fun in the Sun		
Crossword Puzzles Ominibus	0-312-37041-5	$11.95/$15.95 Can.
How to Conquer The New York Times		
Crossword Puzzle	0-312-36554-3	$9.95/$11.95 Can.
Crossword Under the Covers	0-312-37044-x	$6.95/$8.50 Can.
Afternoon Delight Crosswords	0-312-37071-7	$6.95/$8.50 Can.
Favorite Day Crosswords: Tuesday	0-312-37072-5	$6.95/$8.50 Can.
Crosswords for a Mental Edge	0-312-37069-5	$6.95/$8.50 Can.

Special Editions

Brainbuilder Crosswords	0-312-35276-X	$6.95/$9.95 Can.
Fitness for the Mind		
Crosswords Vol. 2	0-312-35278-6	$10.95/$14.95 Can.
Vocabulary Power Crosswords	0-312-35199-2	$10.95/$14.95 Can.
Will Shortz		
Xtreme Xwords Puzzles	0-312-35203-4	$6.95/$9.95 Can.
Will Shortz's Greatest Hits	0-312-34242-X	$8.95/$12.95 Can.
Super Sunday Crosswords	0-312-33115-0	$10.95/$15.95 Can.
Will Shortz's Funniest		
Crosswords Vol. 2	0-312-33960-7	$9.95/$13.95 Can.
Will Shortz's Funniest Crosswords	0-312-32489-8	$9.95/$14.95 Can.
Will Shortz's Sunday Favorites	0-312-32488-X	$9.95/$14.95 Can.
Crosswords for a Brain Workout	0-312-32610-6	$6.95/$9.95 Can.
Crosswords to Boost Your		
Brainpower	0-312-32033-7	$6.95/$9.95 Can.
Crossword All-Stars	0-312-31004-8	$9.95/$14.95 Can.
Will Shortz's Favorites	0-312-30613-X	$9.95/$14.95 Can.
Ultimate Omnibus	0-312-31622-4	$17.95/$25.95 Can.

Daily Crosswords

Daily Crossword Puzzles Vol. 72	0-312-35260-3	$9.95/$14.95 Can.
Fitness for the Mind Vol. 1	0-312-34955-6	$10.95/$14.95 Can.
Crosswords for the Weekend	0-312-34332-9	$9.95/$14.95 Can.
Monday through Friday Vol. 2	0-312-31459-0	$9.95/$14.95 Can.
Monday through Friday	0-312-30058-1	$9.95/$14.95 Can.
Daily Crosswords Vol. 71	0-312-34858-4	$9.95/$14.95 Can.
Daily Crosswords Vol. 70	0-312-34239-X	$9.95/$14.95 Can.
Daily Crosswords Vol. 69	0-312-33956-9	$9.95/$14.95 Can.
Daily Crosswords Vol. 68	0-312-33434-6	$9.95/$14.95 Can.
Daily Crosswords Vol. 67	0-312-32437-5	$9.95/$14.95 Can.
Daily Crosswords Vol. 66	0-312-32436-7	$9.95/$14.95 Can.
Daily Crosswords Vol. 65	0-312-32034-5	$9.95/$14.95 Can.
Daily Crosswords Vol. 64	0-312-31458-2	$9.95/$14.95 Can.

Volumes 57-63 also available

Easy Crosswords

Easy Crossword Puzzles Vol. 7	0-312-35261-1	$9.95/$14.95 Can.
Easy Crosswords Vol. 6	0-312-33957-7	$10.95/$15.95 Can.
Easy Crosswords Vol. 5	0-312-32438-3	$9.95/$14.95 Can.

Volumes 2-4 also available

Tough Crosswords

Tough Crosswords Vol. 13	0-312-34240-3	$10.95/$14.95 Can.
Tough Crosswords Vol. 12	0-312-32442-1	$10.95/$15.95 Can.
Tough Crosswords Vol. 11	0-312-31456-6	$10.95/$15.95 Can.

Volumes 9-10 also available

Sunday Crosswords

Sunday Morning Crossword Puzzles	0-312-35672-2	$6.95/$9.95 Can.
Everyday Sunday	0-312-36106-8	$6.95/$9.95 Can.
Sunday Puzzle Omnibus Vol.32	0-312-36066-5	$6.95/$13.95 Can.
Sunday Morning Crossword Puzzles	0-312-35672-2	$6.95/$9.95 Can.
Sunday In the Park Crosswords	0-312-35197-6	$6.95/$9.95 Can.
Sunday Crosswords Vol. 30	0-312-33538-5	$9.95/$14.95 Can.
Sunday Crosswords Vol. 29	0-312-32038-8	$9.95/$14.95 Can.

Large-Print Crosswords

Large-Print Crosswords for Your		
Bedside	0-312-34245-4	$10.95/$14.95 Can.
Large-Print Will Shortz's		
Favorite Crosswords	0-312-33959-3	$10.95/$15.95 Can.
Large-Print Big Book		
of Easy Crosswords	0-312-33958-5	$12.95/$18.95 Can.
Large-Print Big Book of		
Holiday Crosswords	0-312-33092-8	$12.95/$18.95 Can.
Large-Print Crosswords for		
Your Coffeebreak	0-312-33109-6	$10.95/$15.95 Can.
Large-Print Crosswords for		
a Brain Workout	0-312-32612-2	$10.95/$15.95 Can.
Large Print Crosswords to		
Boost Your Brainpower	0-312-32037-X	$11.95/$17.95 Can.

Large-Print Easy Omnibus	0-312-32439-1	$12.95/$18.95 Can.
Large-Print Daily Crosswords Vol. 2	0-312-33111-8	$10.95/$15.95 Can.
Large-Print Daily Crosswords	0-312-31457-4	$10.95/$15.95 Can.
Large-Print Omnibus Vol. 6	0-312-34861-4	$12.95/$18.95 Can.
Large-Print Omnibus Vol. 5	0-312-32036-1	$12.95/$18.95 Can.

Previous volumes also available

Omnibus

Crosswords for a Long Weekend	0-312-36560-8	$11.95/$15.95 Can.
Crosswords for a Relaxing Vacation	0-312-36696-7	$11.95/$15.95 Can.
Holiday Cheer Crossword Puzzles	0-312-36126-2	$11.95/$15.95 Can.
Supersized Sunday Crosswords	0-312-36122-x	$16.95/$22.95 Can.
Biggest Beach Crossword Omnibus	0-312-35667-6	$11.95/$15.95 Can.
Weekend Away Crossword		
Puzzle Omnibus	0-312-35669-2	$11.95/$15.95 Can.
Weekend at Home Crossword		
Puzzle Omnibus	0-312-35670-6	$11.95/$15.95 Can.
Sunday Crossword Omnibus Volume 9	0-312-35666-8	$11.95/$17.95 Can.
Lazy Sunday Crossword		
Puzzle Omnibus	0-312-35279-4	$11.95/$15.95 Can.
Supersized Book of Easy Crosswords	0-312-35277-8	$14.95/$21.95 Can.
Crosswords for a Weekend Getaway	0-312-35198-4	$11.95/$15.95 Can.
Crossword Challenge	0-312-33951-8	$12.95/$18.95 Can.
Giant Book of Holiday Crosswords	0-312-34927-0	$11.95/$15.95 Can.
Big Book of Holiday Crosswords	0-312-33533-4	$11.95/$16.95 Can.
Tough Omnibus Vol. 1	0-312-32441-3	$11.95/$17.95 Can.
Easy Omnibus Vol. 5	0-312-36123-8	$11.95/$17.95 Can.
Easy Omnibus Vol. 4	0-312-34859-2	$11.95/$17.95 Can.
Easy Omnibus Vol. 3	0-312-33537-7	$11.95/$17.95 Can.
Easy Omnibus Vol. 2	0-312-32035-3	$11.95/$17.95 Can.
Daily Omnibus Vol. 16	0-312-36104-1	$11.95/$17.95 Can.
Daily Omnibus Vol. 15	0-312-34856-8	$11.95/$17.95 Can.
Daily Omnibus Vol. 14	0-312-33534-2	$11.95/$17.95 Can.
Sunday Omnibus Vol. 8	0-312-32440-5	$11.95/$17.95 Can.
Sunday Omnibus Vol. 7	0-312-30950-3	$11.95/$17.95 Can.
Sunday Omnibus Vol. 6	0-312-28913-8	$11.95/$17.95 Can.

Variety Puzzles

Acrostic Puzzles Vol. 10	0-312-34853-3	$9.95/$14.95 Can.
Acrostic Puzzles Vol. 9	0-312-30949-X	$9.95/$14.95 Can.
Sunday Variety Puzzles	0-312-30059-X	$9.95/$14.95 Can.

Previous volumes also available

Portable Size Format

Expand Your Mind Crosswords	0-312-36553-5	$6.95/$8.50 Can.
After Dinner Crosswords	0-312-36559-4	$6.95/$8.50 Can.
Crosswords in the Sun	0-312-36555-1	$6.95/$8.50 Can.
Will Shortz Presents Crosswords To Go	0-312-36694-9	$6.95/$8.50 Can.
Favorite Day Crosswords: Monday	0-312-36556-x	$6.95/$8.50 Can.
Piece of Cake Crosswords	0-312-36124-6	$6.95/$8.50 Can.
Carefree Crosswords	0-312-36102-5	$6.95/$8.50 Can.
Groovy Crosswords from the '60s	0-312-36103-3	$6.95/$8.50 Can.
Little Black (and White)		
Book of Crosswords	0-312-36105-x	$12.95/$17.95 Can.
Will Shortz Presents		
Crosswords for 365 Days	0-312-36121-1	$6.95/$13.95 Can.
Easy Crossword Puzzles for		
Lazy Hazy Crazy Days	0-312-35671-4	$6.95/$9.95 Can.
Backyard Crossword Puzzles	0-312-35668-4	$6.95/$9.95 Can.
Fast and Easy Crossword Puzzles	0-312-35629-3	$6.95/$9.95 Can.
Crosswords for Your Lunch Hour	0-312-34857-6	$6.95/$9.95 Can.
Café Crosswords	0-312-34854-1	$6.95/$9.95 Can.
Easy as Pie Crosswords	0-312-34331-0	$6.95/$9.95 Can.
More Quick Crosswords	0-312-34246-2	$6.95/$9.95 Can.
Crosswords to Soothe Your Soul	0-312-34244-6	$6.95/$9.95 Can.
Beach Blanket Crosswords	0-312-34250-0	$6.95/$9.95 Can.
Simply Sunday Crosswords	0-312-34243-8	$6.95/$9.95 Can.
Crosswords for a Rainy Day	0-312-33952-6	$6.95/$9.95 Can.
Crosswords for Stress Relief	0-312-33953-4	$6.95/$9.95 Can.
Crosswords to Beat the Clock	0-312-33954-2	$6.95/$9.95 Can.
Quick Crosswords	0-312-33114-2	$6.95/$9.95 Can.
More Sun, Sand and Crosswords	0-312-33112-6	$6.95/$9.95 Can.
Planes, Trains and Crosswords	0-312-33113-4	$6.95/$9.95 Can.
Cup of Tea and Crosswords	0-312-32435-9	$6.95/$9.95 Can.

Other volumes also available

For Young Solvers

New York Times on the Web		
Crosswords for Teens	0-312-28911-1	$6.95/$9.95 Can.
Outrageous Crossword Puzzles		
and Word Games for Kids	0-312-28915-1	$6.95/$9.95 Can.
More Outrageous Crossword		
Puzzles for Kids	0-312-30062-X	$6.95/$9.95 Can.

 St. Martin's Griffin